# SOOTHING

--Longtime therapist W. Hans Miller tells two stories: his own, and a broader tale of how "soothing" plays a major role in our ability to cope with everyday life. Miller uses a compelling, almost novelistic storytelling style to help him make sense of his life. Miller not only shows great empathy but a willingness to find creative solutions... Both lay audiences and professional psychologists will learn much from Miller's admirable candor and compassion.
- (From Blue Ink Review)

--*Soothing* is an exceptional memoir that imparts understanding around psychotherapy. Even though the book is based in science, it uses clear everyday language. Miller tells his story and the stories of his patients in a direct and emotional way. His examples are thorough, descriptive, and easy to identify with.
- (From Clarion Review)

--A psychologist looks back on his struggles to quiet the seething minds of his patients – and his own – in this fine, engrossing portrait of mental illness and healing. Miller writes with a nice balance of subtle, searching analysis and warm empathy that vividly evokes psychic pain and embarrassment – especially his own... It's fascinating to watch as he improvises strategies to resolve his patients' problems. The result is a revealing, humane, down to earth look at the day-to-day art of clinical psychology that should give many readers insights into their own problems.
- (From Kirkus Reviews)

--*Soothing* is indeed a gift from Dr. Miller. This fascinating look at his life's work is also a thoughtful tale about Dr. Miller's pilgrimage.
- (From Pacific Review)

--Physician, heal yourself" could be the underlying theme of this book. *Soothing* will interest several reader types: those fascinated by the psychology of the mind, those employed in the field, and anyone who suffered hurtful scenarios in youth.
- (From US Review)

# SOOTHING

## LIVES OF A CHILD PSYCHOLOGIST

# W. HANS MILLER

Library of Congress Control Number:        2016916228
ISBN:               Hardcover            978-1-5245-4630-4
                    Softcover            978-1-5245-4631-1
                    eBook                978-1-5245-4632-8

Rev. date: 04/10/2018

**To order additional copies of this book, contact:**
Xlibris
1-888-795-4274
www.Xlibris.com
Orders@Xlibris.com
703579

# CONTENTS

Preface.............................................................................................i

Introduction: Joanie...........................................................................1

    What Is Soothing?......................................................................10


## PART ONE: *Beginnings*

Luck................................................................................................17

    Ancient Beginnings: Blue and Red...........................................20

    Recent Beginnings: Bulahhead..................................................24

Talking: A Mini Memoir..................................................................27

    Ray.............................................................................................27

    The Missionary.........................................................................29

    The Performer...........................................................................30

    The Reformer............................................................................31

    Sid..............................................................................................37

    Dr. Bill Boardman....................................................................42

    Westward Bound: UCLA...........................................................43

    I Can Do This!..........................................................................46

    Who Am I Kidding?..................................................................47

    Dan............................................................................................49

    My First Wider View................................................................52

More Beginnings..............................................................................54

Learning to Be Afraid.......................................................................56

The Train with the Giant Red Light: Four Years Old ............... 56

The Dynamite Cap: Five Years Old ........................................ 57

Learning to Hope ....................................................................... 58

The Thermometer: Six Years Old ......................................... 58

The Orange Crates: Eight Years Old .................................... 59

Grandma's Lap ..................................................................... 61

Searching for the True Self ........................................................ 65

Mommy, Daddy, and Me Once Again ................................. 68

My Helen Keller Moment: Discovering Abstraction ........... 73

Discovering the Moving Goalpost Syndrome ...................... 81

Escape to Baseball ...................................................................... 86

Living the Dream ................................................................. 87

The Golden Years ................................................................. 89

The Perfect Game ................................................................ 90

The Long Road to Freedom ................................................. 92

## PART TWO: *Practicing*

Learning about Psychotherapy .................................................. 99

"This Fruud Guy" and *The Psychopathology of Everyday Life* .. 99

Dr. Florene Young and Toys Out the Window ..................... 102

Dr. Rick Ward and the Fish-Tank Kid ................................ 104

What Makes Psychotherapy Work, or Not ............................... 107

Model Scenes Can Tell the Story ........................................ 107

Lindsay and Me ............................................................. 109

Getting Well with Empathy: Dr. Kohut and Adolf Hitler ....... 112

Getting Well With Creativity, Insight and Initiative:
Remembering Joanie ........................................................... 116

Rigidity: Michael and "Better the Devil You Know" ............. 125

Paranoia: Kimberly and Her Nervous Therapist .................. 127

What Doesn't Happen in the Therapist's Office ..............................134

   Wagons in the Front Yard ..............................135

   When Sarah Started Talking Again ..............................138

   Westward Bound ..............................143

   Dr. Young, Once Again: Darlene's Story ..............................144

The Parent Training Clinic: An Alternative to
Psychoanalytic Child Therapy ..............................149

   Getting Started: From Outpatient Psychiatry to Navajoland . 149

   The Parent Training Clinic's Greatest Challenge and
   Discovery ..............................155

   You Can Go Home Again ..............................161

Private Practice ..............................163

   DR. MILLER! Honeymooning in Maui ..............................165

   David: A Professional Tragedy ..............................167

   Lynda, Who Taught Me How to Do Therapy ..............................173

   Andrew: The Joke Killer with a Rifle on the Roof ..............................182

   Nobody Doesn't Have Scoldophobia: Sasha's Story ..............................190

Gone! How Charlie Stopped Counting and Started Living ..............................207

   Getting Rinaldo and Ted to Sleep ..............................217

     Rinaldo: Sleeping with Hypnosis ..............................217

     Ted: Sleeping with "Nothing" and "Four Sleepy
     Questions" ..............................222

   Ava: The Manic Defense and the Capacity to Be Alone ..............................231

   Monica: Protecting the True Self at All Costs ..............................245

## PART THREE: *The Mockingbird*

Searching for Integration and the True Self ..............................257

   The Potato Digger ..............................260

   The Bagpipe Professor ..............................264

The White Oleander ....................................................268
The Mockingbird .......................................................272

Acknowledgments .....................................................275
Index ........................................................................277

For Nancy Miller

# PREFACE

*I decided that that although nobody's life makes any sense, if you are going to make a book out of it, you might as well make it into a story... Don't look for strict chronology or tidy connections in the rest of the trip. The journey itself will tell you—as it gradually told me—what the book is about.*

Russell Baker

THERE WAS SOMETHING special about putting my life and work down on paper. No matter how much I have shared with therapists, closest friends, and a soulmate, there was always more that was unshared. I needed a record of the big moments in life to keep from forgetting or repressing them, all the way until I was seventy-four and had gathered enough confidence to go public, which is why this memoir was sixty years in the making.

Writing an extended memoir gives a different kind of freedom than talking; publicly or privately, talking is too guarded by the vigilant social brain. With a memoir all you have to do is find your one-of-a-kind river, jump in, and surrender to the current no matter where it needs to go. I found that in my river I could laugh about what I write without caring if anyone gets the joke; it is me only on my terms. Family members will disagree with my memories, readers will like me or not, but no one else can understand what is going on the way I understand.

Early on I discovered that one of my few talents is a very good memory of the past, from what someone said or did many years ago to the odd ability to recall most of the meals I or my companions had at restaurants. But all memories are imperfect; every time brain circuits containing a memory are activated, they open up like the gates of Troy to the influence of new Trojan horses sneaking in with whatever is meaningful at the moment. The Pulitzer Prize–winning writer Annie Dillard mourned an even greater loss for memoir writers: "After you've written, you can no longer remember anything but the writing." Yet I've learned to trust most of my memories and hope that the stories written here are more fact than wish.

In William Zinsser's wonderful teaching memoir *Writing about One's Life*, he cautions against the urge to tell the comprehensive story, preferring to catch a distinctive moment that can reveal the importance of some life event or life stage. Then, if there is more to say, a different memoir can be written. *Lives of a Child Psychologist* breaks his rule, telling a lifetime of stories about suffering and soothing on the way to self-acceptance and a kind of contentment. I suppose that makes this book an autobiographical memoir. This approach is based on my belief that with enough good stories from enough parts of our lives, common themes emerge that can define anyone.

Because I have been on a lifelong quest to find my 'what-ness and who-ness,' I was extremely lucky to become a therapist for children and their families, since their stories have had such a great influence. I was never taught how this two-way, giving and getting arrangement can make therapy succeed or fail. I was professionally raised in the days of the dominant medical model which meant the doctor diagnoses and the patient gets treated. The importance of a therapeutic partnership was not part of the training.

I learned something else about the stories I tell that stimulated more stories with each telling. I have a strong feeling that by the end of this book my stories will begin to converge on a common theme based on the blurred histories and life experiences of my parents, all of my mentors and relationships, my patients, my choices, and no small amount of luck. I can now see that my life has been a series of returning loops, and that is the only way I can think about it.

But before I began writing, I wanted to make sure someone else hadn't used soothing as a home base for their memoir. In my search I found everything I needed to know about "50 Ways to Soothe Yourself without Food," "Lovers Massage: Soothing Touch for Two," "Chocolate to a Lovers Heart: Soul-Soothing Stories That Celebrate the Power of Love," the self-help book *Recovery: Self-Soothing Techniques* and many similar titles. At least in my small survey, it appeared that I had a memoir about soothing all to myself.

Early on, while describing my book plan to a therapist colleague, he wondered why I was concerned about integrating my professional and personal lives. "Don't most people go to work and then come home to a different life? They don't worry about integration; they just go with the flow. They leave their work at the workplace and it's better that way." I have observed others who are able to do this, but for me, this was a new concept. The problem was that I was competent and mostly conflict-free in my office but had little peace of mind away from work, and I did not know why. Yet I was in the peace of mind business. What was happening to my self-esteem and confidence when I was not helping others?

About the same time, a writer friend saw my idea for the title of this book, shook her head and said, "It's too big a subject. It covers everything. Even evil acts can make some people happy. Everybody needs it. Try to narrow it down by describing how as a child therapist you found ways to soothe patients like yours." I understood the challenge but got excited about describing a subject that might bring together my personal and professional lives. It would also be about how I didn't make much progress anywhere until I started inventing healthier ways to soothe myself.

My version of 'narrowing down' is to find what the psychoanalyst Joseph Lichtenberg called "model scenes," which contain in simple stories the larger picture of life lessons. Model scenes are single episodes, such as an unforgettable interaction with a parent that have great influence throughout life.

Writing about model scenes is the method used throughout this book to describe the major influences that made me and all of my patients who we are, for better or worse. Some scenes are about the general topic of soothing, but most try to capture the essence of the people I am writing about. For these individuals and families, model scenes can help explain how we sometimes get stuck with damaging negative self-beliefs, but with help, can learn something about self-acceptance. With hard work and good fortune, we can even find ways to create more optimistic stories about the future.

In Part 1, "Beginnings," I describe in some detail the events of my early years that organized my beliefs and intentions. More recent influences tell about my emotional extremes and how I handled and failed to handle the challenges of growing up. Part 1 contains the stories of my seemingly endless attempts to self-soothe and find a sense of unity.

Part 2, "Practicing," is about the ways my own problems helped me to invent better ways to soothe others. It tells about the professional strand that for years seemed so alien to the personal strands in Part 1. For example, I spend some time describing my UCLA Parent Training Clinic where I found what I was after: measurable proof that I could not only discover out what good parenting was all about, but see problems coming before anyone knew they existed. I now think that this scientific veil was all about the need to sanitize the disturbing model scenes of my childhood. But I was on autopilot, going after the facts about families in need with my own unexamined motives.

All good therapy eventually soothes, and when the partnership was working, my patients left with the tools and positive beliefs they needed to soothe themselves as they moved forward in their lives. I will constantly emphasize the importance of features of the therapist that are essential for the treatment to work, such as empathy and caring, creativity, and understanding the model scenes in child development.

In addition, I watched as two features of successful patients emerged: the personality traits of *openness to change* and the presence of *internal motivation* to improve. I will also describe patients who seemed to feel soothed just by showing up for their appointment. Yet without being an active participant in their growth, lasting improvements in self-regard, relationships, and mature productivity were unlikely. Also, in Part 2, I have included nine of my most interesting and challenging private practice cases.

Finally, Part 3, "The Mockingbird" is an attempt to braid together the two strands of my competent and conflicted selves. This attempt at integration also showed me how writing about a better understanding of my true self was surprisingly richer than the help I received from my own therapies and hours of mental introspections. I am still looking for this ever-widening view of victories, defeats, and existence itself that together with a loving relationship are the ultimate soothers.

No section of this autobiographical memoir stands alone, although the mini-memoir "Talking" comes close. Just as my memories unfold, each of the stories loop around each other, hopefully on the way to some kind of coherence. Each of them shares patients and interventions, based on whatever idea I was pursuing at the moment. Yet they are all on a common road, hopefully headed toward a larger story in which the parts become "braided so tightly they cannot be separated."

# INTRODUCTION: JOANIE

*Each person deserves a day in which no problems are*
*confronted, no solutions searched for.*

—Maya Angelou

SOOTHING IS WHAT we can't stop needing or giving whenever possible. For all psychotherapists, the goal is not only to relieve discomfort but also to add something to the patient's life: new healthy ways to self-soothe. Yet sometimes, even when we do the best we can and know that we have been helpful, it's not enough.

I had a good idea what was wrong with four-and-a-half-year-old Joanie the first time I saw her clinging to her mother on my waiting room couch. This kind of knowing came partly by having been there; it was about shame and hopelessness. It also came from recognizing the pattern and getting to know many Joanie's with their uncontained suffering. I'm not referring to her chopped off, balding hair, which most people would recognize in photos of the butchered haircuts of Jews in the concentration camps. Joanie clearly had a disorder called *trichotillomania*, or compulsive hair pulling. What I saw that day was a defeated child in the despair that sometimes fill even young lives like hers.

Joanie's mother Adriana was referred by a pediatrician friend. She called and said that like herself, Joanie had always been anxious, but not with the crippling panic attacks that kept her from school when she was young. Joanie had already been in psychoanalytically-oriented play therapy for anxiety but without much success. Adriana wondered if there was any effective treatment other than medication, which is usually not recommended for preschoolers.

After this brief phone interview about Joanie's problems, we set up a time to meet. Joanie's divorced father Larry, who had joint custody, did not come to the meeting.

In the office with her mother, Joanie would not look up from the floor, nor did she allow herself to become unglued from her mother's bosom. I rolled my chair over to a safe distance and said, "Joanie, I don't know you very well but I do know how sad and scared you are right now. What if I told you that with you and your mother working together, we can try to make things better?" I finally got to see her eyes and she asked, "How are you going to do that?"

I explained that her mother had already told me what was going on and asked if we could start by my having a look at her bald spot. It had the medical name of *noncicatricial alopecia areata* on the right side of her head, meaning her hairless scalp was smooth with no scars. This disorder is found in about 3 percent of the population and can be caused by faulty genetic and brain chemistry, as well as chronic life stress. Serious hair pulling even occurs during relaxation when the mind is pleasantly wandering.

All girls play with their hair; with Joanie I would have to answer the question "What does she need that she can only get by pulling her hair out?" It is useless to look to the patient for the answer at almost any age about any symptom; they don't know. For Joanie, it could have been self-punishment, a plea for help, a safe haven from an avalanche of harm, or even a neurological symptom of *obsessive-compulsive disorder* or *Tourette's syndrome*.

I felt better about her motivation for accepting help when Joanie bent down her head so I could have a look. She was clearly using her dominant right thumb and forefinger to pull her hair without injurious scratching or much discomfort. Later she said it happened mostly when she was studying or daydreaming. Because the habit was automatic, occurring when she wasn't aware she was doing it, the therapy would require training her to become much more aware of the urge to move her hand toward her head, and then to interrupt any movement in that direction. The bald spot was about the size of a half-dollar. The rest of her hair appeared to have been twisted off at various lengths.

I told Joanie that I was going to help her the same way I always do when I see little girls who are having trouble letting their blonde hair grow out. I asked her to watch me while I strongly pressed my right thumb and forefinger tightly while pinching a finger on my other hand. I then asked her to show me what her pinching looks like, which after a few moments she did with some intensity and then repeated the exercise several times. Then I flattened out my right hand with fully extended fingers, pressed hard on the right side of my head with my palm, and rubbed a small area of my hair round and round while saying, "Now my itchy scalp feels better." Together we all repeatedly practiced a hard pinch of thumb and forefinger followed by widely opening her hand.

I asked Joanie to carefully watch her mother while she copied everything I did, speaking to her mother exactly as I spoke to Joanie. I told her to copy her mother and me over and over so that she could get the feeling she needed to stop pulling her hair and instead, firmly rubbing her head with her hand. I wanted her to practice this every day with her mother with just one rule. She would show me her hardest pinch with her thumb and finger for the very last time; no more pinching was allowed, only rubbing her bald spot in a circle as hard as she wanted with open palm and stretched-out fingers.

The three of us together practiced in each session spreading her fingers apart widely and using our palms to rub different parts of our scalp. Privately, her mother and I role-played ways to let Joanie know how smart and strong she was to practice this new habit, how this was going to work, and what it would mean for her. I wanted the therapy for hair pulling, the real changes, to occur at home and not in my office. If the treatment was successful, Joanie would learn a new, natural habit that was the opposite of the symptom.

I also wanted to test the seriousness of the problem by first treating only the symptom. What's more, pediatricians have a way of sending their acutely disturbed child patients for symptom relief, not deep psychotherapy. Week by week Joanie's hair slowly started growing again. In six weeks her bald spot was nearly invisible; in four months she had the nearly full head of the blonde hair that she was certain had been lost forever. Her mood had also improved and she no longer felt helpless about her future.

An important issue remained, which is always a child therapist's greatest concern after rapid success with what can be a serious disorder: is there more to this?

As it happened, the successful treatment of Joanie's hair pulling was the first in a series of treatments for other fears and phobias: next was the onset of *encopresis*, or inappropriate bowel elimination often due to fear of the toilet, then terrible nightmares which were only calmed by sleeping with her mother and her boyfriend. Next, she could sleep alone but not without a light on. But with a light in her bedroom she imagined monsters and insects were crawling toward her. Each of these symptoms were treated by a procedure known as *systematic desensitization,* in which Joanie became less sensitive to the source of anxiety by gradually and safely approaching the fearful situation.

Using a 0-3 fear rating scale, Joanie was only allowed to move forward after reporting comfort and low scores at each step. For example, if she reported that she was at a 3 while imagining a strange-looking shape in her bedroom, we would draw all kinds of monster figures that she could look at while taking slow deep breaths and then imagining them with her eyes closed until her number was 1 or 0. Joanie liked this highly structured measurement approach because she was always in control of the pace, and she quickly mastered the steps.

Then came a disabling fear that she would never learn to properly write out her schoolwork; each time she tried at her school she felt everyone was watching her make mistakes. We both had fun with this and Joanie was the only patient I ever taught from scratch to write letters and numbers and spell, homework and all. It took two months to teach her graphic skills, and this was one of the few "treatments" that actually took place in my office.

Each of her panic-causing problems were treated successfully, reminiscent of Freud's famous "symptom substitution" theory. He taught that underneath all symptoms there was some sort of sexual trauma produced—an inner pressure that could only be cured by bringing it to consciousness through dreams and free associations, and that directly treating a superficial symptom would only release another symptom.

Joanie's insecurity was so widespread that it kept finding new ways to show itself, and for a while I wasn't sure where it would end. It soon became clear that Joanie had a form of generalized anxiety disorder just waiting to attach itself to anything that bound up her anxiety. Yet because there were no indications of specific trauma anywhere in her history, I thought of her diagnosis in terms of genetic risks for anxiety disorders and the impact of intense parental fighting which had started the previous year.

In our second year, Joanie's beloved blind dog Chucky passed away, which was immediately followed by the onset of a hysterical fear of all dogs which looked at her, and then all dogs everywhere. I called for a meeting with her mother, her boyfriend, and ex-husband. Again I explained how her genetic risks on both sides of her family and, together with the battles between her mother and father, made it impossible for Joanie to believe that she could be truly safe.

No one liked what I told them next: I would not treat Joanie for her dog phobia for at least six months for two reasons. First, this fear was not completely irrational; years earlier I had successfully treated a number of children who learned to trust dogs, one of which was bitten in the face by the normally friendly dog next door. But most importantly, I wanted Joanie to have a more normal childhood, growing up in peace for a while with all of her anxieties bound up in one neat belief: "I'm okay as long as I'm not around dogs."

Meanwhile, she continued to see me, and we talked about other things. I said that she could bring up the idea of watching kittens and puppies in a nearby animal store anytime she wanted. Then in one unforgettable session, Joanie came in looking tense, standing shoulder to shoulder as usual at my desk with the blank pages she used to draw her weekly picture. Looking down, she said, "I hope you're not going to be mad at me." I said that would never happen, and then she told about her best school friend April, who had complained that day about being afraid of bees.

Joanie described how she explained to April with great precision the step-by-step method she had used for herself. She first had April imagine and then gradually get closer and closer to a bee in a closed jar while taking deep breaths and moving as she wished on the 0-3 fear rating scale. I was flabbergasted: I had never heard anything close to this. Joanie, then six and a half, ended her story by asking if she could keep helping her friend and tell me about her progress.

Things continued to go well and Joanie started coming monthly. However, six months later her younger sister started demanding to get another dog, and Joanie was still unable to visit her friends, all of whom seemed to have dogs around. The parents came in, again upset that I was not treating this fear the way I had with all the others. I told them that if they were willing to be extremely patient and only move forward in tiny steps determined by Joanie herself, I would find a way to at least reduce her fear of dogs. The parents had mixed results in keeping my rules.

Joanie was eight years old before many sessions of *imagined* scenarios of getting close to dogs, together with our *real* trips together to animal stores finally paid off. She made daily Internet searches on her own and found a very shy, miniature cocker spaniel that she allowed in the house and came to trust.

What changed in three years of on and off therapy, and why? Joanie was much worse off than I was between five and eight, but she did slowly change her deepest belief about herself: that something terrible was wrong with her and that she would never feel normal. Only by trying everything that I had learned about my own childhood traumas, learned and invented treatments, and taking advantage of her natural maturation was I able to be useful. It wasn't nondirective psychoanalysis that Joanie needed; it was dedicated, creative guidance, and new skills. There would be time for in-depth psychotherapy later, when Joanie had enough experience to begin making sense of her life. Then there was one additional detail of Joanie's treatment, a back story of my own.

In psychoanalytically-oriented training, the student is taught to be objective about the patient's illnesses, lest he or she commit the forbidden sin of "positive countertransference." This happens when the therapist becomes emotionally involved with the patient, allowing personal feelings to interfere with the necessary objective which was, according to Freud, interpretation of infantile fantasies.

Fortunately, those days are mostly gone and positive countertransference with children has made a big comeback in recent years. All child therapists now know that successful therapy requires demonstrations of genuine caring. I related immediately to Joanie's stories, which made it natural for me to care for her as a person. Also, I was confident about what I was doing; after all, in a way I had been practicing my whole life to help children like Joanie.

If only we could have continued Joanie's childhood search for reliable soothing. This might have happened in my therapy with her, but after the parents finally got back together, the family moved to a city on the East Coast. I never knew if Joanie continued her therapy.

That was the last I knew about this family, although I believe that I helped Joanie prepare for an uncertain future, and that had to be good enough.

Joanie's story contains much of what I know about failing and succeeding at being soothed. She was helpless and then less helpless. She was soothed and then soothed her friend April. Her mother taught her and her younger sister about meditation and then she learned about soothing herself. She believed she was strong enough to take care of a puppy, which would soon be taking care of her.

I had my own challenges with Joanie's treatment. I had to deeply care about Joanie and still keep her in a separate mental "Joanie container" that left plenty of room for other patients to get full attention. Then I and all child therapists have had to accept this reality: too often our patients leave treatment with unfinished business.

Joanie's story also hints at the fever that struck a fourteen-year-old boy about how not just to find out what made people suffer, but to actually *do* something about it. Helping her required nearly a lifetime of accumulating clinical knowledge together with a degree of creativity and determination. Her treatment contains critical information about the genetic influences on our personalities, especially those that can lead to potentially life-wrecking mood and anxiety disorders. And most of all, it explains my lifelong concern with soothing and self-soothing.

I am everywhere in Joanie's story, trouble-causing genes and all. Growing up will be difficult for her as it was for me, and she will likely need help from outside the family for many years. Yet from what I saw, Joanie had the makings of a very good child psychologist herself, recognizing at a glance some troubled child in her waiting room.

# WHAT IS SOOTHING?

*The quiet of the night was more*
*soothing than a sleeping pill.*
—Elisabeth Kubler-Ross

IS THIS STATEMENT true or false? *The mass of men lead lives of quiet desperation.* When I first read this 1849 declaration by the great American writer Henry David Thoreau, I decided it was true and began a lifetime of thinking about soothing. At some point I added this: *And the rest of them lead lives of loud desperation.* I looked for people who did not appear to need soothing in one form or another, and never found such a person. At first, I thought it applied to people who were in big trouble, especially big pain. But when I watched the people I knew up close, or in literature, film, or the most simple interactions, I could see soothing and self-soothing going on everywhere. Just what *is* soothing?

It seemed odd that there were so many people in blue gowns gathered around my oral surgery table. After all, it was just a tooth extraction. There were at least four, including the dental surgeon. He said that preparing for my new implanted tooth would be easy, but then spent the next hour with hammer and chisel hacking away to remove broken tooth roots from the jawbone. The banging was regularly interrupted by some sort of buzz saw. This tooth removal was worse than a previous one, but it didn't bother me very much. At least that's what I thought. Finally, the surgeon said, "That's it, we got it all."

Then one nurse sitting quite close, whose only job seemed to be checking on me, softly placed her palm on my left forearm and every hint of the disturbing operation vanished. It was like suddenly being awash in a bed of warm cotton.

A few minutes later I was signing out at the front desk and she walked up to wish me well. I could've just thanked her, but instead I said, "You're really good at knowing what your patients need. Somehow you knew the perfect moment to put your hand on my arm and end a problem that I didn't even know I had." She smiled and we parted. *Soothing is the right touch at the right moment.*

And then there was Bertha. In my first encounter with psychotic patients, while on a clinical rotation in the old Milledgeville State Hospital in Georgia, a nurse assigned me to "work with" a patient with lifelong schizophrenia named Bertha. According to her chart, Bertha spent her day alone, buried in a corner of the day room. I watched how Bertha, with smooth rhythm, would repeatedly lean forward and gently press her nose into the corner of the two walls for a moment and then sit up very straight. It had the appearance of some kind of Hasidic prayer ritual, except that she wasn't Jewish and had been doing this since her teens when her parents were killed in a car crash. She did this all day without uttering a sound. Whenever she was interrupted for necessary cleaning or feeding, she protested violently. She only showed this bizarre behavior in the daytime when she was in the presence of others.

The nurse told me that without her strong antipsychotic medications, Bertha would try to jump out of a window as she once did when interrupted. My clinical naïveté was quickly revealed when I asked the nurse why Bertha did this ritual. She only said something about how glad the staff was that Bertha had long ago found this nondangerous way of soothing herself and not bothering anyone, including the nurses. Even in our group supervision, the clinical teachers could only repeat that Bertha was a "typical chronic schizophrenic." I was afraid to ask what "work with Bertha" meant. So I just sat with Bertha for a few hours every day looking for signs of psychic life. But I will never forget her strange peacefulness. *Soothing is finding relief, no matter what it takes.*

Daniel Stern's *The Diary of a Baby*, which I have pushed hard to make famous over the years, begins with a six-week-old baby named Joey as he is soothed in his crib by a strong beam of sunlight on the wall. One of the unique features of the book is that throughout Joey's babyhood, Stern seems to have an open window to the child's inner experience of what is going on. In the form of a poem, here is how he described the opening scene as Joey is soothed by the light and the warmth.

> *Joey has just awakened. He stares at a patch of sunshine on the wall beside his crib.*

> *A space glows over there, A gentle magnet pulls to capture. The space is growing warmer and coming to life. Inside it, forces start to turn around one another in a slow dance. The*

*dance comes closer and closer. Everything rises to meet it. It keeps coming. But it never arrives. The thrill ebbs away.*

*Joey has been born with strong preferences about what he wants to look at, about what pleases him. If it is moderately intense, like the patch of sunshine, Joey is spellbound . . . He immediately alters in response to it. It increases his animation, activates his whole being. His attention is sharper. The patch of sunshine is a "gentle magnet," whose force he feels.*

There are two answers the question *what is soothing*? One is a definition, and the other is about whatever it takes for a person to feel soothed. In this book, I want to bring together some of the ways that "soothing" is used in everyday language, as well as more personal meanings that soothing has for me. In this book I will look for the many different emotional states that people find themselves in, for which they need comfort or just to enjoy themselves because something special is happening.

Soothing brings short and long feelings of peace, quiet, and freedom. It is what happens when arriving back home at the end of a long trip. It is also the right music at the right moment in an already good day, and the perfect sunset bringing a treasured moment of awe. When I felt the perfectly timed nurse's hand on my arm, I was soothed in the most wonderful way; when a patch of warm sunshine next to Joey kept him peacefully gazing for a long time, he was also soothed in an awe-filled way. *Soothing is soft pleasure.*

One day my wife Nancy came home from a party where everyone walked away with the gift of their own: a small round plastic device with a big red button on top. All you had to do to be instantly soothed was to press the button and hear a gentle baritone voice saying, "That was easy." This little gizmo stayed in our presence for years as a shortcut soother and a perfect definition of soothing: *whatever you do or whatever happens to you that goes your way.*

All these ways of self-and-other reassurance return, sooner or later, to my emotions about the surgeon's nurse, Bertha's winning way to deal with what was going on in the real world, Joey's calm delight with his own special sunbeam, and Nancy's magic red button.

# PART ONE
# Beginnings

# LUCK

*Everything in life is luck.*

—Donald Winnicott

*Good writers make their own luck.*

—William Zinsser

LIFE IS A series of beginnings. I have noticed at least eight likely beginnings for my selfhood that we all seem to share: my mother's genetic and developmental history and the way she experienced her life, and the same three sources of my father's personality. Then there is what I, as a unique individual, brought to the mixture. Finally, there is the much undervalued role of unexpected happenings, which include everything from having an abusive older brother and an all-inspiring tenth grade English teacher, to whole life-changing freak occurrences like that in the movie *Sliding Doors.*

In that film, Gwyneth Paltrow plays the role of Helen Quilley, a young Englishwoman who one day either makes it to work on the London "tube," or misses the train by a half second as the door slides shut. Her world splits into two parallel universes, one in which she returns home to find her fiancé in bed with his old girlfriend, but eventually starts life over and finds happiness. In the other universe she makes it on the train, goes to work and for a while lives a wacky cuckolded life. In modern cosmology, there's no convincing argument why existence and the laws of physics cannot work like this. Well-established fields such as quantum physics, complex adaptive systems, and chaos theory are showing that very little things can mean a lot. There may even be different universes for every decision and accident.

I was surprised at the number of stories in this book in which a few minutes or even seconds made the difference between someone's well-being or impairment. Or in my own life, being a mostly thriving psychologist-neuroscientist instead of an over-the-hill high school baseball coach, or marrying Nancy instead of Chris.

There are many opinions about the role of luck in life. My view, which I have rarely questioned, is exactly how the philosopher Paul Feyerabend once described his: "My life has been the result of accidents, not goals or principles." It is not that I am without willpower; I have choices about how to get to my office, but fortune determines which route will be available. So not everything is possible and luck is limited. I cannot get to my office tomorrow morning by way of Alaska. Little in life is ever predetermined or controlled.

If everything in life is luck, early in life something very unlucky crashed my self-confidence. The therapies I tried sooner or later focused on a failed and traumatic childhood attachment experience, which for years has been the prevailing psychological gospel. At first this was quite soothing as in "Aha, maybe it's not all my fault." But I came to resent anything sounding like a criticism of the only mother and father I'll ever have. My parents were who they were and did the best they could, especially since they had more serious matters to worry about than my extreme sensitivity. I needed to rethink my origins, and it did not take long to come up with a new view of my life.

My fears are explained in part by at least three generations of men on my father's side with widespread feelings of inadequacy, insecurity, and anxiety. Meanwhile, my apparent resilience in the face of so much worry and emotional hypersensitivity would be understandable by anyone who ever knew my mother or any of her four older sisters. With the best of intentions, Dad helplessly destabilized the family while Mom kept us all afloat. Mother was a master of detached efficiency even if she was sometimes too cool. Meanwhile, father was too often in a state of collapse, not an ideal model for a sensitive, needy little boy. There were many other sources of trauma and soothing, with bad and good luck. And as I said, there was what I brought to the mix. None of this had a purpose, plan, or intention; it's just what happened.

Randomness and luck and our failure to be certain about anything are not well tolerated in psychological practice because it is messy and cannot be predicted. The economist Satyjat Das, agreeing with many scientists, put it this way: Inexactness (and randomness) marks an end to certainty, undermines scientific determinism, questions all methodology, challenges causality, and shows that we cannot know all of the determining elements of the present." The science writer Jacob Aron said it simply: "Your existence is unbelievably unlikely."

This is not what people who teach or practice psychotherapy want to hear. Surely thoughts, feelings, and behavior, even personality traits, can be predicted. The trend in psychoanalysis and child development has always been to put the heaviest weight of suffering on our individual early years and a belief in the awesome power of psychotherapy. A current exception is in the growing amount of consideration given to our genetic history, which is full of randomness.

Even though much research suggests that personality is about 50 percent inherited, it's unlikely that anyone will ever figure precisely out how much weight to give to the origins of who we turn out to be. All I can do is make guesses about who I am and how I got this way.

It was growing up in a confused and uncertain world that I came to make better guesses about how the mixing of *nature* in the form of genetics and *nurture* in the form of childhood influences made me who I am. Again, there was no one to blame, but there were plenty of places to look for the influence of genes and my environment. This new search began with a surprising event that would take me back not just to my start but to that of every person on earth.

## Ancient Beginnings: Blue and Red

One day I got an unexpected email, over four months after I had submitted a DNA sample to National Geographic's "genomics" survey. When I first sent in my DNA, they said it would take a long time to analyze the results and I had basically forgotten about it. This survey compared my female and male genetic influences with thousands of others, and traced out the genetic changes that took place nearly one hundred thousand years during the human pilgrimage out of Africa, all the way to south Georgia in the USA.

I spent most of the night reading the report and marking on a world globe my parents' known journeys step-by-step through the millennia with blue (liberal mom) and red (conservative dad) magic marker dots. The DNA findings were extremely compelling, but I wasn't sure how it could become a flesh and blood story. But the personal impact of the report since that night has been so great that I don't believe anyone's full story can be told without it.

Who are those people? This image causes a chill each time I imagine one of my ancestors walking on that fragile rock bridge as they made their way out of Africa. For sure, his and her terror could only be soothed by hoping to make it all the way across and imagining a better life somewhere ahead. The image also reminds me that compared with their more than *one hundred thousand years* of marginal lives and early, bloody deaths, our civilization today may be in an age of trumped-up ways to soothe hurt feelings and headaches. Or, perhaps it's all relative to our time on earth and nothing about suffering and soothing should ever be minimized.

A less personal story would show the big picture of our journey out of Africa. The first home of humanity, well over 100,000 years ago, was in northeastern Africa, the starting place for colonizing nearly every spot on earth where there was available food. We know this because the first carefully designed stone tools, ornaments, and human bones were found in that general area. Nearly all maps describing the directions taken by these colonizing humans show the spread north into the Middle East, and then westward toward southern Europe.

Other migrating pathways include northern Europe and Asia all the way into North America and the extremes of South America. For example, I have friends Sonia, whose people are from Spain, and her mate Robin, who is a Native American Cherokee Indian. Their children will grow up with the genes that first left Africa and headed west to Spain and then Mexico and California (Sonia), and then east all the way to the Appalachian Mountains of North America and eventually California (Robin).

It was about that time that large numbers of humans, including my ancient parents, ended their trip in Eastern Europe and then Ireland, where there must have been food aplenty because they stayed there a very long time.

My genomics report described how anyone alive today is an evolutionary success story, beginning somewhere around two hundred thousand years ago with a very famous lady called "*Mitochondrial Eve.*" Fifty thousand generations later of mothers mixing with near-human people such as *Neanderthals* (1.8%) and *Denisovans* (2.7%), wandering from the eastern Ethiopia through the Middle East, and then Europe, landing around ten thousand years ago in Ireland after the last ice age finally retreated, there she is, leaving for America, the great-great-great-grandmother of Georgie O'Quinn Miller.

The O'Quinns had migrated to North Carolina in the late 1700s, and then found their way to the south Georgia town of Adel before the Civil War. My father also arrived in Ireland but later by way of a much longer journey. Remarkably, his folks also migrated to North Carolina and then to Richland, Georgia (just seventeen miles from Plains and my grandfather's friend Earl Carter, father of Jimmy) and less than one hundred miles away from my father's wife-to-be. My grandmother Mattie used to say that her son Thomas and Georgie were destined to find each other. How could she know?

Overall, my genetic history showed that I am mostly of British and German descent. The average of my DNA concentrations for both of my parents is about equal: 47% northern European, 33% Mediterranean, and 17% Southwest Asian, all containing genetic influences from related populations. What this means is that my ancestry was dominated by the population genes of people in northern Europe after many genetic mutations during the long trip out of Africa. Most importantly, as final proof of my Irish oddities, the available samples of DNA tracked my father's journey to one genetic subgroup and my mother's to a different subgroup, which together account for 90 percent of all people in Ireland today.

So at the end of one hundred thousand years of wandering and genetic variations, all I really I know is this: I am unique and one of a breed at the same time, most recently because of the genetic mixing from my parents' ova and sperm. I can and cannot be fully compared with any living soul. I will never know the exact origins of any of my mental and emotional traits. The only certainty is that I am the partial result of an accumulation of all those mutations that survived and made up my mother's natural strengths and my father's unfortunate weaknesses. My genetic line will end with the lives of my sister, brother, and my own because none of us have biological offspring, unlike the good fortune of the writer Thomas Hardy and most people: "I am the family face; Flesh perishes, I live on."

We now know that genes are not fate. Genes only load up the future with potential while our lived-in environments pull the trigger, which is why I now have to look into my more recent past. Somewhere in these pages I hope to get clues about the blurred forces of nature and nurture that produced a confidant helper of children like Joanie.

## Recent Beginnings: Bulahhead

I cannot possibly understand the full source of my insecurities without confronting an event of October 3, 1941. That was my birthdate, and it was memorable for two more or less interesting reasons. First, on the day after I was born, Patterson Hospital III, in the small south Georgia town of Cuthbert, burned flat to the ground. Also, during my birth it was clear that I had an unusually large head from which I never fully recovered psychologically. Physically I've always been in excellent health, even after two cancer surgeries. But running through most days of my life has been an attention-getting profile that constantly drove my search for compensatory soothing wherever I could find it. I still have unanswered questions about why this mattered so much.

Here are some of the labels I often failed to deal with, but did have the advantage of bringing much mirth to my tormentors: Eight years old, first away-camp in the mountains, the camp leader yells at me for all to hear: "Bulahhead, what are you doing here?" Twelve years old, walking by some kid on the porch, "Mom, come look—a midget." Fourteen, skipping church service as usual with best friend

Sam as he refers to his girlfriend Julie, "There's nothing either of us can do about it but she calls you 'big head, little body'." Fifteen years old, unrepeatable slurs from the opposing dugout while pitching in the championship Pony League baseball game, my only saving grace was that no one could hit the knuckleball my father taught me, and we won.

Twenty-one-year-old graduate student, teaching an introductory psychology course with the football jocks lined up on the back row of the amphitheater, all snickering as the university star quarterback reads his essay, "Pygmies." I gave him a *C-*, citing his poor research, which led to a hilarious over-the-top phone call from the football coach, but the grade stuck. Perhaps the jock needed a higher grade to undo some recent *F*s and bring his grade-point average above a *C* so he could graduate and move on to the pros, which he did.

Looking back, vicious name-calling may have actually been rare, perhaps because a little humiliation for me went a very long way. Also, I worked very hard to keep everyone's gaze directed toward my clever storytelling, but I still often see "the look" in strangers.

I never learned what a bulahhead was. I don't recall being teased anymore while I was at that summer camp but again I had the last word. On the ceremonial evening before going home, everyone made small boats with a sail and a lit candle on board and gently pushed them away from the shoreline of the lake. Somehow mine caught the night breeze and was the first to make it to the opposite shore, lit candle intact. For some people, little victories go a long way.

❧

This book is in part the story of how my often laughable struggles to ward off this shame and rejection led to positive attention-getting accomplishments of many kinds. None were so rewarding, and as troublemaking, as my much over-practiced thinking and verbal skills, both of which showed up as unstoppable talking.

# TALKING: A MINI MEMOIR

*I have noticed that nothing I never said did me any harm.*
Calvin Coolidge

**Ray**

UNTIL RAY SAID "pass" it had never occurred to me not to talk when called upon. In fact it rarely occurred to me not to talk when I *wasn't* called on; one of my most difficult life challenges has been when I tried looking for things not to say. At last, I am beginning to understand something about this habit, rightly called "prolix" from Latin, "pouring forth," how it got its start and then was so heavily rewarded that it became a way of life.

I became aware of Ray at my first meeting with the Unitarian Church men's group. I had known about the group for some time. But I stayed away to avoid being asked to relive the years since my wife Nancy developed dementia and moved to a board and care facility, but that's another story. Knowing about the serious effects of social isolation and with nothing to lose, I went to a meeting.

As the newbie, I was asked by the group leader Nathan to introduce myself. I was very conscious about trying to keep it short, telling the group I was a clinical psychologist and glad to be in a group just like theirs. I told them about the losses of Nancy and two of my grandchildren, but how I was doing okay by keeping busy writing a memoir. Nine men then gave brief summaries of the previous two weeks' highlights, ending with Ray on my right.

My first thought about Ray was curiosity because he was so brief. After he said "pass," there was a silence for a moment and he added, "All okay for me in the last two weeks," but I wondered if there was more to his reluctance to talk since everyone else had lots to say about themselves. After the next meeting, he called after me as I was walking to my car and we instantly bonded, talking on a very cold Santa Monica street corner for almost two hours. By the time we parted, I had a hint about his reluctance to talk about himself in the group: Ray had already embarked on a nonego driven path and was putting it into practice. It was Ray who started my comeback from isolation with a new friendship, especially with someone who seemed to share my goals.

At the time I met Ray, I had already written a number of stories for this book. I had temporarily given up trying to describe how those different stories could be woven together. I got only as far as the obvious and stark contrast between mostly effective clinical work and personal struggles, which is how the book got its subtitle about the two lives of a child psychologist. But that level of integration turned out to be too big a project in the early days. I decided to start with my beginnings and many attempts at self-cure, which later led to a lifetime of work with children and their families. Any braiding of my two lives would have to come from stories yet to be told.

Yet only a few weeks after Ray's disciplined response in the group, I found one common denominator for some of the stories I had completed. It was *talking* and then talking some more but always about talking. Even after many therapies I still could only speculate about causes and possible cures for my verbal compulsion; maybe writing about my life in chunks could give me more clues.

## The Missionary

One Christmas at my grandparents' house in Richland, Georgia when I was seven, I found myself surrounded by grandma Mattie and her two sisters. They held the real power in my family. I didn't know what was happening, but they were definitely closing in with a message. Aunt Dora, my favorite aunt with the shiny new black Buick spoke, "God has a plan for you, young man. You are the best talker in this family and you're going to be a medical missionary to China, taking care of people and spreading the word of God." Very frightened, I managed to say, "I am?" I recall grandma helping out by saying something like "It's okay, we'll help you, but this is your mission." Nowadays I wish I had at least been able to say, "*China?*"

In the summer of the following year it happened that a medical missionary to Africa, making his dutiful rounds back home to convert sinners, came to the First Baptist Church in the town where we lived for what was called a "Revival." Kids always looked forward to these summer Revivals because it meant that something interesting might actually happen in church. I rushed to get a seat in the front to find out about this amazing explorer who knew all about the world. The traveling preacher did not disappoint. Foreign adventures and helping others anywhere in the world suddenly seemed like a real possibility for me.

That was the night I understood what my aunts and grandmother were talking about. Watching others get a warm embrace from the missionary after being "born again," I tearfully stepped forward and "accepted Jesus as my Lord and Savior." Somehow the next day my mother arranged for the good reverend to come to our house for lunch. As a new Christian follower, I was very excited and got up the nerve to ask him how I could learn to be like him. His words are still as clear today as they were back then:

"The most important thing of all is to learn everything you can about everything—all knowledge is valid for a missionary." I did not know what "valid" meant except that it sounded really important. Little did anyone know that I was going to take him so seriously that I would become an insatiable, searching missionary but of a very different kind. My mission was going to be fixing people by knowing everything so I could tell them what to do about their troubles. I soon found a way to put my new credo to work. The first step was to learn and then learn some more.

## The Performer

It did not take long for me to focus my spare time, spending hours in the city library of whichever town we happened to be living in, reading anything related to world history, cultural differences, and especially all those unsaved Africans. And because I could talk a little about almost anything, people began to notice. Teachers often called on me first, which was a mistake because then they had to say, "Does anyone else have something to say?" I didn't know when or how to stop. But I had discovered the art of entertaining by guessing, often correctly, what was most likely to interest people and keep others focused on what I *said* instead of me.

The good reverend may not have appreciated that I took nearly a year off my library research in the eighth grade when I got completely hooked by science fiction, equipped with binoculars and searching the skies every night for UFOs with Jay Hook, my smoking buddy. My father called him "Jay Hood." The missionary would've especially been troubled when I shifted from science fiction to studying astronomy, then real science, and soon after altogether rejecting churchly gospel and the idea of an all-knowing God.

Yet back then I never stopped feeling soothed by reciting the soft words in the Bible's twenty-third Psalm, or memorizing a few more verses in the New Testament book of Romans at bedtime until I could recite whole chapters. The attention I got for my performances of these recitations again led me to believe that I had found an escape from insecurity. As I write this, I still am both challenged and soothed by the humility in St. Paul's Epistle to the Romans, as in "For I say, through the grace given unto me, to every man that is among you, not to think of himself more highly than he ought to think . . ." and so on.

Then at age fifteen, someone decided I should be the master of ceremonies of the annual Bull Street Baptist Church teen party. I memorized some acceptable jokes and led our band in singing the songs of Fats Domino. I actually got to perform my very first encore, which was Fats' deep-South accented "I found my threeuill . . . on blueburry heeull." I liked being the center of attention without any limits on talking.

## The Reformer

At age seventeen, as a senior in high school, talking got me both the big prize and a devastating surprise. Four senior girls and I put together a grand conspiracy in a group we called "The Gang of Five" to secretly undermine the city council's efforts to cut high school funding for a nurse, physical education, and a few of our favorite teachers. The girls picked me because all of them had seen me do my thing in classes many times and thought I would be a good group spokesperson. With one exception we all half-lied to our parents, telling them we had formed a study group to do school work. The exception was that one of the gang named Lisa, in whose house we met several times a week typing and making copies of propaganda and slanderous attacks on the city administration. We secretly deposited our work late in the night at city buildings and even the city library.

City authorities suspected someone in our senior class was behind this mischief and at one point actually brought in an FBI agent who tried unsuccessfully to track down the typewriter and its owner. We vowed to keep our secret, no matter what, and had the full support of Lisa's parents in more ways than one. Every time I went in their house there was a case of Jack Daniel's whiskey by the front door, available to everyone, which meant that after only a few hours we felt very free to express ourselves.

Our plan was to get everybody riled up and then crash one of the city council meetings and present them with our righteous demands. One morning all of us, fully dedicated but not fully confident, went to city hall and told someone we had an urgent message for the council. The receptionist knocked on the conference door, and suddenly we faced some very serious grown-ups. I was about to begin but my speech was quickly interrupted. The council chairman stood up and said, "Okay kids, just tell us what you want and we will decide what to do with you."

One of the girls, the typist and also the leading activist in the group, had agreed to read from our previous night's work, she told them we wanted all students to have a day off from school to march *en*

*masse* downtown to the city hall in a show of the unity and importance
of our mission. We wanted them to do away with their cuts in school
funding. Finally, we wanted access to the city auditorium to present
our case directly to the people and by way of radio to everyone in
Savannah. After some silence with the board members looking at
each other, the chairman ask us to wait outside while they discussed
our "demands."

Someone came out of the room after about only fifteen minutes
and invited us back inside. We never knew why, but the council
agreed to everything we wanted. They even told us we could select the
date for the auditorium debate. Jack Daniels would've been pleased
at the gathering that night at Lisa's.

So the entire high school got the day off to march and wander
around the city, gathering at the steps of the city hall and chanting
the demands of the Gang of Five. A few nights later we sat on the
stage of the auditorium facing an awful lot of people. Again, we were
all nervous but determined—almost. I had a friend named Gilbert
Kulik who was captain of the school debate team and asked him to
join us. It was a good idea because Gilbert was able to answer some
very sticky questions from city officials about who was going to pay
for the cuts. Then our revolution was over.

There was some fallout back at school: our friends and most of
the school body came at us with backslapping support and thanks
for preventing the cuts and showing up the authorities. Many others
were disdainful conservatives. Some were just envious. One person
shouted "hooligans," a term that today would be close to "terrorists."
My best friend Sam Underwood confronted me in front of a large
group in the hall while he yelled "Dictator, Dictator!" I guess he had
to because his father was the embarrassed superintendent of schools
in Savannah. Or more likely, Sam was just angry or envious that I

had kept such a big secret from him. He came too close, and when I told him to back off, he slapped me hard in the face.

In an unconscious reflex, I hit him hard in the mouth. I only recall him sliding on his behind on the polished hallway floor and me rushing up to see if he was all right. This was only the second time in my whole life that I responded violently when I felt humiliated. The first was when I forever ended my brother's torture by flattening him in the kitchen one year earlier. I was only proud of shutting down my brother; Sam and I made up the next day.

The excitement was over in weeks, but not before I got a reality check that would change my life. The day after the march, our school principal put us on notice that if we did not gather in his office and apologize over the school sound system for disrupting the much-needed education of his pupils, we would be suspended. This was no big decision for the gang; he knew that we had won and he couldn't undo our work. Again I was elected to address the student body and I was ready. I was a king among queens and had my cynicism of authority carefully hidden in my speech.

But when we conspirators entered his office there were no microphones, only a large black cloth that covered part of the wall the size of a door. I was told to stand in front of whatever the thing was and publicly repent for the entire school to hear.

I stepped forward and suddenly all the lights went out in my head: I absolutely froze and only knew what I said when the girls told me later. They were all puzzled that at our proudest moment, I suddenly looked very strange and spoke like a zombie. Most fortunately for me, the principal gave us the day off to think about our misbehavior and come back the next day ready to "get serious about why you are at school." I left the gang to go home and tried to sleep it off. But to this day I never fully recovered and ended up with a public speaking phobia and a near life-wrecking generalized anxiety disorder, which I managed to hide from almost everyone. A giant part of me that had no name seemed destroyed. The "best talker in the family" was exposed for what he was and would never again talk to a large audience without stage fright.

Less than one year later, I was the front-runner for president of freshman class at Mercer University in Macon, Georgia, but gave a shaky campaign speech in the auditorium and lost the election. For a long time, my closest and most valuable friends, problem-solving smarts and talking, deserted me. During the remainder of undergraduate school at the University of Georgia, I played the role of a shy student, holding out hope that I could learn enough to get by on knowledge while faking my way through class presentations.

My new malady was not a total loss because much later, while still early in my career in the Department of Psychiatry at UCLA, I conducted a three-year study of young and old patients who had been incapacitated by panic attacks and phobias of all kinds. I wrote a well-received paper on "Phobias and the Pre-Phobic Hypothesis" describing how phobic experiences occur when an individual catastrophically re-encounters early life traumas. Nearly all of these patients had been carrying around private, unconscious negative beliefs about themselves for many years. And then one day, in a moment of terrifying public exposure, a phobia was born and possessed its victim. Word got out about my paper and suddenly my part-time private practice was filled with all kinds of fearful patients.

Children with OCD came with sudden panic attacks. Moms were afraid to drive with their kids on the freeway (an understandable fear

in Los Angeles). Many more kids were brought in by parents fearful
of their not being accepted in University of California universities,
which naturally showed up as crippling test-taking anxiety in the
child. Wiley, a young patient's father, came in after the elevator in
his twenty-second floor downtown business suddenly dropped ten
floors. In my office, at first he could not even imagine the sound of
the elevator door closing without panic and was on the verge of losing
his job, but was able to go back to work in less than two months, but
not before we spent a lot of time on his elevator. A well-to-do lady
with a pigeon phobia, whose Italian fiancé insisted on a honeymoon
in Rome, the world's greatest haven for pigeons, gave me five weeks
to cure her, and a surprising number of all-aged people came in with
needle phobias.

Three crew members and a CEO passenger survived the crash of
a private jet at the Santa Monica airport; interestingly, only the pilot
and the passenger were unaffected. Was it a coincidence that for the
crew, the amount of trauma lined up perfectly with the amount of
perceived control that each of them had over the fate of the airplane?
Was the CEO so cool because he was a CEO, or was he a CEO because
he was the coolest guy? The flight attendant needed a year of treatment
for PTSD before she could go back to work, and ended up suing the
airlines, which meant a lot of court time for me.

I knew about the most successful treatments for all these patients
and many others, but could not have been nearly as effective without
that disastrous speech at Savannah high school. I knew exactly what
all of these patients went through, and what I had to do in order to
begin to recover. I secretly included myself in the paper as a patient
named "Claude" who had an ability to describe in great detail his
phobia of public speaking, and how his nonstop conflicts about

talking only made things worse. Claude was the only "patient" in the study who struggled with the "treatment."

## Sid

When I lost confidence in my lifelong friend of talking, I needed to find a real live one, and for me this was Sid Jordon. Sid has always been one of the most wonderful, reliable, and unusual people I ever knew. Even with years of not talking with each other, one of us would get a call out of the blue and just pick up right where we had left off. That is not so uncommon, but on two occasions he made me seriously question the value of endless talking when the only thing needed was the brief expression of simple feelings.

On the day after I last saw my thirteen-year-old grandson Veda as he lay dying of brain cancer in a Honolulu hospital, Nancy and I had to briefly return home because of scheduled presentations. Even though Veda's death was inevitable, we were still in shock on learning he passed away the night that we left him. The house phone rang but there were no words, only a man uncontrollably sobbing. All of my attention and concerns suddenly shifted to these woeful sounds and their owner. It turned out to be Sid, who finally was able to ask "What just happened?" We had not talked in over a year.

Years later, Veda's older brother Ari, then living with us, suffered a life-threatening injury in an auto accident. Ari and I had been very close since his birth and I was devastated. While grieving with Nancy, the phone rang again; it was Sid and once more he did the impossible. Crying, he said that he had a sudden overwhelming feeling of grief connected to me and made a desperate call to find out what happened. Then Sid then had a long talk comforting Nancy, Ari's biological grandmother.

Sid and I spoke about these strange incidents many times without any clues whatsoever about how they happened. Sid did not seem to need an explanation. He is gifted in ways that do not have words, something I still have trouble understanding.

Sid and I spoke about these strange incidents many times without any clues whatsoever about how they happened. Sid did not seem to need an explanation. He is gifted in ways that do not have words, something I still have trouble understanding.

I met Sid on my first day in graduate school, and together we became lifelong sources of mutual support. We sat that day with all incoming grads in the university chapel auditorium and were inseparable for the next five years. Much of this time was spent solving the problems of the universe in our tiny basement office underneath the psychology building. Among other things, we created our own two-person religion called the Cosmological Unifying Principle, or CUP, which of course required a much used and unwashed coffee cup on the top shelf in our office for motivation. In time, Sid became my most worthy match at endless verbiage as we traded sermons about neurobiology and the CUP.

Sid and graduate school were the means for me to safely get my talking protector back, because of a new strategy. I would do whatever it took to learn enough so that when I did speak I didn't have to say much to impress the professors. On the first day of classes, the new department head with a new draconian curriculum, Dr. Hammock, addressed our class of forty doctoral students with something like this: "Today there are forty of you. In four years perhaps a dozen of you will still be here. Good luck."

At first, this was terrifying for everyone, which was Dr. Hammock's purpose. But when I recovered, I realize that it was also my cue to do exactly what I needed. Sid and I, together with a few carefully selected others, would band together in a study group and eliminate the competition by learning more and faster with the help of some awful trickery. For example, the faculty made it clear from the start that the way to impress them was to summarize all the related psychological and physiological experiments about a particular subject. So before an important exam, with Sid on one side of the room and me on the other and another planted conspirator in the back, one of us would shout out to another "How many studies did you memorize for the reward centers in the brain?" And another would answer "Nine" followed by another: "You guys are in trouble, I've got thirteen."

Sid and I never stop believing that the faculty had purposefully arranged the curriculum to be as intimidating as possible. First we had to be general psychologists, then experimental psychologists, then physiological psychologists, and then if we made it that far, either academic experimentalists or clinicians. This was a breeding ground for cutthroat competitiveness, and the faculty got what they wanted. Sure enough, each September there were fewer in the class. One of my highly qualified friends left after two years and another went to a different graduate school.

Meanwhile, I had found myself. All I had to do was keep my professors happy in their seminars, go for the best grades using all kinds of invented shortcuts, keep my eyes on whatever step they next laid out for me, and hope that graduate school would never end. That was the scariest part for me; I was seriously worried about an unstructured future. But somewhere about halfway through graduate school I got shocked in ways that I never could have anticipated.

All I wanted was to be a good student and join in terrific group discussions with very bright comrades while avoiding performance anxiety and embarrassment. I thought I had solved these problems by being way over-prepared and ready for anything. But in the space of two days I took a giant dive backward, for very different reasons.

In one seminar with a famous visiting scientist and a group of fifteen fellow students, I was very excited about the high quality of the presentation. Toward the end of the meeting I tried to summarize the implications of the speaker's research, which was followed by total group silence. Sid and I walked out together and I asked him what happened at the end of the meeting. He said, "You intimidated the shit out of everybody."

I was blown away without a clue that I had done something wrong—I could not even get it right when I was just trying to contribute and making a real effort to not show off. My attempt to participate completely backfired and I was filled with regret, shame, and confusion. I was decades away from knowing about healthy self-soothing at times like this.

Looking back after that meeting and talking with Sid, it seemed that our excessive competition strategy had left me with learning and thinking too much, and then once again I was the odd ball in the group. There was no safe haven; what felt natural was unnatural and brought back my worst fear, which was that the people on which I most depended were having bad thoughts about me. For the first time, standing out only meant another set-up for rejection. A pattern was developing.

The other reason for my dive was also unpredictable in the worst possible way. I worked my way through graduate school by teaching undergraduate classes in psychology and stayed in control of stage fright by using every prop I could think of: blackboards, handouts to keep the student's eyes off of me, and any time I felt nervous turning the lecture into a group discussion.

The very day after my disturbing experience in the seminar, I was well into elaborating on a point in the textbook when a sassy and sexy girl in the front row interrupted and asked a question. Somewhat confused, without warning once again, the lights went out and my mind went completely blank. I got the usual concerned and frightened faces that everyone displays when reminded of their own public speaking anxieties. As I looked out at them I could almost hear their prayer: "Come on, get it together, please get it together."

I walked back and forth across the stage in the amphitheater with head down not knowing what to do. I remember finally settling down, murmuring some apology, remembered to direct the class's attention to notes on the blackboard behind me and got through the class. Sid and I often attended each other's lectures, and on our way to lunch he said, "What the hell was that?" I just told him that I lost it for a few minutes. But my problem had returned and I feared that talking, my greatest strength, was again becoming my biggest threat. I thought I could trust Sid with anything but I never pursued this with him. I did mention it later to Dr. Hammock, who had become a much-needed mentor. All he said was "I don't know, Hans, but once you panic that's it."

I realized then that knowledge was not enough to prevent humiliation, and could even cause embarrassment. Without any other safe way to impress others, I also knew that life out in the world was going to be difficult. In class we had learned about the so-called epileptoid personality in which the individual lives in fear, never knowing when the next seizure would strike, and therefore never being able to relax. Perhaps, just as people with epilepsy take their Dilantin three times a day to prevent seizures, there might be some drug for me. It was about that time that my new best soother Valium was invented. I took the tiniest dose, and even if it was only a placebo effect, ever since then I have nervously made it through public presentations, but without another crippling panic attack.

## Dr. Bill Boardman

Sometimes, with the not so good, something good can come. Without possessing the skills to *self*-regulate my anxiety and compulsive talking, it again had no boundaries. I had long postponed the strong recommendation that all doctoral students receive their own psychotherapy. But now it was time for my therapy. My own father figure-therapist, Bill Boardman at Emory University in Atlanta, had much earlier named this potentially life-changing opportunity "a psychological surrender."

Dr. Boardman was widely known as the expert on using the Rorschach ink blot test to diagnose and predict the behaviors of seriously impaired psychiatric patients. In one demonstration at the Georgia State Hospital for mentally ill, he asked someone in a large group to present only a patient's complete and exact responses, including their observed behavior, to the first two cards of the inkblot test. He then asked the group to guess what the patient said on the third card, which only the student examiner had seen. When satisfied with his analysis of the patient's words and behavior, Dr. Boardman gave an almost literal account of the third inkblot's verbal content, and explained how he was able to make his predictions.

His formula was simple, at least for him, and took me decades to develop a degree of his expertise in using the Rorschach. He said to the group, "Studying the patient's behavior, language, and choice of words, what does he *have* to be like, where does he have to come from, and what had to happen to him in order for him to talk this way on the first two cards?" It was the most exciting challenge I was ever to have as a psychologist, and the most useful understanding of how good psychological diagnosis works. He also pointed out that similar to the challenge he gave us that day, unless a diagnosis accurately predicts the future behavior of the patient, even on the next card of the Rorschach, it is clinically useless. His teaching guided all of my own and my students' diagnoses ever since then.

## Westward Bound: UCLA

Dr. Boardman got me through the doctoral program mostly by convincing me that I was not crazy. We remained close even after I moved to California. Before I left, he half-jokingly suggested the ultimate soother for my nervousness: "Get a two-way ticket to Los Angeles and come home if you can't handle it." Yet never having been out of the southeast, I was still uncomfortable about driving all the way to the Pacific in my little Volkswagen, headed for UCLA and my postdoctoral fellowship at the Brain Research Institute. My knowledge about the West was immediately exposed when I drove to the very end of old Route 66 in Santa Monica where it ran into the Pacific Ocean, stopped someone on the street, and asked "Where is the Golden Gate Bridge?" It appeared again the next morning at a café when I ordered scrambled eggs and grits and got back the question "Vasisgrrits?" Neither of us knew what the other was talking about, and I had to wait for a trip home to get my grits.

A year later I found myself in another life-determining crisis. I had done good work in my postdoc on the cardiophysiology of autism and also working with one of the few experts at the time in parent training as a possible alternative to psychoanalysis for children.

I had applied for a number of faculty positions in San Francisco, Pennsylvania, and New York, already with a sensational offer in hand to develop a new department of psychophysiology at the South Carolina Medical Center. I had given a talk there describing my research, and Charleston was where Sid had already taken a job.

One day Dr. Jim Simmons, the chief of UCLA Child Psychiatry, called me in his office for an unknown reason; I did not know him but he seemed to know me, or at least my reputation for sometimes useful blather. Four new tenure-track positions were opening up supported by the massive influx of California funding for mental retardation. I was confused when he asked if I was interested in any of them. Why me? I told him about my dilemma but said that if I did stay in Los Angeles (where at that time the smog was at its worst and I just wanted to see some trees and breathe clean air) I would prefer the outpatient child psychiatry position.

I sent a tape recording describing this meeting to Dr. Boardman after reducing my choices to the awesome-sounding freedom and prestige at UCLA or South Carolina at age twenty-seven. I could develop my own department in the Charleston research hospital, or start at the bottom of the ladder with a potential career at UCLA. I had already made many friends, but the opportunity back east offered a reconnection with Sid and wide recognition, without the smog.

In his usual quippy style, Dr. Boardman's only words on the tape were "Do you want to be a little fish in a big pond or a big fish in a little pond?" I didn't know why he thought that having a whole research wing in a new hospital all of my own was a little pond, but he had made his point. It was the feeling of once again being a "big fish" that bothered me. I was not ready. It also may have had something to do with my earlier quote from St. Paul: ". . . to every man that is among you, not to think of himself more highly than he ought to think . . ." And that's why I stayed put.

Another important reason I accepted the academic position at UCLA was the result of a random meeting with a senior faculty member in the hospital cafeteria. I told him about my conflicts and what I wanted to accomplish. He had graduated from the Department of Psychology at UCLA and knew the whole system, including the medical center, very well. I can't forget his words. "All I can tell you is this: I'm sure you have good offers somewhere else but there's one thing very special about being on the faculty at UCLA. No matter what you want to know, or when you need to know it, you can pick up a telephone that connects you to someone a short walk away on this campus who can answer your question." Amazing! What could possibly be better somewhere else? He seemed so convincing. I was so concerned about how little I knew, and there I was being told about the ultimate soother: quick, informed, and free answers for my little and big questions decades before Jimmy Wales dreamed up Wikipedia.

Armed with this intoxicating news, and then later what sounded like unlimited funding, and then Dr. Boardman's wisdom about being a little fish in a big pond, I was all set.

Dr. Boardman and I remained in touch, but three years later Nancy woke me before daybreak with a call from his wife. Bill had been broadsided on his way to campus by a drunk, red light-running college student, and was dead. For a long time I could not believe this had actually happened. He guided me and taught me many of the things I have gotten credit for in my professional life. And many of my clinical skills come from trying to imitate his genius as a diagnostician and therapist, which gave him a kind of immortality.

## I Can Do This!

It was in my first year in the child psychiatry outpatient department at UCLA Medical Center that I got an important new clue about the talking problem. At the Tuesday morning staff meetings I always sat in the back, listening to the usual difficulties and squabbles that occupy the staff of major hospitals in a very large city. I gradually got a handle on the repeating troublesome issues, but as the latest hire, contributed very little. Then one day the chief asked my opinion about some issue and the group found my answer helpful. After the meeting several staff social workers, nurses other doctors thanked me for my contribution. Suddenly I felt better. Perhaps my problem wasn't out-of-control talking; what if one of the reasons I talked so much because no one else in the room had something really interesting or important to contribute? Fortunately, this arrogance didn't last.

Yet after that, my demeanor in each meeting for a while was the same: sizing up the problems with controlled patience and then occasionally ending the meeting with something useful. I was on the way back to the initial strategy of trying to protect both the group and myself with modesty and refraining. It really felt like I could make an important contribution and experience an appropriate level of pride – at first.

But then I gradually slipped, without knowing about it, back to the role of a highly verbal consultant on many issues in the department. I was asked to take over the position of lecturer for third year medical students rotating through psychiatry. It was the easiest job I ever had because I had been so overtrained at the University of Georgia that I was able to give nearly the same lectures on child psychopathology for several years, each time with the same level of enthusiasm and good feedback.

So now the solution to my talking problem was again to teach while staying connected to the students, which meant at any time I wanted the focus off of me I could get them asking questions and then take the expert consultant role. I had temporarily conquered the panic problem with over-rehearsed, authoritative answers. Once again I would teach while staying closely connected to the small student group, which for me meant security, covered up by appearing to be more knowledgeable than I really was. And I got away with it.

Meanwhile, I was gaining increased animosity from my own Medical Psychology department staff because of the special research support and funding I was getting from Dr. Simmons. His indulgence made possible the creation of the very first Medical Center Parent Training Clinic. Since I was able to screen nearly every child coming through the outpatient clinic for potential treatment and research in my own clinic, I developed a very large database of troubled children and their troubled families. Within a couple of years I was asked to write a book, which became one of the first widely used parent training manuals. What followed were lots of anxious but well-received lectures and interesting travel adventures at home and abroad. Life finally seem to be settling down.

## Who Am I Kidding?

Why neither Dr. Simmons nor I saw our arrangement as a recipe for departmental administrative trouble I will never know. Because of my administrative lapses, I was actually contributing to my department's internal disharmony and time-wasting bickering that I openly complained about. Eventually I flunked out of academic

administration with the reputation of "not a good team member."
I left what was already a part-time academic position and joined
the clinical faculty, which meant that I could maintain my private
practice and supervise clinical psychologists and child psychiatry
fellows while holding onto my UCLA faculty status.

Years later, my final promotion was a plum job because it
meant I could do anything I wanted as "Associate Professor and
Permanent Clinical Faculty" in the Department of Psychiatry, and
I still occasionally teach, treat medical students and contribute at
promotion committees. What I did not anticipate was that when I
stopped accepting regular class teaching assignments and no longer
had any structure or outlet to speak without strict time limits, things
got worse. I started to rethink the whole problem of talking.

I was asked to join a group of psychoanalytically-oriented child
and adult therapists, led by the senior child analyst Joe Palombo who
flew into LA every three months from Chicago for all day meetings.
Many members were very involved and had much to contribute,
while others just came for social reasons and to be entertained. When
I joined I offered to make a presentation on "the biological basis of
the self," a hot topic at the time. It was very well received and again I
took it as license to have a lot to say in the group.

Then after a few years the group somehow started feeling stale
and Joe suggested we take time out in one meeting to talk about our
interest in the group and what we liked that kept us coming. Most
everyone spoke. For me the wisest member of the group was a San
Diego psychoanalyst, Sandy Shapiro, and I was eager to hear his
appraisal of the group process. Shockingly he said, "I come to hear
Hans talk," words that still evoke a full-bodied blow of embarrassment.

I knew Sandy was offering a compliment but that was the very
last thing I wanted to hear. That meeting was the official beginning

of the hate that still I associate with my lack of self-control even if I managed to impress some people. My whole life had been spent trying to find ways to be accepted and likable, to protect against self-loathing and defectiveness. I somehow always found these benefits even with the long history of setbacks and occasional psychological catastrophes. Now the benefits were far outweighed by the costs. Two members of the group, both old friends, stopped coming to the meetings, and I heard that one of them left because he was "tired of Miller dominating the discussions." I was beginning to seriously think that I might be ill with some kind of untreatable disorder.

## Dan

I made a lunch date with Dan Auerbach, my very first psychiatric resident when I joined the UCLA faculty. Dan had come to my office at the beginning of his third residency year, which was one of many options for residents. At first I thought he just wanted an easy ride in his last year, working in my Parent Training Clinic. Instead he became a major contributor both clinically and in a larger research project. His contribution was enough to get a publication and add to his academic profile. At last, I was able to be in the background while my students did the public talking.

By the time Dan came to work with me, he had already established himself as an expert in the field of Consultation Liaison. This meant he was equally skilled in medicine and psychiatry and was a go-to guy in any part of the hospital that needed complementary psychiatric and medical guidance. Emergency calls from various medical units would interrupt our meetings and in a few seconds I would shift from mentoring to admiring a real expert at work. I especially like the way he only spoke about what was immediately relevant, something always hard for me. If my talking was excessive, his was concise with no wasted words.

Over the years we stayed close as we lived our lives in parallel with mutual referrals of patients, diagnostic consultations, and many dinners. Similar to my relationship with Sid, Dan and I are always somewhere in the background as needed.

So with great expectations about getting help for my little problem, I took Dan to lunch. I told him what had been troubling me for years, which would have been hard for him and his wife to miss whenever we went out to dinner, though he never mentioned it. I told him my history of attempts to deal with the conflicts about needing to contribute, self-inflation, and recurring psychological distresses. He listened and then said, "Look, Hans, you are an overshooter who thinks too much." He was placing the emphasis on my nonstop thinking, not my speech, but somehow I couldn't separate the two. I had never heard of an "overshooter." It certainly sounded right, but was it a treatable illness?

We spent lunch going over a "differential diagnosis" which means thinking of everything that might contribute to the symptom and then dismissing anything that did not fit. In his usual quiet style, he listened as I went on about atypical OCD symptoms because of the compulsive part of my talking. I mentioned the neurological problem called "disinhibition" which occurs most often in elderly individuals with poorly functioning areas in the front of the brain. These patients simply do not have the ability to inhibit impulses. Supporting this idea, there was a positive finding on a brainwave EEG test when I was twenty-two.

Then we talked about brainstem overarousal of the motor cortex in the brain, which causes increased physical movement, poor regulation of impulses, and often goes along with attention deficit hyperactive disorder and manic states. Maybe something went wrong in my brain chemistry before birth. I described my old theory of overcompensation for feelings of inferiority. I even threw in the possibility of a genetic factor because my sister Martha also loved to talk (imagine a conversation between the two of us). But neither of us knew about other big talkers in the family, although recently I wondered if on the ancient human journey out of Africa we picked up a few genes from talkative Armenians or unstoppable Irish storytellers.

Then it was time for Dan's specialty, psychopharmacology. I had previously told him about my use of Valium for anxiety, which was only partially helpful for emotional overshooting. Of course he knew all about the latest medications for ADHD, OCD, mania, impulse control disorder, overexcitability, and all the rest. I tried them all in various doses. Each medication I tried definitely slowed me down but produced a sense of dullness with an unacceptable loss of vitality, creativity, and especially spontaneity. So much for my brain's match with modern chemistry.

So there it was. I either had an unusual medical, likely neurological issue, without an acceptable treatment, or a brain that had been permanently rewired by the soothing rewards of social success. As I mentioned earlier, I had a noticeable increase in compulsive talking after I stopped teaching. Perhaps my talking brain just needed an outlet. Also, things seemed to get worse as I got older. Whatever the cause, Dan tried his best but could do no better than give a name to my problem. He concluded by wondering if I had a "weird" brain chemistry that did not respond normally to the usual medications.

As a last resort I also tried a procedure called neurofeedback which can reduce overactive brain waves, but with no helpful results. I remembered what Dr. Boardman taught us about diagnosis. To be useful, it had to predict the future behavior of the patient. Dan's diagnosis certainly did that, because I am still an overshooter. But his conclusion never suggested what to do about it. I'm still looking.

At least I finally understood why Nancy's attempts to give me the discrete "timeout" signal rarely worked when she was in one of my audiences. After one talk, Nancy asked me if I knew how many times I had announced the ending of my lecture. I didn't know so she told me: four times I had said something like "now we need to wrap this up" but kept talking anyway. I also learned why I was at first frightened whenever taking the podium, then irritated if not enough people showed up, and then again worried when the auditorium filled up. When this happens now, it seems so ludicrous that I can laugh about it. What was not laughable was the likelihood that I would forever be stuck between both needing and fearing a lot of attention.

## My First Wider View

But what if my deepest theory about myself was flawed? I was coming to think that my ability to often appear entertaining and useful was not just a cover up. The problem could be a neurologically-based lack of normal restraint, and not only a defensive self-inflation habit. If so, the problem could shift to "So why am I so determined to believe I am defective? Where did I get my real problem, which was an extreme sensitivity to shame? Could the traumatic summer camp as a child and 'bullahead' still be at work"?

Then I came across a book by the Buddhist teacher Tara Brach called *Radical Acceptance*.

There, she teaches that the best cure for what feels like hopeless suffering is to embrace whatever is before you with an open mind and use it as an opportunity to be compassionate toward others and yourself. Tara and other teachers also taught how to just notice what is happening without judgment. I could understand the wisdom of this, but it was just too hard to put into practice. For whatever reason I could attach no meaning to this kind of self-compassion.

Tara also said that with practice, any compulsive behavior can often be reduced with mindfulness meditation and just becoming comfortable with the natural, unjudged flow of mental activity. With practice, mindfulness can allow quicker awareness of impulses, leading to more conscious options for self-control. So far, mindfulness has been my most successful effort to slow down and talk less. It is working but is very hard work because I have learned that my real problem is *thinking* too much. Excessive talking is just showing off in public. On the inside door of my writing studio are displayed two words in very large print from the Buddhist teacher Pema Chodron, who wrote *When Things Fall Apart*:

## REFRAIN, REFRAIN

# MORE BEGINNINGS

TALKING HAS TAKEN me a long way in life, but with very mixed blessings. Yet it was another of my compensatory skills that became my real salvation: the ability to quickly understand and predict other's feelings with confidence about what to say before I started talking. This same hard-earned degree of empathy, applied with all-out efforts to reduce the suffering of others I cared about, gave me a career and standard of living I never dreamed possible.

As far back as I can recall I had a knack for understanding the problems of people and especially children, and what it took to help. It probably got its start somewhere around age 6, when I regularly heard my mother and father arguing. Following my mother's favorite admonishment, "If you can't say something nice, don't say anything at all", a rule that she herself sometimes broke, I would just stand quietly between my parents and wait it out. It worked – I was a good soother but was left with problems later on anytime there was social conflict directed at me.

Also, others have mostly liked what I could do well, whether it throwing a knuckleball, playing tennis, the guitar and cello or being a good debater because I tried to make sure I was one step ahead of the opposition. But I continued to make talking mistakes, such as saying the wrong things at the wrong times and alienating people with unnecessary arrogance. Either I was successfully *impressing* others under the self-serving pretense of *expressing* myself, or punishing those who suffered the misfortune of teasing or criticizing me. You were either charmed or turned off by scared little Hans.

With another look to the past, I can find many model scenes that shaped my personality. Most of them are my versions of what every person encounters: fear and hope.

# LEARNING TO BE AFRAID

*Tell me what you fear and I will tell
you what has happened to you.*

—D. W. Winnicott

## The Train with the Giant Red Light: Four Years Old

I WAS LIVING on Ponce de Leon Avenue in Atlanta in an old and
dark apartment. I was trying to get out of my mind a really bad dream
from the previous night; a very loud train with a giant red light and
the front of the engine was coming through the walls. I did not know
why, but I was much more frightened by the red light than the train
itself. Before I went to bed that night, I knew I did something terrible
because my father had to take out his belt. When that was over my
mother led me outside in the night, crossed the street, and sat on the
steps of a large public park. Under a streetlight at the entrance, she
explained that my father was very angry because he drank too much
beer and maybe he would be settled down when we got back. It was
very cold, but I didn't want to go home.

## The Dynamite Cap: Five Years Old

I was the great explorer, happily looking for something new to do with my older brother in the front yard of my father's friend on a Sunday afternoon. He was building something a few feet away and I began to get bored. I climbed around in the backseat of my father's car and found three little copper tubes, pinched together at the ends. I had no idea what they were for, so I kept looking and there was a hammer on the floor of the car. I took the hammer and the tubes outside, laid one of them on a brick, hit it hard on one side until it was flat, then the other side, and then smacked it hard in its bloated middle. It exploded with a *BAMM!* and I was suddenly lying on my back with my face covered with blood. Fully conscious, I ran screaming into the house; my father saw me and yelled, picked me up like a football, rushed to the car, and then to some hospital.

All this I remember perfectly. I had ignited a blasting cap which my father used to blow tree stumps out of the way of the road he was building as a civil engineer. A piece of metal shaped like a "W" had lodged in my skull a half inch above my left eye. A lot of people kept talking about how lucky I was to be alive. My next memory is sometime later, being in the kitchen of our little apartment as my mother, a nurse, expertly helped the dynamite cap work its way out of my forehead. She washed it and put it in a little jar by the window so I got to look at it every day. But I was still in trouble. How could I be a great explorer if I might die at any moment?

# LEARNING TO HOPE

*Once you choose hope, anything is possible.*

—*Christopher Reeve*

## The Thermometer: Six Years Old

I WAS LIVING in Lakeland, Florida, and one morning woke up late, hurting all over with no desire to go to school. My older brother was already up and gone. I clearly remember having difficulty getting out of the bed and calling for my mother in the kitchen fixing breakfast. I yelled out something like, "Mommy, I don't feel good," hoping she would come. Instead, I heard her yell back, "Sonny, you know where the thermometer is" without ever seeing her face. I dutifully dragged myself into the bathroom, found the thermometer, shook it out the way she had taught me, stuck it under my tongue, and went back to bed. I have no memory of what happened next, but I know this: as usual, I did what I was told because whatever she said must've been the right thing to do.

For years I did not know what I was really after when I tried to get my mother's attention, because as the trauma therapist Bessel van der Kolk and others have emphasized, *the body keeps the score.* An unconscious tally was being kept on the number of neglected basic needs that would weigh heavily on my future; *self-soothing* was fast becoming *self-care by compliance*. This was the beginning of hope. But I was already at risk for later suffering from a growing accumulation of little traumas.

## The Orange Crates: Eight Years Old

It took Christopher Reeve only minutes to go from *Superman* to a special needs cripple. And it wasn't kryptonite that did him in; on May 27, 1995, Reeve was thrown from his horse, which caused an injury resulting in complete paralysis from his neck down. Yet in his quote above about hope, he revealed his super courage and determination that hope can be an active rejection of being a victim.

I had never thought of hope this way, but it reminded me of my most influential psychoanalytic teacher Donald Winnicott when he said "Hopeless is what happens when the only thing left is hope." I now believe Reeve and Winnicott were right. But looking back, long before I was mature enough to understand the power of choice, the closest I could come to feeling hope was relying on overlearned resignation and duty.

I was in the third grade in Douglas, Georgia. The year was about half over, and six months before we had moved, because my father had to change jobs. I always assumed it was to build a new road or bridge somewhere in Georgia. Six months before that, the same thing happened, so this was a pattern. I didn't know it at the time, but I was about to learn something new about why we had to move twice every year. It was dinnertime and I was hanging out as usual by the front door where our small bookcase contained the World Book Encyclopedias. One evening I was absorbed with a picture of a very funny-looking man sneezing out a cloud of water vapor that the label said was over a hundred miles an hour.

Suddenly I was alerted by the familiar sound of my father driving up and approaching the front door. One glance at his face and I was already scared about what would surely happen next. A loud argument followed in the kitchen and then I knew exactly what to do: get out the orange crates and start packing the encyclopedias. My father walked by me mumbling something about "going up the street for a minute," always his code for getting a beer in the local pub.

Mother collected me and my brother and said that daddy was upset about something bad happening with someone at work and he could not go back there. So we had to move. I went to my room and started drawing more pictures of flying saucers. It was about then that I began to feel the self-soothing value of living on autopilot, and trying to stay calm until a new problem showed up. Then I would find a new solution. It felt good to be able to handle things like this. Maybe I could be something like a missionary after all. Or maybe, I thought much later, a philosopher.

I suppose that because my mother grew up in the depression era, she survived and succeeded early on by being independent, which became her philosophy for raising children. It's not a bad philosophy when it is matched by enough up-close soothing and positive guidance. But looking back, somehow soothing events like my orange crate routine only intensified the yearning for another moment of perfect, devoted soothing that I could hold on to, like a few years before in my grandmother's lap on her front porch.

## Grandma's Lap

Christmas, mid-1980s. I was on a Delta flight from Los Angeles to Atlanta to spend the holidays with my mother and sister, envying the very classy African American woman who happened to have the window seat. I also could not help noticing that she was reading Psychology Today magazine. After a while I asked her something about it and before long learned that her son was about to get his PhD in psychology. I told her that I was a psychologist; we got into Christmas talk and going home, and then a very strange thing happened.

Charlene was a lawyer living in Chicago but her childhood home was in Richland, Georgia, where after visiting Los Angeles, she was headed for a family reunion to celebrate the season. I clearly remember the stunned stare between the two of us when I told her how I spent Christmases, summers, and my entire second grade living with my grandparents in Richland.

Before long I got up the courage to ask Charlene about her childhood in Richland, and wanting to hear about her journey from Richland to Chicago. She got a bigger shock when I introduced myself as Hans Miller. She said, "You are Tom Miller's boy? Do you remember my grandmother Freddie?" When I said yes it was all we could do to keep from shouting and hugging. Charlene's grandmother was my father's nanny and then years later, still working for my grandmother, she took care of my brother and me when we lived with my grandmother. All those stories flashed back.

Not only did I remember Freddie, but I had once spent a very hot summer day in her sharecropper's home in the middle of a giant cotton field. It must have been very special because as Charlene was talking, I recalled the unforgettable sweet kitchen smells of her cabin, which brought back memories of Freddie cooking fried chicken for Sunday dinner at my grandmother's house. Sometimes when I got home from Sunday school she would even let me help out. Where else could a seven-year-old town kid learn how to chase down and tackle a fat barnyard hen, wring its neck, and pluck its feathers?

And then there were Freddie's grandchildren, one of which was a boy my age ready to go out and play. Hiding behind him was a little girl, who could only have been Charlene. Now on the plane, she recalled wonderful memories about her grandmother's life with "Miss Mattie" and my father. Sometimes the odds don't matter.

Everyone's grandmother is somehow special. Grandma Mattie Miller always favored my older brother Tommy because he was named after her real favorite, my father Thomas. I remember how strange it seemed that she spoiled him one minute and switched him the next. But none of this mattered to me: my grandmother was the ultimate authority in the family and to her I was the sweet and quiet grandson who always obeyed. In return, grandma taught me the difference between love and duty, something I had somehow missed at home.

Every night at sundown after dinner, I would find myself on her front porch swing with my head in her lap, a feeling that would take years to fully recapture. Someone on the porch would ritually say, "Now don't you to go to sleep" and my grandma would ritually reply, "Hans is just resting his eyes." No other childhood memory was so perfect and it became my very private Holy Grail. All mothers and grandmothers soothe, tease, tolerate, and sometimes punish. As far as it mattered to me, my grandma just soothed, a model scene that kept me going for years.

The problem of course is the scarcity of perfect warm laps. Every psychology student is expected to learn why this mostly unsuccessful search for a much valued reward is so persistent, in the hope that it will later be useful in a life of science or clinical practice. The topic especially appealed to me. I spent many graduate school nights planning new experiments for my undergraduate students and trying new approaches. One effect of scarce soothing and the inflated fantasies it causes is famously known to students as the "Zeigarnik Effect" after its discoverer, which in the simplest terms just means that *unfinished business is never forgotten.* This rang many bells for me.

Another explanation for human's excessive emotional craving is straight out of the much more famous "Skinner box." We used this apparatus to perform experiments on animals to find out how learning and forgetting occurs. It starts out by having a very hungry rodent or pigeon press a bar or peck a button to get a much needed food reward. However, after initial training the animal is only rewarded on a *random* basis. The animal can never again predict when it will be satisfied.

This was one of those lessons with a lifetime payoff for me as a student-scientist, patient, and then psychotherapist. Needs that are unpredictably satisfied make the perfect recipe for this automatic and deep belief: *"Just keep pressing the bar, maybe next time you'll get it."* Replace the rat with an aging woman using her Social Security money to waste quarters in a Las Vegas slot machine, or any addict or loved-starved person, and you've got the picture.

My grandmother and mother didn't know they had an oversensitive little boy or intend any harm, but for different reasons they both trained a grandchild and child destined to become addicted to a lifetime of unsuccessful foraging for love. It was many years later that I was able to learn about the physical basis for this addiction, and all others.

Addictions result from the brain's natural pleasure-related chemical *dopamine* being unnaturally hijacked by any excessive need, such as craving devoted care. When this pattern is repeated, there comes a time when no amount of dopamine is enough to be satisfying. The person is hooked. What then happens is an otherwise free-willed individual is turned into a puppet, controlled by temporary self-soothing which is never enough and often becomes a self-destructive habit. This one finding from the laboratories of psychologists and neuroscientists may explain more about unhealthy emotional lifestyles, including mine, than any other.

# Searching for the True Self

THESE STORIES OF my mother and grandmother contain two of this book's story themes: a once-known salvation from unmet yearnings and the addictive search to recover the moment in any form. They helped me to understand how people like me and a lot of others became so filled with unfinished business, self-loathing, and private yearnings that we became self-protection experts. Anything I could do that brought me closer to the soothing feeling of being cared for, whether it was a nurse's warm hand on my arm after surgery, the gratitude of a successfully treated family, or even the applause of baseball fans, was also biologically rewarded and permanently installed in my nervous system as hope.

Is the resulting change in the child's body-brain more of the positive or negative kind? How does this parental implant show itself in the child's daily life and long-term self-beliefs? It took many years, much therapy, writing this book, and the enduring influence of the British child psychoanalyst Donald Winnicott for me to find answers for some of these questions about my life.

Winnicott's new approach to child development in the 1950s and '60s was based on what he called the "true" and "false" self. Psychological health is only possible when parents, especially the "good-enough mother", regardless of gender, understand the importance of the infant's spontaneous gestures on the way to establishing his or her own selfhood.

When this "true" self is facilitated and guided to generally conform to the norms of the local culture, its natural abilities and creativity flourish and contentment is possible. But too much forced compliance robs the child of his or her unique existence. It can become a setup for extreme versions of protesting noncompliance, or worse, an unfulfilling, nonauthentic life and even suicide. This is the "false" self. Sadly, this is the cultural norm for many places I have been. This may be because the true selves of many parents have themselves been discouraged by overcontrolling parents and cultures.

Winnicott repeatedly emphasized that the diagnosis of a false self is often more important than the patient's traditional psychiatric diagnosis. This was a lesson that influenced a great deal of my psychotherapy with young and old people. Later, in Part 2, "Practicing," I will describe the treatment of a suicidal teenage cello player named Monica. I am sure that I could not have helped her as well without understanding, and helping her parents understand, her emptiness and emotional nonexistence as a "false self." Yet I did my best work with Monica when I followed one of Winnicott's biographers, who said, Winnicott's genius as a child therapist was not just because he understood his patients, but because his patients could understand him."

After Winnicott, the psychiatrist Daniel Stern again changed the landscape of psychoanalysis in his 1985 book *The Interpersonal World of the Infant*. There he forever ended prescientific speculations about infant obsessions with sex and aggressive instincts by confirming the power of infants to actively organize their human attachments in the social world. This instinct for pursuing soothing interactions with others is now believed to determine the way we respond to sexual and aggressive impulses. Most sexually addicted or violent patients did not start out that way. They started out with normal yearnings for a secure connection with a mature and healthy person and it didn't work out the way it was supposed to; the child after that was derailed by short-term addictive solutions for despair.

Stern also wrote the book that has always been required reading for my psychology interns and child psychiatry fellows: *The Diary of a Baby*. As I described earlier, the book begins with the story of a six-months old child, safely alone in the crib, completely absorbed and soothed by a patch of early-morning warm sunlight. The child is already self-soothing, but only because he or she feels safe, thanks to a steady diet of dedicated soothing by devoted others.

I also prescribe *The Diary of a Baby* for all parents of young children. I tell them how much they and their children will profit if they keep the book close by, taking in and regularly applying its messages. Here is how Stern described what my group therapist Dr. Gordon Saver once referred to as psychological "chunks":

*I see striking evidence not only of the power of such parental constructions to affect a child, but the strength of the parents' need to invent the child's inner experience . . . They compose for their baby an ongoing biography, which they constantly consult . . . Psychological problems may arise when a parent's fantasy of a child is, and what that child actually experiences, are contradictory.*

Saver, Winnicott, and Stern were referring to the parents' self-beliefs and behavioral habits that produce their child's greatest longings and fears, which then become part of the child's basic personality structure.

These quickly hardened parental signatures present themselves at different times in the child's early life. I wasn't conscious of my father's most important influences until I was studying psychology in college, and I never stopped feeling the effects of my mother's emotional lessons.

In my case, I grew up with a mostly successful false self, made up of a compliant self and a smart-talking personality, driven to please everyone. My true self only showed itself in moments of protesting, despair, and spontaneous joy in things like playing baseball. Many people make it through their entire lives as psychological phonies, protecting their fragile true selves with a strong intellect and a nonending collection of daily hassles that keep them from looking inward.

## Mommy, Daddy, and Me Once Again

> *We come from a tribe of fallible people, prisoners of our*
> *own destructiveness, and we have endured to tell the story*
> *without judgment and to get on with our lives.*
>
> —William Zinsser

As I just mentioned, moms and dads unknowingly implant what Dr. Saver called a "chunk of themselves" into every little boy and girl. The exceptions are parents who consciously attempt to preplan their child's destiny, often before birth, which almost never works out for anyone. Either way, every little boy and girl actively takes in and holds parts of their parents' personality forever.

In any case, the child has no choice but to digest his or her parents, with their most meaningful good and bad influences, even if he or she later rebels. Usually it's real, but this happens also with orphans who only have stories and fantasies about their unknown parents. The reality-based *model scenes* that shape our lives can only do their work because of these underlying and unconscious parental chunks that create our expectations.

The model scenes and chunks that I think about are: How much of the child's mind and brain is being influenced? Do the results from healthy or harsh parental chunks make children stronger or weaker?

Once after winning some playground contest on a summer morning I came bursting in the back screen door of our apartment, sat in my father's seat at the lunch table, and loudly announced, "Got any half-decent food for lunch today?" The next thing I knew I was on my back on the floor with a stinging face and my mother standing over me. "Listen here, in my house we don't have half-decent food, everything I make for you all is *always decent*, never half-decent. You can get up from the floor when you apologize."

It was the only time my mother ever struck me, and one of the best lessons I ever got from anyone. Years later when I described this to my therapist Dr. Boardman, he said, "Good for her, every child needs one good whack sooner or later to really understand right and wrong." The model scene built by this chunk of my mother taught me a lifetime lesson about how to treat people with decency.

A very different kind of model scene happened close to that apartment's screen door from the kitchen to the backyard. Mother and I were in the midst of some argument, probably about me wanting to go play ball instead of doing my homework. Words were passed and something she said hurt my feelings. I opened the screen door and headed out. She asked me where I was going and I said, "Leave me alone." What happened next still rings in my ears; she said, "Okay, you're alone," and slammed the door. I was terrified. There was no later discussion of what happened. But I learned everything I would ever need to know about feelings of abandonment.

Then years later in college while spending the weekend at home, I had my first full-blown panic attack in the middle of the night; difficulty breathing, sweating, and trembling after being screamed at by an angry girlfriend earlier. I remember being certain that I was about to die. All I knew to do was to go in and wake up my mother. She took one look at me, asked me to sit on her bed and wait, and brought back a half pint of whiskey from the kitchen cabinet. A few swallows and I quickly settled down. She told me to stay on her bed until I felt okay and got back to sleep, which I did. Then she woke me and told me to go back to my room, but to call her if I got scared again. The best nurse I ever knew did it again. Perfect soothing. As a bonus, I learned that anyone of the opposite sex whom I depended on could be the source of both hurt and salvation.

At another time, while traveling from our home to visit our grandparents, it was my father who did something that kept my head spinning for years. Even though Dad grew up in a totally segregated town, I once heard that as a youngster he was friends with a black boy "on the other side of the tracks." But all I remember was extreme racism and the worst kind of bigotry; he hated Jews, Catholics, Italians, gypsies and especially African Americans. In graduate school I even invented the term "negative identification" to describe my total disgust with Dad's minority hatreds, and the origin of my own extremely liberal thinking.

On this trip to visit Grandma, my brother and I were sitting in the backseat traveling along a blacktop highway while Mom and Dad were arguing about something in the front seat. Perhaps because of the tension I became very disturbed when he suddenly pulled off the road onto the red clay and hit the brakes hard. He jumped out of the car, ran across the road and down a hill to an old sharecropper's shack. Frightened, I leaned forward and asked my mom what was going on. She said something like "just watch." Then to my utter disbelief, he banged on the screen door until a huge black man met him and after a brief conversation invited him in the house. Within minutes the two men exited a rear door, both with shotguns headed into the woods. A short while later came the sounds of shotguns booming.

After another long time they appeared in a meadow casually toting their weapons on their shoulders and laughing together. He stayed in the house for a while and finally came back to the car, got in, and without a word off we went down the road to Richland. I could not relax until later that night on grandma's front porch when my mother explained that Dad had seen a large antlered deer dash across the road in front of the car into the woods behind the house. How did going after the deer interrupt his rabid racism? It was all very, very confusing.

Parental chunks can have their unconscious effect almost immediately, but often become fully conscious only during self-exploration, such as therapy, meditation, or honest conversations with trusted others. Sometimes all someone needs to say is "Tell me about your parents." This is how I learned about my mommy and daddy chunks, with many of their influences remaining unconscious, but causing fear and hope, for years.

Other model scenes found their way into my bones and stand out in my mind today. Many of them greatly helped in trying to understand my parents' good and not so good influences.

My father was a prince among paupers not by wealth but popularity. He grew up in one of the most important families in Richland with his sister Leah. Thanks to his genes and a proud, over-indulging mother, he was not only the best looking and brightest boy in town, but something of a playboy in college. As told to us by our mother, Dad's best friend and fraternity brother at the University of Georgia was Herman Talmadge, later governor and the son of the state Governor Eugene Talmadge.

In the spring of his senior year, Thomas and Herman embarked on a "panty raid" in the girls' dorm by climbing up the wall to their bedroom. Things went bad; the boys were hauled into the dean's office; Herman's dad got him off; my father took the hit for the whole misadventure and was expelled from college only two months before graduation.

Dad moved from Athens over to Atlanta, enrolled in Georgia Tech and became an engineer with the national Core of Engineers, and spent World War II building the infrastructure of Puerto Rico.

Then years later my grandma Mattie Miller collapsed and died in the new Richland, Georgia hospital kitchen where she was the dietitian. Much like a near-total energy power shutdown, my father's spirit collapsed and he never fully recovered. For the remainder of my childhood and beyond, he was in a state of psychological weakness and dependency with few defenses except flashes of false pride and his latest beer. I could see that he wanted to do fatherly things, but even with all of his intelligence, he just didn't seem to understand much about parenting, which unsurprisingly became my professional specialty. Or perhaps his own emotional needs were so great that he couldn't focus on much of anything else. But he did have his moments.

For example, on some occasions he would round up us boys and sit before us in the living room with palms together, full of different coins. Money was very scarce then and I think he did this on payday. It was always a surprising peak experience for both of us. With blindfolds on and taking turns, he instructed us to pick the first coin we touched from his cupped hands. We would then go into our bedroom and compare riches. I don't recall any other time when my father seemed so happy.

## My Helen Keller Moment: Discovering Abstraction

On another occasion of Dad's fatherly intentions when I was eleven, he asked if I wanted to be his carpenter assistant on a construction project. But even before the work started, he introduced me to an idea so powerful that it still organizes much of my life whenever I am solving problems as a clinician, philosopher-neuroscientist, or in my personal life.

We never owned a home, so I can only guess that he got special permission to add a small extra room onto our house. One night before the construction was to begin, I found a large blue sheet of paper spread out on his desk with the perfect printing style I've never seen except in engineers. When I asked him about the drawing, he said it was the "blueprint" plan for the room. This seemed like magic to me. How could this drawing be the same as a playroom?

He explained that everything about the room had been shrunk down to fit the paper covering his desk, but I still didn't make the link to the real room. Dad said, "Just imagine that one inch on the blueprint will be the same as one foot in the real room. The drawing is an abstract model for the real thing." I think I said something really dumb like, "But how can you be sure it will work?" He mentioned some new words to describe the leap from paper to the real room, but all I later wrote down was "abstract model." I knew all about building model airplanes, but didn't know why models were "abstract." I later found that this was because I had definite mental pictures and feelings about models, but *no feelings* for "abstract."

I do know that when he went to work the next day, I took a yardstick and measured one inch on the drawing and then one foot in length where the room was going to be. Still confused, I looked up the word *abstract* in our Encyclopedia Americana. I don't remember much except something like, "hard to understand because it is only an idea in the mind" and something about a *general idea* that had many examples, like "money" and "tree." There was a picture of different-looking trees, followed by a simple sketch of a tree with all its basic parts: roots, trunk, branches, and leaves. Somehow, the "tree" word was about an *idea*, not about actual trees.

Dad's model of the room was abstract because it wasn't the real thing; it was just an idea that with some changes could be a model for any room. The blueprint was an "abstract idea" and "model" for our room that would soon be physically real.

Somehow I started to have a vague feeling about the blueprint. As I studied it, I could almost feel the presence of a room in my imagination, because I could attach a small feeling to it. To really understand "abstraction," I had to learn how to have the same feeling about the blueprint that I had for the imagined new room. Abstraction suddenly seemed to have a lot of power.

It occurred to me that anytime I could make a good model that felt like something I already knew about, like our idea of the playroom, I could imagine and maybe build anything. I had discovered abstract thinking and immediately loved the thought that everything was open to being modeled and expanded to something greater.

I could barely contain my excitement about this new mental leap, but when I tried to tell my father about it, he just said, "Yup, that's the way it works." My ideas about abstraction all finally came together when I told a teacher at school about the blueprint and the real room. Reconstructing today what he said back then, he seemed to repeat what the encyclopedia said. Abstraction is hard to learn about because abstract ideas, like my father's idea of what he could do with the blueprint, are in the mind and not in the world.

Many years later I learned that the abstract idea of "money" included all real coins and banknotes, and the "coin" idea contained pennies and silver dollars, and so on (there are many kinds of pennies). After all that sunk in, my imagination went wild because learning about abstraction became a whole new way about thinking about how the world works. I could never again see a single car, or person, or even planet without knowing and feeling something about all cars and people and planets. I could feel my perception stretching to include more and more things in the world. By then, I had discovered *categories* as well as abstractions.

Actually, I already knew about abstract thinking and categories, I just didn't know that I knew. Monkeys quickly learn that any red fruit means edible. Water is just another idea and word that people made up to describe clear drinkable wet stuff. Three-year-olds can say "I want some candy" and settle for a wide variety of specific candies. Every six-year-old knows that all balls and oranges are "round," and that a hammer and saw are both "tools." "Roundness" and "tools" are both abstract category names with many examples. But it takes several more years before a child *knows that he knows* about "roundness" and can talk in terms of categories made up of many familiar possibilities, such as "Can *we* go to the *movies* and get some *pizza*."

Many years later, while writing a chapter on the origins of abstract reasoning and language, I remembered Helen Keller. She was a blind, deaf, and speechless eight-year-old who expressed in her autobiography the joyful discovery of abstraction much better than I ever could.

*We walked down the path to the well house, attracted by the fragrance of the honeysuckle with which it was covered. Someone was drawing water and my teacher placed my hand under the spout. As the cool stream gushed over one hand she spelled out in the other palm the other the word "water," first slowly, and then rapidly. I stood still, my whole attention fixed upon the motions of her fingers.*

*Suddenly I felt the misty consciousness of something forgotten - a thrill of returning thoughts; and somehow the mystery of language was revealed to me. I knew then that "w-a-t-e-r" meant the wonderful cool something that was flowing over my hand. That living word awakened my soul, gave it flight, hope, joy, set it free! . . . I learned a great many new words that day... In a flash I knew that the word was the name of the process that was going on in my head. This was my first conscious perception of an abstract idea.*

An image below shows Helen's teacher Anne Sullivan making letter marks on her left palm.

My own model scene at age eleven was just as touching because I could feel myself absorbing something wonderful from my father. And it was equally explosive and lasting in its effects, right up to the present time. It even became a way to understand the leap that made us fully human, something I had been researching for two decades. Like Helen, we all mentally jumped from unnamed things in the world to a system of named *symbols* that allowed us to communicate with whole sentences of linked words.

So these are the steps that made possible the human "Great Leap Forward" some 40,000 years ago. Once we could assign agreed-upon labels for thinking and talking about things like water, we could also share ideas about ways to store water in containers, increasing our chances for survival. Our thinking, imagination, and language were jumpstarted onto a road with no end.

When I was first studying neuroscience, what I had learned about abstraction also explained the birth of self-consciousness and how the brain together with social living makes the idea of a "self"

possible. For example, one part of my brain is specialized to become
aware of the simple feel of a raw physical sensation such as a touch.
Another close-by brain area picks up this sensation and announces
to my conscious brain that the sensation of being touched belongs to
me and no one else. *I exist*. The feeling of possessing a "self" pops into
consciousness; this is "self-awareness."

As for me, knowing about higher and higher levels of abstract
thinking was the perfect antidote for my lifelong feeling of
powerlessness. There was great strength in understanding the big
picture, and I vowed to never stop looking for it.

For example, abstraction gave me a model to build a wider view
of my personal angels and demons, allowing me to begin the quest
to embrace all good and bad intentions as a single idea about "being
human." I was no longer puzzled by my dad's mixture of kinship
and racial hatred; both were features of his humanness. Sooner or
later, almost everyone learns about abstraction, but my exciting and
soothing discoveries got their start because a boy wanted to think
like his father.

An even more powerful scene hit home long after it actually
happened, but when it did, it felt like a doomsday prediction from my
mother, which I took to be a prediction about me. It would not have
had so much force without what came before.

Sometime after the room was built when I was about twelve years
old, I got to see what my mother had often described as my father's
"weakness." One night I answered the door of our modest apartment

in some Georgia town and a man asked for him. Here's what I recall when my father heard about the visitor.

Father: "I can't."

Mother: "Thomas, you have to, he'll take the car if you don't talk to him right now"!

Father: (Flailing his arms, shaking, collapsing on the floor against the wall holding his head) "I can't, I can't do it."

I went to my room and covered my ears and then it was over. I'm pretty sure he went to work the next day, even without the family car, because I was waiting for him to come home so I could see if he was okay, which he was. Somehow he retained his southern aristocratic endurance to rebound, even if briefly.

Then, seven years later when I was a junior at the University of Georgia, I got a call from my mother. She lived in Atlanta close to my older brother Tommy and I lived about sixty miles away. She calmly said, "Your father has finally cracked up. Hitchhike home as soon as you can and use my car to take him to the State Hospital at Milledgeville." I didn't give it much thought except to ask, "Tommy is right there with his car, why can't he do it?" She said my brother could not do things like that and it had to be me.

So I hitchhiked to Atlanta, picked up her car and my father and drove him down to the mental hospital, and checked him in as a voluntary admission. As usual, he was in good spirits and had no objections. I'm fairly sure he was thinking in terms of the free room and board and some kind of brief oasis from his life on the road. I went back to the car and for a moment glanced back at the building entrance, I think for the purpose of saying good-bye. But then something very weird happened.

Suddenly, it was as if I had some sort of zoom lenses in my eyes. I could see the red bricks in the building, and one in particular in the greatest detail, right down to the individual grains of sand and clay in the brick. My vision was extraordinary and was never more sharp and clear before or since that moment. I was more fascinated than anything else and did not relate the strange eyesight to what was going on. I spent some time on the trip back home not analyzing, but just marveling at what seemed like some extraordinary ability.

It was not until later, in graduate school, that I bragged about my remarkable vision to a clinical supervisor, who said it was a classic example of the supersensory symptoms of acute dissociation. In other words, the only way I could handle the events at the hospital was to psychologically escape from what was going on with a momentary superpower. The "hit" that unintentionally came from my mother took its toll later when I started thinking about a very scary chunk of my father that might be somewhere inside me, waiting to explode.

Dad stayed in the mental hospital for about two weeks and then once again hit the road, regularly cycling through the places my mother was living at the time. Several times a year I would get another call from Mom to meet Dad at some down-and-out hotel coffee shop in a Greyhound bus stop. I never said no. There he would be, smoking a Camel cigarette with head up high, working on a fresh legal pad with a newly sharpened #2 pencil, optimistically planning his next move.

We would talk for a while and I would buy him a bus ticket to another town with a hopeful part-time job at an engineering office. I developed a habit of always glancing back at him after we parted, and sure enough there he would always be, practically marching toward the bus, chin up. Now, as I write this, a very odd question comes to mind: "Who was this guy?"

What I am sure about are my father's inadequate, anxious traits and bouts of fragility that stayed with me. Once at UCLA I was dating a very well-off occupational therapist, who was accustomed to a living style that eventually played a role in our breakup. We took off one weekend for San Francisco, but because I had discovered a flophouse hotel in Oakland that I was drawn to, we went there for the night. She objected but I persisted, excusing it as an adventure in the old way of traveling.

I never told her how comfortable I was with the old beds, spacious high ceilings, and yellowing window drapes, and most of all the coffee shop with cigarette and fresh bacon smells from the past. I still don't know if I loved my father because no matter how he tried, he needed a lot of protection from the world. Or maybe it was because every son must find some way to stay connected to his father.

## Discovering the Moving Goalpost Syndrome

The only thing I learned about mother's early life was, according to her, the only important thing. She spoke often about how she worshiped her father, "The best man who ever lived." When she was twenty-four, he suddenly died of a heart attack, and based on what I later realized, no other man would ever be able to match up to him. The only time she ever wavered was when she sorrowfully talked about being a nurse at Warm Springs, Georgia when her new hero, Franklin Roosevelt, died there in 1945. What I got from this was that no other man should ever apply for the job of trying to fully please her. But for my first twenty-five years, I never stopped trying.

I got other doses of her high standards. After I became very fond of a girl sitting next to me in class in high school, she gave me a picture of herself and I brought it home to show Mother. I was hoping that my new friend would also be my very first real girlfriend, but Mom said in words I can never forget, "What is that little mole down on her chin? I think you can do better than that."

So there we have a fully loaded chunk of my mom: a force that would keep me scouring the earth in search of the good enough girl or woman, and always left with unmet yearnings. I lost count of the psychoanalytic meanings given to Mother's words by different therapists as they tried to understand my troubled love life.

I did get something good from this unsolvable frustration: it was the discovery of the "moving goalpost syndrome." Here's how the syndrome works: son gets lots of degrees and attention, always moving up. Then one day not long after arriving in California, he receives his PhD diploma in the mail and proudly calls Mom, knowing that at last he has made her happy. She says, "Good for you, sonny, now what's next?" Son can't talk except to say, "Talk to you later," hangs up, grabs a beer, and takes a long walk on the beach.

It wasn't all bad. I knew at some point I would have to set my own standards. And there came a time when I accepted my mom for who she was and then was able to make very good use of what I learned from her.

The moving goalpost syndrome comes up regularly in my treatment of patients who often live their lives in frustration and confusion. Only a few days ago, a seventeen-year-old patient named Justin asked me if I could get his mother to cut him "some slack." Before the session ended, he decided that what he really needed from his mom was only some kind of recognition for his efforts. No matter what he did, his mom wanted more. Justin kept asking "What's so bad about making Bs in school?" He had always thought of himself as a B student but neither of his parents thought that was good enough.

When I described the moving goalpost syndrome, he said, "You mean there's a name for this? Why is she like that?" He was quick to make a link between his nagging mother and her failed attempts to help Justin's older brother, whom I had treated years earlier. The brother had an extreme version of mental and emotional lethargy, which prevented him from doing almost any of his work or caring about anything. His parents tried, but even with clear evidence from neuropsychological testing about his learning problems, they could never give up on the notion that he was lazy and capable of much more. But none of this insight about his family helped Justin. He just wanted to find a way to feel good enough for his mother.

The syndrome came up again for me in my fifties, when I fell madly in love with the cello. I took many lessons and even was invited to play in a small chamber music group, where I was determined to perform well enough to please our group's director. My first problem was something called "musical dyslexia," which meant that I am basically blind to the meanings of musical symbols on the page.

Fortunately, I was good at learning by ear so that if a teacher played the piece once, I could quickly memorize it and fake my way through performances using the printed notes to tell me *when* to play. Of course the inevitable time came, when just before a performance our director handed us new music and said she had changed her mind about the program. Thankfully it was a predictable chamber piece by Bach. At one point in the performance the violist sitting next to me leaned over and whispered, "Are you ad-libbing?" But I survived that evening because of my ability to make a chosen few distinct and correct notes.

My second problem was that this ability for good musical note making came by way of cello boot camp. It was drilled in by my teacher, a cellist with the Los Angeles Symphony. This was his somewhat less than loving style: "Okay, Hans, you hit the middle of the note. Now hit the *middle of the middle* of the note!" No matter how hard I tried, there was absolutely nothing I could do to please this man. Next time I will get a teacher's name off the wall at the cello store and take my chances.

For many of my patients, I never found much of a cure for the moving goalpost syndrome. However, I may have discovered a reason for the lack of cure in the middle of a long run up our canyon road: it occurred to me that in my mother's case, she never had any *intention* to stop moving the goalpost. I never had a chance. But more importantly, even when my patients were somewhat helped by finding nonparent sources of reassurance and approval, the critical chunk of the real parent was already in their bones, just as it was for me.

I can only hope that some of these people also got the additional mother chunk that I got: the refusal to quit, no matter what. When I look at what I have been able to achieve, I sometimes want to say, "Thank you, Mom." Where would I be today without the relentless drive to prove myself to my mother and others?

It's not hard to find parent sources for unhappiness, even misery. But Mommy and Daddy got the most important thing right; in my earliest memories, they both were extremely attentive to every ache and injury. From this I learned to take for granted that soothing was possible and even predictable if it was about being physically ill.

Now, looking back with senior eyes, I can understand that even their disturbing misreads of an overly sensitive child were well meant.

As a youngster, I did find one way to not to worry so much about pleasing others. For the very first time, my only goal was going to be achieving something just for me.

# ESCAPE TO BASEBALL

*I really love the togetherness in baseball.*
*That's a real true love.*

—Billy Martin

*Once I entered that world of flanneled*
*heroes I thought about little else.*

—William Zinsser

*I believe in the Church of Baseball.*

—Ron Shelton

## Living the Dream

BEFORE THE DARK, before the crowd, with the sweetest fragrance of fresh cut grass and cigar smells and linseed oil rubbed into baseball gloves still lingering in the air, I would climb over the outfield fence and step onto the pitcher's mound. I loved pretending that I was professional ballplayer, but I couldn't stay there long because the groundskeeper at Grayson Stadium in Savannah would soon arrive and holler me away. This happened many times during my baseball years.

Then, in yet another unreal world I would lean forward, look for the knuckleball sign from my catcher, check the runner on first, and set sail with my unhittable dancing butterfly pitch. The helpless batter's legs would freeze and he would never even lift his bat. At the last fraction of a second, my floater would dart over the plate for the last out of the game. One of my screaming hometown fans behind home plate would hold up another giant K, the scorekeeper's sign for a strikeout.

Suddenly I'm again on the mound, but no longer in the minor-minor leagues. I am now warming up in the bullpen down the left field line at Dodger Stadium. Instead of a small crowd, there are fifty thousand screaming Dodger Blues on their feet in the top of the ninth inning in the last game of the World Series with the New York Yankees. One run ahead; one more out to go and the World Championship would be ours. The public address announcer introduces the Yankee's cleanup hitter with the bases loaded and then calls my name. To the roar of "Game over" I begin my trot to the mound from the bullpen to get the final out against the best hitter in the major leagues. This guy is good; he works the count to three balls

and two strikes. Either I walk in the tying run, likely lose the World
Series with a base hit, or get him out.

Long forgotten is my knuckleball, replaced by the nastiest
outside-in cutter in the game, taught personally to me by the great
Greg Maddux of the Atlanta Braves. Everybody in the ballpark knows
what's coming but it won't matter. The batter cannot afford to let the
pitch go, because it's coming right down the middle of the plate, belt
high. But if he swings at the ball, he will either miss altogether or it
will attack his wrist with a fury and explode his bat into a half dozen
pieces. He will still be feeling the vibrating shock the next morning.

I grip the ball on the two seams and start squeezing as hard as I
can with my first finger and thumb on the left side of the ball. This
will reduce the pressure on the right side, causing it to "cut" down and
to the right, off the plate. Opposing right-handed batters know this
so well that they no longer bring their favorite bats when they have
to face my cutter. They also know they *have* to swing at it; now, with
one more strike, the Yankees will have a long winter.

I throw hard at the heart of the plate, at the last possible moment
the ball cuts down and in at his knee, the swinging bat hits a lot of air
and the giant flashing neon sign on the centerfield wall finally obeys
the crowd: "GAME OVER!" My only problem is that I am smothering
at the bottom of two dozen piled-up wild and crazy Dodger players.
Self-inflating fantasy wins again.

## The Golden Years

My parents refused to give me permission to join Little League when I was ten years old, but I went for tryouts anyway. I then lucked out and got on a winning team with mostly the same guys for eight straight summers. My disobedience was to become a glorious escape from home.

Only a few feet from where I'm sitting right now with my laptop is a very old handmade wooden box full of ragged baseballs with faded inscriptions like *"With this ball I pitched a no-hitter and beat the First Federal Bankers in the playoffs 4 – 1 on August 5, 1953. Three walks, 5 strikeouts."* This should've been enough, even for a kid like me.

But shortly after I moved up from Little League ball to the Pony League in the next age bracket, I developed an irresistible urge not only to get better at baseball but to do something no one else I knew had done. We lived two blocks away from my junior high school, which had a red brick wall on the side of the school next to a large playground. I measured the right distance between the wall and my homemade pitcher's mound, then carefully chalked out the strike zone on the wall. Almost every day after school and on Sundays after church I would put my baseball glove on my right hand so that I could throw with my left arm. I destroyed many baseballs against those red bricks, pitching left-handed at imagined batters, and even developed a fair curveball.

Then came my big day. Before a real game I begged the manager to let me play first base, which at that time was completely owned by lanky left-handers. I borrowed the regular first baseman's glove and played six innings using my left hand to throw, with only a couple of errors. I don't remember anyone making any comments. All of that practice must've paid off, because most of this took place on autopilot. It just seemed like something I was going to do no matter what. I asked if I could pitch in the last inning with us ahead, and it was a disaster. I walked four straight batters, threw a total of three strikes, and it almost cost us the game. Even so, I felt great.

What the heck was that all about? Later it occurred to me that I was trying to prove something, or maybe *disprove* something, but it was a long while before I could find a name for what I was after. And even though I was the best hitter, this venture didn't do anything to improve my reputation as an oddball on the team (all knuckleball pitchers are considered to be oddballs). But what would be the prize once I became a famous left-handed pitcher? Did a prize really exist? Was the moving goalpost chunk from my mother on the move again?

## The Perfect Game

In the long months surrounding our baseball summers, various ballplayers in our neighborhood would gather at Roger Benton's living room after school. By the end of the 1956 major-league baseball season and the first hard month of school, we had perfected a baseball-like game played on Roger's oversized hardwood floor with a marble for the baseball, baseball cards for players in the field, and a pencil for a bat. What we were after was the *idea* of baseball and the *feeling* we got when we were actually on the field. The rules just made it possible to actually play.

So with a boyhood love of baseball and a mixture of imagination and invention, our games were played out like a real game; three outs per inning, nine innings per game. Whoever was there that day had his turn as marble-thumping pitcher, catcher, outfielder and umpire to settle disputes. Each game usually lasted about an hour, and because it was in October, in the background on Roger's television during one game was the World Series between my Brooklyn Dodgers and the New York Yankees favored by the rest of the non-Brooklyn bums.

At first, we only paid partial attention to the World Series because we felt like we were doing the *real* thing and everything else was being played out far away. I was having a very good day, already scoring a bunch of runs by the late innings and suddenly the television grabbed our attention.

A mediocre Yankee pitcher named Don Larson suddenly found himself throwing a no-hitter in the fifth inning of a World Series game, and the announcer was beginning to use the sacred baseball words, "Larson's got a no-no going." A possible no-hitter was sacred on the field and in the pitcher's dugout because any mention of it was considered to be bad luck. Ever since the first World Series game in the early 1900s, there had never been a no-hitter, but Larson kept it going into the seventh-inning.

Then all of a sudden, on October 7, 1956, four days after my fifteenth birthday, Mr. Nobody Larson, with two strikes and two outs in the top of the ninth inning, threw a way-too-high fastball that the umpire called a strike for the one and only *perfect* game in World Series history. Twenty-seven batters up, twenty-seven batters down. It was unbelievable.

The guys went nuts but the Dodgers and I got cheated—no way was that a strike. At least they didn't rub it in, turning off the TV so we could finish our game and I could pretend that the Dodgers didn't get skunked. To make it worse, partly because of Larson, the Dodgers eventually lost the World Series four games to three.

Many floor baseball games later, when the guys would talk about how we lucked out and got to watch "The Perfect Game," I would remind them all of the *real* perfect game, the one we made up to keep our minds off homework, get us through the winter, and back on the field.

## The Long Road to Freedom

In our last year of high school, four of our players signed professional baseball contracts and one, Kenny Harrelson, became the most valuable player for the Boston Red Sox and is still the stormy announcer for the Chicago White Sox. We were good and I was good, usually the smallest but often the best hitter on the team. After I pitched and won a playoff game one year, the professional scouts came down from the stands to the dugout to talk with some players. I had high hopes, but heard from no one except our plain-spoken coach: "Sorry, Hans, they just don't take little guys in the pros (professional minor leagues)." At the time this hurt, but it wasn't all bad: four inches taller and I might today be coaching baseball back in Savannah instead of writing this memoir about the lives of a child psychologist.

For those eight years, no one in my family ever came to a single game or saw me swing a bat or even said anything about baseball, except on one occasion by my dad. One night he came in with a photograph of Lou Gehrig, with all the identifications taped over. He eagerly said something like, "I'll bet you can't name this guy." I was immediately put off; how could he even *think* that I did not know Lou Gehrig? He could not have felt good when I waved him away and dismissed his attempt to make a connection. Looking back, I recall a vague sense of feeling "Too little, too late," although that reaction was the cause of intense guilt and sadness about the way I treated my father. After all, even before Little League, he was the one who taught me how to throw a knuckleball.

Yet I don't have many memories of thinking about home whenever I was practicing or playing a game. When I did think of home, I tried not to let it matter because at some level I really needed for those two worlds to never meet, and my parents, older brother, and little sister made it easy. My escape from home troubles and low self-esteem into baseball was complete, almost.

Then on a long trip to the state high school championships, our Savannah high school team lost in nine innings to end the year. Somehow a team from north Georgia had come up with a professional prospect with a killer fastball and we got beat 4–0. I struck out three times, and never saw the ball but have a distinct memory of hearing it as it whistled by. At least he wasn't wild; there were no helmets back in those days. As all teams do at times like this, we were all grieving, some with tears. We thought we were unbeatable.

Devastated, I quickly left the field, went to the back of our bus alone and completely lost it. I remember the sound of my voice screaming out of an open window in the direction of the stadium, "KISS MY ASS YOU DAMN HICKS!" The team piled on to the bus and coach Terp stood for a moment staring at us from the side of his driver seat. He calmly said, "If anyone on this team thinks he is big enough or bad enough to take on a team that was better than us tonight, get off this bus right now and be man enough to go cuss them to their faces." Everyone knew who he was talking about. I had no regrets and didn't move. Unlike everyone else, I didn't sleep on the all-night ride back to Savannah, staring out the window into the night, trying to figure out why I was the only one who could not control the pain.

Long after my baseball days, I got serious about playing tennis. Unlike baseball, I had very little natural ability, so to compete I had to take many lessons. After about a dozen years I became a very good player, but again, it wasn't enough. A Swiss player named Roger Federer had developed a shocking, unreturnable backhand swing suitable for the Bolshoi Ballet. He was becoming the greatest professional tennis player of all time and his backhand was a very big reason.

One day Nancy was in Santa Monica at the mall and picked up the small local newspaper, circled one of the ads, and brought it home for me. The previous top player on the UCLA men's team was now teaching on a private court only a few miles from my house. He had Roger's backhand.

My best stroke had always been my backhand because even though I am right-handed, I always hit from the left side of home plate in baseball, so I had a natural, powerful follow-through with any swing: ax, baseball bat, or tennis racket. Happily, my new coach didn't laugh when I said I wanted Roger's backhand stroke. My usually victorious twenty-five year tennis partner would no longer have a chance if I could master it. But it wasn't just about winning; I could get the feeling I wanted with one winning Roger smash per game, or even one in the whole match. If I could have recorded that one beauty, I would still be watching it.

Then a thousand backhands later in our practice drills, one Sunday morning I swung harder than usual and felt a lightning bolt in my neck. My tennis career was over, and so was my ability to sleep through the night without serious pain killers and tranquilizers.

All this because of my endless search for just a few more moments of glory on the tennis court, on the ski slopes, playing the flamenco guitar and cello, or on the baseball field. But it was living the life of a ballplayer from ten to seventeen, together with much success at talking, that started my successful escape from a depressing home, both in reality and in a fantasy life that is still very active.

Most of the time the pills are not enough to do the job, so years ago I started putting myself to sleep by playing out, in great detail, the two Walter Mitty fantasy scenes above in which I had total control: winning-pitch glory at Grayson or Dodger Stadiums. Somehow the feeling that I was in control helped more to get me asleep than the stories kept me awake. After a while, it was not even about glory, just making that one perfect pitch, all by myself. One of my many secrets is that I still sleep with a new official major league baseball on a bedside shelf. My slumber begins with the soothing, fresh rawhide smell of that greatest of fragrances as I dream the impossible; finding a way to keep the goalpost from again moving back.

It was in the middle of one of those long nights with ball in hand that I had my big breakup; not break*down* but break*up* as in "breakaway" from the lifelong tether of mother's remote control. Any good baseball pitcher spends hours, especially in the night before he's about to pitch the next day, with a new baseball, rubbing it up and practicing the different squeezes that will produce the right kind of spin when he later takes the mound.

That's what I was doing one night in my as-if world, when it occurred to me that just like I owned the baseball and could at one time control its movements, it was now time to claim ownership of the moving goalpost. After many years of helping others understand that *the only lasting solution to victimhood is healthy action*, such as refusing to quit and accepting who they are instead of who they are not, I finally grasped the real source of my patients' problems. Without treatment, many of them lived a doomed life, fated to be forever jerked around and tethered to a long-accepted chunk from their most influential parent. What they did not know was that by the time they came to see a psychologist they had already taken the first step toward seeing their parental chunks as a choice.

This long and practiced solution for my patients and me at last became clear: if I can make choices, then with practice I can then choose what I want to believe. Someone or something else used to be in control of my choices and self-beliefs, but no longer. The goalpost would never again move back unless I wanted it to move. All those therapies were finally paying off. In one of my most soothing moments ever, I was getting closer to a new beginning.

# PART TWO
# Practicing

*Live usefully; nothing in your life will be as satisfying as making a difference in someone else's life.*

—William Zinsser

# LEARNING ABOUT PSYCHOTHERAPY

FOR A CHILD psychologist, the search for personal fulfillment and helping others is about practicing good psychotherapy. I know this is so, but I am making it sound much more simple and easy than it was in the beginning. For a long time, I knew I wanted to make others feel better, but it was a dream without a plan. How does someone change someone else for the better? Are there times when therapy requires struggling with painful problems and the soothing must come later? Can you actually be taught to practice good child psychotherapy? If so, can you really help children and their families and make a living doing it?

## "This Fruud Guy" and *The Psychopathology of Everyday Life*

I was fourteen when I discovered clinical psychology in an act of defiance. My brother Tommy had a large cardboard box full of paperback books under his bed, which I was strictly forbidden to touch. Of course at the first opportunity I pulled the box out and saw dozens of tightly packed science fiction books. One stood out but it couldn't be about science fiction because it had a big word I'd never seen before; I carefully memorized its position and took it from the box. On the worn cover were the strange words *The Psychopathology of Everyday Life* by someone named Sigmund Freud. I hid the book and later spent all night reading it, dreading the moment that I would be discovered.

The next morning I waited for my brother to leave, and became aware of the cooking sounds and smells in the kitchen. I ran there and told my mother about the book. I remember holding it up and asking her, "Who is this Fruud guy?" Because of her nursing training, she recognized the writer and said, "No, you're talking about Sigmund Freud—he was the first doctor who helped people with their emotional problems. Where did you find that?" I changed the subject and said, "Mom, this is it! I want to be like him—what do I have to do?" I don't remember what happened after that except that I kept the book and never got caught. I read it many times and begin to have fantasies about being able to think like this Freud guy, who seem to have an answer for my biggest questions.

Why do people do what they do? Why is my brother so mean? Why do my parents fight so much? Why did the man in Freud's book, coming home late from work, dreading a confrontation with his wife, try to open the front door of his house with his office key? Freud's famous explanation for this and all other so-called accidents: "*There are no psychological accidents.*" The man wanted so much to be back at work and anywhere but home that his unconscious mind, for a moment, soothed him with an escape plan.

If Freud was right, most of the time we have no idea why we do what we do. But there is always a possible explanation if we know how our unconscious minds work and how at different times they torment and soothe us. This is what the neuroscientist David Eagleman explained so well in his recent book *Incognito*. It's true, at least according to Eagleman's research, that there are always nonconscious causes for our behavior. This leads us to make up self-serving reasons for what we do as we go along. Without increasing our awareness of our motives, our autopilot, self-protective unconscious motivation rules and soothes our inner and outer lives.

After discovering Freud, the path seemed simple and clear. I would continue to learn how to box and play baseball and try to get a girlfriend and learn everything I could in and out of school. But one day I would be a psychologist like Freud, who invented the tool I most needed. It took a while to realize that my true calling was child clinical psychology, which I finally did as a psychology major in college.

If soothing was invented by evolution, clinical child psychology was invented in our culture for the children and families who needed outside help from highly skilled guides. Also, the child psychologists that I have known and known about, including myself, all had our own unmet emotional needs, with no less need for soothing than most others (and sometimes more). So actually, our profession chose us.

This helps me understand why, throughout my life as a child psychologist, I never gave much thought to my career choice. The closest I ever came to a conscious answer was "I like working with kids and their families." But I learned that strangers at a party or an airplane seatmate always left me alone whenever I told them that I was an expert in nuclear hydroponics. (When pushed, I would disguise my baloney as "It's a new field with a lot of math," which worked every time.) For whatever reason, I rarely went much deeper in my own search for answers.

It was only when I was well into this memoir about my two conflicted lives that I began to find clues about their origins. Writing can do this: motivations can be looked at with clarity, as if from afar. What I learned was that I could not fully understand my own career motives until I was actually doing child psychotherapy, and doing it well. Then I had to escape my training and rethink the whole process of therapy as two humans collaborating, not just an "expert" helping some troubled "patient." Each new case was seen in the light of mutual growth. I also learned that somewhere in the therapy process, the child and the parents must feel valued as persons with much to offer the treatment process.

Yet in the beginning, I had no idea what I was doing. I assumed that my graduate classmates in school knew something I didn't. Only a few showed any interest in treating children. Some were just afraid of kids; some complained that they only wanted patients with whom they could actually carry on a conversation. With little or no insight, I kept requesting supervisors and child patients I could learn from.

## Dr. Florene Young and Toys Out the Window

"The child leads the way, and the therapist follows" is the first rule in the once-popular 1960s child therapy classic, *Play Therapy* by Virginia May Axline. Famously known as "The first female child psychologist south of the Mason-Dixon Line," Dr. Florene Young was also the only full-time child psychologist at the University of Georgia. She had us read Axline's book and talk about ways to make the rule work.

One of my first university clinic patients was a seven-year-old boy who I think was called Jimmy, and I was determined for him to "lead the way" so I could follow. Within the first ten minutes, Jimmy began throwing the blocks and toys out of the open window onto unsuspecting students below in the parking lot. Now I had a problem. What would Dr. Young do? Should I take her literally and toss out a few wooden blocks of my own, proving to the child that I really cared?

Back then I might have been a little concrete, so Dr. Young told me that I should have simply said, without judgment, "Jimmy, I am noticing that you are throwing the toys out of the window." Even after trying to integrate Dr. Young's version of "the child leads the way" into normal conversation, I never became very good at this and mostly abandoned it a little later when an eleven-year-old girl screamed at me, "Stop repeating what I am saying and doing!"

Because Dr. Young was known throughout the southland for her expert treatment of children and families, I always assumed that I just didn't understand how to properly do child therapy. If this situation with my patient had occurred only a few years later when supervisors began watching the action through a one-way mirror, or used a video recorder for recording with "pause" for training, perhaps I could have done better.

Dr. Young also famously repeated her biblical mantra at least once in each of her lectures, which was all about soothing at its best: "Temper the wind to the shorn lamb." I remember picturing a young naked lamb which recently had its wool chopped off out in a snow storm, but rescued by a farmer's blanket. Dr. Young meant for the therapist to change things in the environment that supported a fragile child rather than expecting the child to match up to excessive expectations.

After class at Happy Hour, many of us tried in beer-soaked failure to imitate Dr. Young's commanding voice as she repeated many times in each lecture, "The goal in therapy is to strengthen the eggo (for ego)." Yet years later I was still thinking about her teachings, applying them most directly in my UCLA Parent Training Clinic, where the goal was to improve the family environments of our child patients. Dr. Young will always be famous in my mind and she remains the only professor I ever knew who used biblical instructions for student clinicians.

## Dr. Rick Ward and the Fish-Tank Kid

Just by the luck of the draw, in a pre-doctoral summer clerkship in the Department of Child Psychiatry at Emory University, I was assigned to the department head Dr. Rick Ward for supervision. He asked for a short meeting to describe my first outpatient child for therapy. The next day I met a red-haired eight-year-old boy in the waiting room and he followed me to my little upstairs office.

Back then, the Emory hospital outpatient Child Psychiatry Department was located in purchased old Decatur homes across the street from the university campus. I have never liked modern child outpatient clinics since then because of the change I saw in children when they could no longer go to an old-fashioned house that was something like where they lived.

Our "therapy offices" were sections of upstairs bedrooms. I had made sure that plenty of toys were around for play therapy, the only child therapy method that I knew anything about at that time. My patient, whom I will call Bobby, had been brought to the clinic by his mother because of extreme social withdrawal. He cautiously followed me into the room, and I tried to make him comfortable. I thought I was well-trained in interview skills, but all I got from Bobby was a downward gaze and brief mumbled answers to my standard mental status questions.

One of my prepared questions was to ask about the child's hobbies, and I duly noted his responses. Bobby softly said he liked his pet fish and playing catch with his father. Just as I was trained to do, I then showed him all of our toys and asked him where he would like to start. He fooled around with some of the toys but still would not spontaneously talk. I was less disappointed than confused. The only thing I was sure about was to avoid repeating everything he did and said.

But how could I do therapy if the child would not talk to me? Dare I lead the way myself and make suggestions about playing with the toys? For a while, I sat across from him and pushed around a few blocks of my own. Nothing else happened. No wonder my buddies back at school chose adult psychotherapy. I wondered if I should request a different patient.

The following day, I met with Dr. Ward for my first supervision session and confessed my complete failure to "do" therapy with Bobby. He asked a few questions about Bobby's interests. When I told him that Bobby had a pet fish, Dr. Ward interrupted and told me to inform his mother that the following week our time would be spent at a pet store in the nearby campus village. But before that session, I was to learn everything there was to know about pet fish and fish tanks. I really wanted to ask what this advice had to do with therapy, but Dr. Ward left no room for discussion. So I did what I was told.

After that, what happened can be guessed. Bobby not only became my teacher, but over the summer also became more outgoing and made a new friend his own age. His comfort with me also greatly improved when I told him about my life in baseball. We had managed to teach each other about the security and soothing that comes with shared interests and teamwork. I learned that sometimes child therapy only gets real when it gets personal.

As one bonus of helping Bobby, I got my own fish tank, which after a leak became a terrarium that is still in my office today, nearly a half century later. Another bonus was learning what it meant to follow my mother's mandate once I decided to become a clinical psychologist: "Sonny, no matter who comes to you and needs your help, you must never turn them away." But to make this work, first I had to first learn how to listen and watch for the little stories my patients told about themselves that revealed what kind of soothing they needed for whatever troubled them. As it turned out, the stories told a lot more; I learned how and why psychotherapy can sometimes make a real difference in someone's life.

# What Makes Psychotherapy Work, or Not

OVER THE YEARS I learned about the therapist and patient qualities which for me have been essential for successful therapy, and those qualities which can cause therapy to fail. High on the list of valued therapist qualities I have mentioned are understanding model scenes and knowing and the difference between *empathy* and *caring*. Qualities in my patients that seem to be most important for successful outcomes are creativity, insight, and initiative, or the self-motivated hard work that makes learning about self-soothing possible. Heading up the list of troubling patient qualities are inflexibility (rigidity) and unconscious, acted out hostility toward the therapist (paranoia).

## Model Scenes Can Tell the Story

Gradually, I learned more and more from my patient's stories about how to ease a child's negative self-beliefs before they settled in as a fixed identity. Freud famously said that the royal road to the unconscious was the analysis of dreams; listening carefully to the stories of children and parents tell me what I need to know about their self-beliefs.

I learned to look for answers in the stories we tell ourselves and others. I like the stories I write about here because when they are true, they reveal much about our true nature. If they are false, they reveal what we don't like about reality. Either way, they tell a lot about how insecure we feel and what kind of soothing we need. What really matters are our convictions and how they can get a very early grip on the way we think and talk about our lives.

When these told or remembered events about our past are spontaneously expressed in an open and safe setting, they are especially important. This is because they can take the form of 'model scenes' that summarize and reveal much more information than is apparent. These are pregnant stories, full of disturbance and hope, waiting to be safely told. And because they play such crucial roles in the creation of our personalities, it is sometimes possible for a trained listener to reconstruct a person's developing selfhood from the emotions in these special stories as they appear in dreams, fantasies, and symptoms. I am reminded of the earlier quote by Donald Winnicott: "*Tell me what you fear and I will tell you what has happened to you.*"

So even if they are rarely conscious, model scenes are the way our minds remain fixed on important periods in our lives, like little linked islands in the sea. They often reveal to the therapist much about what is wrong and what must be done. For example, in Joanie's case at the beginning of this book her single worried story about 'treating' her schoolmate Alice told me about her compassionate nature and her assertiveness, her intelligence and her belief that help and hope was possible. Perhaps there was even something there about resilience in the presence of a difficult life and a high risk future.

Another model scene that influenced a good portion of my clinical philosophy was the time when my mother announced my mandate to never refuse a patient for any reason. What she left out was the risk of burning out. This book returns time and again to these influences from my mother and father. But it was a patient named Lindsay who reminded me of a most important model scene with my mother, which then turned out to be very useful for Lindsay's therapy.

## Lindsay and Me

A mother brought in her sixteen-year-old daughter Lindsay, describing her as "disgracefully fat." Not long after that, my teenage patient told me about a memory involving her lawyer-mother who worked in her home office so she could be close to her children during the day. Without any emotion, she described how as a four-year-old she once really wanted her mother's attention and crawled under the mother's desk to touch her shoe. After 12 years, she still recalled her mother jerking her foot away, apparently busy and not wanting to be disturbed. Lindsay said that it happened often and had no importance. But the memory had a mind of its own.

There was no denial of the event, only self-soothing *disavowal* that wiped out the emotional meaning of what happened. Lindsay had mastered a kind of dissociative reaction, except that her mind also stayed close enough to the facts to be believable.

Lindsay had a second, even more powerful and unconscious weapon to fight will off her sense of being unworthy of her mother's love. At one point I referred her for medication evaluation to my former student Jeffrey, then a child psychiatrist in private practice near UCLA. He had been the chief resident of his child psychiatry fellowship group and was remarkably sensitive and empathic, already with a full private practice. Our goal was to intervene more aggressively with Lindsay's recent panic attacks. He prescribed *Paxil,* a cousin of Prozac with antidepressant and anti-anxiety benefits.

After he saw her he called and said, "Hans, you have sent me the most interesting patient. I rarely hear of someone her age with such a dramatic life full of so many near-death experiences. Has she told you about last weekend when she was in the middle of a gun battle in Watts, holding a friend's head in her lap with a bleeding wound, waiting for the police and paramedics? Do her parents know about this? How are you handling situations like these?"

In truth, according to her parents, Lindsay had spent the entire weekend with them on the weekend of the alleged gang shootout in south-central LA. When I ask her about it, she came up with an elaborate story about how easy it was to sneak out and get herself cleaned up and back into bed before daybreak. But nothing like this ever happened.

Years earlier I had encountered my first patient at Emory with the odd-sounding diagnosis of *pseudo-logica fantastica,* or seemingly logical fantasy, which means the patient earnestly but wrongly tells the doctor about outrageously improbable events. Yet the story is perfectly logical, and is told in such a way that if it is an encounter with a new doctor, it has a good chance of being believed. Lindsay was good at this and had completely flummoxed a very sharp child psychiatrist with a story that could have easily been passed on a lie detector test. In Lindsay's mind there was no doubt that it happened exactly the way she told Jeffrey and then me. When I mentioned the disorder to Jeffrey, there was a long pause. He said, "Oh my God, how did I miss this?" I reassured my friend that it took a while for me to sort this out, another testimony to the power of this strange malady.

Later, while discussing this kind of grandiose defensiveness in paranoid and sensational storytellers of model scenes like Lindsay's with another group of psychiatric residents, something triggered a new idea. I drew a vertical line on the blackboard with two arrows going horizontally right and left out from the center of the vertical line. At the left end of one arrow I wrote "degree of insecurity and self-loathing" and at the other arrow wrote "degree of grandiosity." I suggested that the length of the two opposing arrows was normally equal; if you're very *insecure* you are likely to be equally creative in faking *security*, usually by grandiose thoughts and claims.

Patients like Lindsay have long lines going in both directions: great stories and great insecurity. The average person is the same except their arrows are much shorter. These are the healthy "defense mechanisms" we use to safeguard our security, soothing our weaknesses with prideful self-reports. I asked the group if they bought the theory and if so to give clinical examples, which they did. Because others have also liked the idea I not only use it in teaching but use it to watch my own emotional and behavioral extremes.

Lindsay's trauma of rejection (actually *re*-trauma) by her mother represented dozens of later scenes that maintained her poorly disguised low self-esteem. In her original model scene she had unconsciously and skillfully managed to bind up the hurt into one story about her mother, and then convince herself that it was without importance. With me, she wrote off the scene about touching her mother's shoe under the table as "just a silly memory" and didn't know why it came up. This meant that my challenge was to help Lindsay learn to confront, and then accept, what was real about her feelings of being neglected and then try to move on in her present life.

But first, I had to demonstrate to Lindsay that I understood what she was going through by staying in touch with the rejected child within myself. Only then could she trust me enough to risk being honest in therapy.

The lessons learned from Jimmy, Bobby, and Lindsay were model scenes for me as a beginning therapist. Jimmy throwing toys out of the playroom window was one of the most lasting. He was the little guy who showed me how little I knew and how much I needed to learn in order to succeed in the business of clinical child psychology.

But it was Bobby, with Dr. Ward's help, who taught me how to put aside everything about me and really listen. This kind of empathy is the primary requirement for any therapist applying for the job, no matter how long it takes to learn it. But beware: putting oneself in someone else's shoes can become very uncomfortable.

## Getting Well with Empathy: Dr. Kohut and Adolf Hitler

WHAT DID IT add to my treatment of Lindsay for me to have intimate knowledge of her despair? Once in a session with a group of psychotherapy trainees, I emphasized the importance of delaying clinical thinking long enough to feel exactly what their patients were feeling, no matter how painful. Perhaps because momentarily identifying with their patients' despair was a new idea, one young doctor's response was, "There has to be another way—I can understand psychiatric illnesses without having to be ill myself."

Surely, another group member offered, patients can get what they need from any well-trained listener and clarifier without sharing in the suffering. Surely, patients need for their therapist to remain objective at all times. But this is wrong. These therapists of the future will hopefully accept that they are sufferers too. They must identify enough with someone else's troubles so the patient knows they are actually in a room with another human being. Empathy does not mean failing to safeguard that which is most dear about oneself.

Some degree of empathy is a natural biological reflex in all humans, because of special cells called "mirror neurons" in the front of the brain that automatically detect the intentions of others. For some reason, mirror neurons have never gotten credit for being our "sixth" sense of empathy, even though they meet all of the requirements for our other senses. However, for many therapists (and best friends) *sustaining* empathy is the most difficult skill to master and requires a lot of practice. This is because it requires them to defy nature and learn to *keep their own self interests in the background* for an abnormal amount of time, an ability which may only come naturally to mothers of newborns who experience an obsessive "primary maternal preoccupation."

For some of us, who as children had the ability to soothe grown-ups, it can feel like the inborn expertise of the young mother. Yet listening and making good guesses about others' feelings and intentions is not unique to humans; my springer spaniel Gus and Burmese cat Daisy Bell could do this. As a human, I just have many more and faster imagined options to choose from when deciding what's going on inside someone else.

It took me a long time to understand that empathy does not mean caring; it just means listening and understanding before making a decision and acting. This distinction escapes many people who have not been trained in psychoanalytic psychotherapy. The therapist literally has to control and bracket nearly everything about him or herself with full focus on the patient's inner world.

In the past, Bobby and Dr. Young taught me that I did not have a clue about how to use this skill, and that I had no chance of being a successful therapist with any patient until I understood the difference between empathy and caring. Empathy is the *selfless investigation of another's thoughts and feelings*, while *caring* is about one human sincerely wanting to soothe another human, or any living thing. Empathy is detective work, not love.

Dr. Heinz Kohut was perhaps the most influential psychoanalyst at the end of the last century, because he turned Freudian classical psychoanalysis on its head. No longer would up-to-date therapists only search for misguided infantile instincts of sex and aggression underlying neurotic symptoms. Kohut taught that before the therapist could make an interpretation about their patient's problems, he or she must work to make the patient feel *understood* with the use of empathy. And the only way this could happen was by a kind of indirect, "vicarious" introspection.

Instead of introspectively searching one's own mind for its mental and emotional contents, the therapist must first be objective in the search for whatever his or her patient was experiencing at the moment. The old theory of curing blocked instincts was abandoned, and replaced by the need for a sustained empathic meeting of the minds. The new theory went too far, dismissing our aggressive and sexual instincts almost totally, but it opened up psychoanalytic treatment to vast numbers of new therapists and unhappy patients.

Shortly before his passing, Dr. Kohut gave a lecture at a psychoanalytic meeting in San Francisco, and told this story. He said that many times in his Chicago psychoanalytic study group he would refer to the importance of empathy in all therapies. At some point he realized that a crucial understanding was missing and he asked each of his fellow analysts to privately write down the meaning of "empathy." As he suspected, there was much disagreement and debate. According to a close friend who was a member of the original group, Kohut told them what he later presented in his San Francisco lecture. It was a story for which no one was prepared.

At one point in 1944 and 1945 when Hitler's V1 rockets were bombing London and the countryside villages, he complained that the explosions were not killing enough British citizens. He ordered his engineers to build a new V2 rocket containing a screaming siren that came on at a certain altitude as it descended on London. Hitler's insightful invention would cause suspense and terror among the population, with the hope that the victims would either die of fear or the chaos would further disrupt life and the economy.

Kohut acknowledged Hitler for his extraordinary empathy, which thoroughly confused his audience. And then he reminded them that empathy is not about caring, but is simply a tool to investigate the inner life of another. Perhaps Hitler got where he was in part because he was so good at reading minds and feelings. Like a surgeon's scalpel, this information could then be available for whatever use any person wanted to make of it. Then compassion, caring, or even torture could become much more effective.

Today the average person can be excused for not making a distinction between empathy and caring, but it is disappointing to hear therapists make the same mistake. This error can severely limit the therapist's ability to collect and test reported information about the patient's inner world *before* he or she reacts with clarifications and interpretations.

Empathy is the closest thing we have to an overall philosophy about practicing one-to-one psychotherapy, especially when it leaves ample space for the patient's own discovery of new insights. It is this back-and-forth dialogue between *objective* assessment and *subjective* connection between therapist and patient that makes treatment effective, and it is especially true for very difficult patients.

The same approach is true for child patients like Joanie, described earlier, who sometimes needed individual attention. The only difference is that children, and seriously ill adults stuck in early childhood, require a display of empathy-based caring from beginning to end, even while the therapist is silently assessing the child's mental and emotional state.

The great psychologist Alfred Bandura long ago described a critical role of empathy in therapy with this analogy: First, ease your way into the patient's river, regardless of the current. Later, when the time is right, make small changes in the course of the river.

The importance of empathy comes up a lot in this book. Later I will describe how at one point, in the UCLA Parent Training Clinic students had to learn to improve their own empathy skills before they could help self-centered and inflexible parents become more empathic.

## Getting Well With Creativity, Insight and Initiative: Remembering Joanie

IN THIS BOOK, I keep referring to Joanie, who was truly unforgettable, and not just because unfinished business is never forgotten. She had a creative inner drive and spirit that could save her if she emotionally survived her childhood. Hopefully, every therapist, early in his or her career, encounters a patient like Joanie or Solomon or Bethany.

Seventy-two-year-old Solomon's story was very simple, at least by the time he came to see me. He described a life of frustration and failure, long periods of despair, and then a wake-up call that he linked to his grandson's bar mitzvah. He told of many failures in his own therapy with many therapists and rabbis. I asked him what difference he thought I could make. He said, "A friend said you helped him with a really bad habit, so I thought I would give therapy one more chance. I think I'm ready to do whatever it takes to feel better."

Solomon described a half dozen troublesome personality traits and habits that other therapists had identified and explained, but without any of them being changed much. I asked him to pick one and he described his multiyear habit of being unable to pass by record stores without going in and spending a lot of money which was becoming increasingly dear in his retirement.

To his wife's unending frustration and grief, Solomon had already filled two storage lockers with unopened CDs that he might never listen to. He said he started with that habit because he felt so out of control, that if he could fix that compulsion, maybe he could change some of the others on his own. Yet it's not the nature of a habit to be open to change on its own. I thought he had a long way to go, but we had to start somewhere.

I asked Solomon if he was willing to do something entirely new, just as an experiment to learn about the strange power that buying records had over him. At first, he shouldn't worry about changing anything. Without pause he said, "Don't forget, I said I'm going to try anything you say."

I told Solomon that when he left the office he was to drive back and forth a few times in front of Tower Records, and then park and walk by the entrance. Only this time, he had to force himself to walk all the way to the end of the block, stop and ask himself how he survived that previously impossible goal. This could quickly tell us if buying CDs was a good place to start, or if he was truly enslaved and a long way from getting well. We both needed to first test the power of his new self-determination when it went up against a twenty-five-year-old fixed habit.

Solomon returned the next week, smiling and at one point laughing about being noncompliant with my suggestion to only do a walk-by. He told how as he forcefully marched up to the door of Tower Records, looked inside and said to himself, "What's it going to be, Solomon? Consider this to be the biggest moment of your life." He then gritted his teeth, directed some curse words at all those rows of CDs inside the store, and rapidly walked on. Then, so he could curse his tempting devils some more, he said that he had walked back to the store, going up and down the aisles, and found himself laughing at what he called his own stupidity. On the way home all he could think about was what to do with two storage bins full of "that crap."

Solomon could never fully explain why he had such a dramatic shift in his attitude about what was important to him, but again said he thought it was about his grandson's bar mitzvah speech, in which the youngster singled out his grandfather as the greatest influence on his life. Old dogs can learn new tricks; the timing just has to be right.

My neuroscience training never had anything to say about these kinds of unexpected transitions. Habits and memories are the result of brain circuits that had been long overwired, and are by their very nature resistant to change. This "hardwiring" in the brain is essential for children to learn stable ways of acting and thinking, but is easily hijacked by unhealthy habits.

However, with Solomon these overlearned habits and their underlying brain circuits were no match for his intense self-motivation. I just facilitated what was already in motion. I could never have made him walk past that Tower Records store on his own. That was all Solomon. But the implications of Solomon's case were profound. Psychological problems could no longer be explained only by the history or strength of unhealthy habits and deep-seated negative parental chunks. Something more important was at play when people change and my word for that emotional-mental state is *initiative.*

A woman named Bethany took it several steps further than Solomon: in his therapy, I was a baffled, admiring bystander. I saw Bethany for the better part of a year, treating her for a complex grief reaction with only modest results. Nearly nine months following the death of her husband of forty years, she had become a recluse to the great despair of her nearby clan of relatives.

As a nurse, she knew that grieving and mourning were essential when the average person suffers a major loss. Yet she also knew that something was wrong with her version of grieving, but for a prolonged time refused to get help. She felt that "properly" mourning her loss would be the same as abandoning her final link to her husband. Then nearby relatives came to her house and literally dragged her out of bed, insisting that she talk to someone. They found me and I began seeing her weekly.

Bethany was a sloppy dresser, quite fragile and sad from the beginning, saying that she was willing to come in but wanted no deep therapy, only time to recover in a safe environment. This was a start because at least she was hinting at a light at the end of the tunnel. So my only role was to sit with her and be available whenever she felt like talking.

At some point Bethany came in and said that I had helped her, and that she was beginning to think there was something deeper causing her prolonged incapacitation. This desire to understand her deep feelings was another sign of her self-motivation, and I asked where she would like to start. She said that she was ready to look hard at her past and see what could come out of that.

After a few months of her own surprising insights about her father, who died when she was young, she came in one day with a look that I did not recognize. She was no longer slumping over, her voice was stronger and her face was soft with a slight smile. Most unusual for her, she wore brightly colored casual clothes, like someone going out to lunch with a friend on a spring day. Something big had changed.

I had to contain myself to keep from asking what had happened, but this was her show. She said that the day following her last session, she woke up with what was for her a most unusual idea. With only the briefest message to her sister about not worrying, Bethany checked into a quiet local hotel with a few supplies for an overnight stay.

Bethany said that she had no particular goals except for a vague notion that she needed to "go to the very bottom of a deep black hole and just sit there for a while." She described how she checked in, left all the lights off, plopped into a soft chair by the shuttered window, and for over an hour just cried. Then somewhat later, she felt something strange and decided it was the quiet solitude that began to ease her mind. This surprised her because she expected to be flooded with a deep sense of self-loathing for all the mistakes she had made.

With no knowledge of mindfulness meditation and silent retreats or cognitive therapy, Bethany described in great detail how after just a few hours sitting in the quiet room alone, she started to feel "lighter." She said it was as if all grief was mysteriously lifting from her chest. When she had had some negative thoughts in the night, she told herself to put them off until the next day when she could think more clearly.

She slept well that night and woke the next morning without speaking or hearing a single word since she checked into the hotel the previous morning. After getting something to eat, she went back to her sitting, waiting for painful thoughts and feelings, but none came that she could not dismiss with a few deep breaths. Almost unbelievably, Bethany had fast-tracked months of learning the therapeutic tools for conditions such as hers.

Bethany said it was the only time in her life that her mind was completely empty of jobs, problems, daily hassles, and a "much too noisy world." However, when she said "I felt nothing at all," I could not help but consider that she might have experienced a pathological dissociative reaction, in which some people escape from crisis by mental and physical numbing. I also had to consider an acute schizoid depressive reaction with emotional blunting, like the hopeless zombielike Meursault in Albert Camus' 1942 existentialist novel "The Stranger." Hers could even be a rare case of "flight into reality" sometimes seen in patients in an acute state of psychosis.

Bethany quickly ended my mistaken diagnostic guesses by describing her "odd but wonderful ability to just be in the moment," noticing things in her room and her body sensations. Nothing was being blunted. She also looked very healthy, had a genuine soft smile and excellent eye contact. I could only think that with some help feeling safe and open, she had found the peace she was looking for, even if just for a while.

She had planned for a late checkout from the hotel in the afternoon, and maintained her peaceful spirit right up to the time of our appointment. I momentarily gave into an impulse to ask her if she had felt anything like a blast of reality when she stepped out on to the sidewalk. Bethany thought for a minute and said, "At first I felt the temptation to get caught up again with everything going on out there. Things were happening all around, but I just told myself that they were not such a big deal anymore."

So what happened with Bethany? I was first thinking that she had somehow escaped from her overstimulating environment, even her beloved children and grandchildren, by dismissing unwanted feelings. Perhaps all she needed was a rest, like Japanese doctors have provided for centuries in what they call "Morita therapy." There, patients with any emotional affliction (recently, burnout from work pressures) are sent to countryside setting where they lived in solitude with all their needs taken care of until they felt like rejoining society. But could this work overnight?

No matter what actually happened, Bethany had found a new perspective on life. She wanted to continue therapy for a while, and came in for a few sessions for clarification and satisfactory closure on her "deeper issue." She said something like "I guess I'm like everybody else with problems, but somehow now I just kind of accept things that used to kill me." Yet I was not completely surprised when several years after I first treated her, she made a poor choice for her second marriage and came in for more counseling.

I should add that Bethany was not a patient that therapists should for. I've seen a few Solomons, but I never saw any other patient could self-soothe in a crisis as did Bethany.

nd Freud and one of his major adversaries, Alfred Adler, er Adler's theory that emotional illness is not about wayward childhood sexual and aggressive instincts but about what is now known as "self-actualization." Freud won the political struggle but Adler's theories made good sense for a lot of therapists. In his writings, he described our greatest psychological need to be "the desire we all have to take charge of our own lives, fulfill our potential, and realize our ideals."

Freud's instinct theory dominated psychoanalysis for the better part of a century, but I have consistently found that in nearly every successful treatment, patient initiative and real-life success also play a major role. If there is no internal motivation, then all the psychotherapy in the world can't help.

I've already mentioned the value of internal motivation in a number of my cases and how it is especially important in self-soothing. *How can you self-soothe without making an effort to self-initiate?* We saw this in Joanie's completely original impulse to re-create her therapy with a close friend and in my own unceasing attempts to learn about self-soothing from therapists with more experience and different orientations.

Often the therapist's greatest challenge is to search for ways to "turn on" their patients' motivation to take charge of their own treatment. There is no known formula for activating self-initiative. Some even say this is one of those traits that you either have or you don't, although this theory doesn't fit Solomon, who didn't make his move until he was in his seventies. I've seen many patients who got very little from my attempts to help them follow through, even with their own good ideas. Yet I would like to believe that some degree of internal self-motivation to be happier exists for everyone.

As I mentioned earlier, I have been telling patients victimized by depression and all sorts of abusive and unkind people that the only solution is some kind of healthy *action*. I even made up something

I call "activity therapy" for depression. The reasoning is simple: victimization and *healthy assertion* cannot go together. It once took nearly a year to get a morbidly depressed nineteen-year-old patient, who was nonresponsive to medication and cognitive therapy, to finally attend a yoga session.

My first goal was just to get her up and moving, out of bed. I tried everything I knew, even buying her a little squeegee ball and helping her put increasing amounts of pressure on it to prove there was something she could actually do. Then in a little more than one year, she took over her therapy and in another year became a yoga teacher with her own studio. She had become free at last to do her own thing and get beyond family expectations to succeed in college. One more checkmark for Alfred Adler's personal achievement motive.

So in some cases like this young woman and Bethany, I have learned that sometimes therapy can actually ignite, or reignite, or just facilitate the spark to healthy living. This is very good news, and somehow should be part of any therapist's training. It is not true that "you can lead a horse to water but you cannot make him drink." Instead it seems to be more true that in the right therapeutic environment the therapist may be able to help a patient become thirsty enough to take action for him or herself.

In Bethany's case, a remaining issue was how long her "cure" would last. The last time I talked with her, I wondered out loud what would happen if in the future she did not wait for some black hole to rise up and seize her, but rather explored some local well-established center that offered occasional daylong silent retreats. She said she would think about that.

Her parting remark to me with a wry smile was something like "If the word about what I did gets out, you therapists may be in trouble." But the enterprise of psychotherapy is unlikely to be in trouble. In our own research at UCLA we found that less than 25 percent of our clinic population had Bethany's and Solomon's kind of intense self-motivation. All they needed was a start and then they took over their own therapy. My concern is the sad flaw inhabiting almost all psychotherapies that do not include active guidance; in many cases it is ongoing dependence, not independence that is encouraged.

## Rigidity: Michael and "Better the Devil You Know"

AT THE OTHER extreme from healthy internal motivation to do what's needed to be well is *rigidity*: resistance to change. Later I will describe how in the UCLA Parent Training Clinic we discovered a reliable way to determine in advance which parents were likely to be in a "poor outcome" category. Using a broad-spectrum personality analysis, we even found out *why* individuals in this category made it so hard for them to change (and so frustrating for our students); it was their rigidity.

What is this personality trait of inflexibility, even in the midst of a patient's yearnings and pleas for help? There is some evidence that it is an inherited cognitive style, which can make life very difficult for someone confronted with a need to change. It is often associated with a lack of creativity, and can earn someone the reputation for being "stubborn," "hardheaded," or "oppositional." In therapy the patient may know all of this and wish to be different, but presents a difficult task to the therapist: "Help me feel better without doing anything that will shake up my life."

If Bethany's initiative was what made her therapy work, then the deep behavioral trait of rigidity can foil the best efforts of any therapist. Some individuals come in with pretty much everyday troubles, complaints, and histories of joys and sorrows, but then the years go by and nothing significant changes. Others are even more difficult: they assertively demand help for their despairing lives and then find ways to sabotage all efforts.

On the surface, Michael and his parents appeared to be in the midst of fighting about a common problem. Michael was one of my many "rebound" young patients who were happily sent off to college by frustrated parents eager to have their sons find their way in the world. In each case their son or daughter found reasons to "take some time off" and return to their childhood bedrooms and what their parents had hoped was going to be an empty nest.

In most cases, the reasons were valid, at least from one point of view. Some youngsters had untreated depression and severe anxiety; some were ill-prepared and set up to fail the social or educational demands of college life. And most parents were supportive, at least at first. When the family problems escalated, they came to see therapists like me.

I was very accustomed to intensive therapy for my patients, nearly all of whom had some version of long-standing negative beliefs about themselves. But there was something I was not ready for in Michael's case. This was how hard he and each of his parents worked to *undo* every plan we came up with for him to get a job, register for a class, clean up the backyard mess of automobile parts, or even make a schedule for himself.

Typically, I would ask Michael to name one thing that would make it possible for him to move forward in life. He would say he wanted to work in construction but had to have a particular kind of pickup truck, and nothing else would do. I would negotiate a workable solution with him and his well-off parents, who then on a whim decided they could not afford to buy him the truck of his choice. I would assure them that the money would be a loan which Michael could repay based on an existing job offer. They would then ignore his pleas and demands about following through with getting the truck. Michael would again start punching holes in walls and threatening to kill himself. This would bring them all back into my office demanding that I "do something." They all seem to both love and hate the status quo.

I began to suspect that they also hated each other. How else to understand unending mutual punishments? A call to the referring therapist confirmed this idea, and he finally explained why he gave up on this sad family. I understood exactly what he was saying, but didn't thank him for the referral. My work ended one day when Michael, who had always been very respectful and superficially did his part in following my suggestions, called in a screaming rage and fired me for lying to him about "promising" to change his parents.

Michael and his family were an unusual case, but every career therapist will sooner or later encounter *rigidity*: a patient's unwillingness or inability to change.

## Paranoia: Kimberly and Her Nervous Therapist

HOPEFULLY, THERAPISTS DON'T often have to deal with a blockade worse than their patients' inflexible bad habits. Yet there is another obstruction, which is the inevitable result of working with certain paranoid patients. It is the constant undercurrent of threat to the therapist's own well-being.

Years ago at an annual psychoanalytic convention in San Diego, I had the great fortune of attending a small workshop with one of my most influential psychotherapy teachers. This was Michael Basch, whose every comment about working with difficult patients was filled with clinical wisdom and compassion.

At the time, I was still young and struggling to develop a working relationship with a controlling patient who demanded my full attention to her endless whims and crises. She felt like a constant invasion. I thought this was the perfect time to get a few words of wisdom from the master.

During one of the workshop breaks, I approached Dr. Basch and asked for a brief consultation. He agreed, but after only about three sentences describing my patient, he interrupted with "I'm afraid I can't help you—I don't work with paranoid patients." I was so dumbfounded that all I could say was, "That's okay, thanks anyway."

How could this be? If Dr. Basch couldn't help with a case like this, then who could? Shouldn't the most ill patients get the most expert help? It took several years to shift my opinion of Dr. Basch from disappointment to admiration for his healthy sense of boundaries. I realized that he had been around long enough to fully understand the limitations of talk therapy with some people.

The problem was that many disturbed patients don't show up in the beginning as troublemakers, so by the time an unhealthy dependent relationship developed, it was too late. That's what happened with Kimberly.

I was already working with patients who had what was known as a "borderline personality organization" which I'll describe in detail later. Features of this very serious disorder are extreme emotional immaturity, conflicted relationships, self-hatred and self-destructive behaviors, and a powerful tendency to make others feel every bit of their pain. "Borderline" originally referred to the ability of these patients to behave appropriately and appear quite normal at times, while living just this side of the border of psychosis. Only a few of these patients are paranoid and dangerous, but it can often take a long time to sort this out.

The therapist's problem is inevitably the breakdown of boundaries between him or her and the patient, almost as if the patient needs to inhabit or sometimes even invade and control the inner life of the therapist. What this means in practice is that a great deal of time and effort has to be spent reasserting boundaries, which can often inflame the patient even more.

This is an odd situation: many therapists spend years learning how to help the patient talk about their feelings toward the therapist. The goal is to build a strong "transference" that can allow the patient to have "a second chance" and finally succeed by feeling safe with a parent figure. But with many patients who have the features of a borderline personality organization, the therapist finds him or herself struggling to get the therapy focus on the patient's life, and *off* of the therapist's.

At the close of a workshop I was leading on treating impasses with severe personality disorders for professionals at UCLA, several members approached me for private supervision, and one of them was Kimberly. I agreed, and later she presented a few cases with whom I was helpful. Then at the end of one session she asked if I would take her on as a private patient.

She seemed to be sincere, with promising clinical skills, so I agreed to see her. Unfortunately, this was before I learned to say, "Let's meet for a few times and see if we are a good match." Even more unfortunately, this encounter happened before my consultation with Dr. Basch.

It wasn't long after that that I began to question my decision to take Kimberly on as a patient. Increasingly, she asked personal questions and assertively requested odd favors, such as rearranging lamps and objects in the office to make her more comfortable. She began wanting me to reveal my motivation for everything I said. Once she wanted me to use the entire session to read aloud her poetry. Because of her earnestness, I made the mistake of reading one of her poems while she relaxed on the couch. Soon afterward, following an insensitive question from Kimberly about my wife, I said, "That's too personal, let's talk about you."

That's when I saw the real Kimberly's Dr. Jekyll and Mr. Hyde for the first time. Nancy and I walked to our separate cars after work, and that afternoon she called me over to ask about a note under her van's windshield wiper. It said "You stay the hell away from my therapist!"

I had two options: I could call Kimberly that night and say that I could not treat her under the present circumstances, but would try to find her another therapist. Or, I could hope that she would apologize and we could then use this episode as a starting point in understanding more about her paranoid rage. I chose the second option, partly out of concern for her, partly out of my grandiosity at the time that I could handle just about anything in therapy, and partly out of concern about Kimberly's possible psychotic retaliation against Nancy if I should send her away.

The following week I showed Kimberly the note and asked her if it was hers. She said she did write the note and begged me to forgive her, promising that nothing like that would happen again. I agreed to continue, but from that moment on I was on guard.

Over the course of the next few months, Kimberly focused more on her childhood traumas. She described how between the age of eleven and thirteen, her father would take her downstairs to the house basement and coerce her into various sexual acts. She told the stories of sexual abuse in a matter-of-fact way, strangely void of emotion, like many patients with severe personality disorders. But she also described how she would pause at the top step and imagine him walking ahead of her as she pulled out a gun and shot him in the back of the head.

For reasons she never understood, her father left the home when she was thirteen and never returned. Also, because of the threats by her father, she never told anyone about the basement business but never stopped worrying that one day he would show up again. The family moved several times. After college she received a master's degree in social work, hoping that by becoming a therapist she could understand enough about her childhood to overcome her love-hate feelings about men. Once she heard a lecture about the link between child sexual abuse and the so-called borderline personality syndrome, learned about my seminar, and that's how we met.

One day I commented on her lack of emotion while describing her father's actions, and her facial expression shifted to a distorted posture that I had never seen: grimacing with murderous glare in her eyes. I remained quiet but became increasingly uncomfortable when she would not take her eyes off me. I wanted to ask what she was feeling, but stopped myself. Kimberly then demanded, "Are you just going to sit there for the rest of the session and not say anything?" I said "I'm waiting to see what you would like to talk about."

Kimberly's face then softened with an almost bizarre smile. She unexpectedly shifted again, this time, talking about her patients. She said, "You know, I'm only seeing female patients—I can never predict what's going to happen when I'm trying to understand a man." I said, "Yet you chose a man for a therapist." As we ran out of time, Kimberly sharply said, "You'll see, I'm not the kind to give up." I had trouble fully focusing on my next patient because of a lingering chill on the back of my neck.

During the week I tried to plan a strategy of dealing with whatever happened in the next session. I knew that my feeling of being trapped, invaded, and threatened were part of Kimberly's semiconscious or unconscious intentions. I have found that in a great many abused and untreated people like Kimberly, their driving force in life is to find a situation in which they can at last elevate themselves from victimhood to dominance. This may require putting inside someone else the same degree of terror and impotence they once felt. Many psychoanalysts believe that there is a yearning in these patients for someone who can contain their poisonous self-hate. But what the patient really fears is that their behavior will be intolerable and push the other person away, confirming their own hopeless condition. Perhaps Kimberly was testing the power of her poison with me.

So much for the analysis; I had a real-life issue and I was frightened. I spoke to two colleagues about my situation, but neither of them had much to offer. A week later I went out to greet Kimberly in the waiting room.

My eyes immediately went to a new bag she had brought in, and based on its weight when she lifted it, there was clearly something heavy in the bag. In the office, Kimberly sat in her usual place tightly holding the bag on the floor between her legs. She resumed her glare at me and began describing the need to "get out some closure" about her relationship with me. I pictured her reaching into the bag and pulling out some sort of weapon. I began to imagine my options if she did this, then remembered who I was dealing with.

Kimberly was no longer having a "normal" transference; she was having a *psychotic* transference. I was no longer like her terrible father, I *was* her father. What I had to do was bring her back into reality. I said, "Kimberly, you went through hell with your father and you survived. He physically left but I know he is still with you mentally. Have I, your therapist, ever reminded you of him?" With that, her body seemed to relax and she slumped back onto the couch.

Kimberly quietly said, "All men remind me of my father. Will it always be this way?" I said, "You once told me that you are not a quitter. I believe that if you keep working on the question you just asked me, you can get relief from all those traumatic memories." Kimberly asked, "Will you help me?" I reminded her that I was not a trauma specialist, but I would make sure she saw someone who could. A few weeks later, she said that she had lost confidence that I could help her and that she wanted to see someone else, which was okay with me.

# WHAT DOESN'T HAPPEN IN
# THE THERAPIST'S OFFICE

I GOT MY first clues about the limitations of office-bound therapy for many children and families from Dr. Young and Dr. Ward. I also saw the potential benefits of physically and psychologically getting out of the office. Dr. Young counseled parents to change things in the child's environment; Dr. Ward told me to take Bobby to a store with lots of fishes, and whenever possible to go out and get into the world of my patients. These different ways of understanding the real-life context of patients was another legacy of Alfred Adler.

When I began to understand the wisdom of that philosophy, I knew that my entire career would directly or indirectly be based on what happens in the world in which children actually live. The office would be a place to get things started and clinically monitored. Traditional psychotherapy would be reserved to treat the deeper problems of parents and children only when they were blockades that prevented making positive changes in their everyday lives.

Yet therapists are trained to work within an environment where they have control. How can they influence what happens outside of the office? A new philosophy and new interventions were needed. The clinical internship at the Emory University Medical Center was the beginning, and it was in the very first week that I got what sounded like an impossible overdose of getting out of the office.

## Wagons in the Front Yard

As it happened, a new Emory University psychiatric hospital opened its doors to patients and psychiatric trainees the same year Sid and I finished our university course work. Because of the updated setting, the faculty supervisors apparently took this to mean that they were free to experiment with new approaches to training psychologists.

On the first day, I was one of eight nervous interns who were given an overview of the year by the department director. Some thought it was just the next obvious step on the way to a career as a practicing psychologist. Others, like me, saw it as a place where I would mostly be in over my head. This was not another summer clerkship under the sharp eyes of many supervisors. We had to at least act like grown-ups.

The director confirmed my suspicions when he paired us off into two-person teams to go into the country outside of Atlanta and put together rural mental health free clinics from scratch. The only help we would get was the name of the town, a faculty psychologist to visit and supervise us once a week, and a map of how to get there. It never occurred to any of us to ask what we were supposed to learn from such an overwhelming task. When you feel like a hapless newbie you just do what you're told.

Apparently, the plan was for us to learn to provide efficient family care to those folks who wouldn't normally seek help or could not afford therapy; our supervisor just forgot to tell us how to do it.

My town was a place called Jonesboro about forty miles south of Atlanta, and my companion Carl (unfortunately not Sid) spent the next couple of days trying to swipe ideas from others who might know a little more about where to start. But Carl turned out to be a bonus because his mother had relatives in Jonesboro. One of them suggested we contact the local Baptist preacher. Perhaps he would let us begin to meet in the church basement after Wednesday night prayer meeting. So we met with the pastor and even got his blessing. He said he would announce "our new mental health service and free family counseling" before Sunday service. But at least he told them that it would take us a few weeks to get up and running.

Our "practice" was full from the first day. We then spent long Fridays taking all comers and learning how to severely budget our time with each family. At first, we just stayed at the church until people stopped coming.

One of the church members had just moved from a small house and donated it the church to be used as the "clinic." I was very anxious when I arrived one morning and saw the large front yard filled with pickup trucks and one horse-drawn wagon. A church lady had agreed to be a receptionist, keep track of arrivals, and help us get familiar with whoever showed up. Perhaps her greatest gift was to put up a notice saying that she would not accept any new families after five o'clock, but even then we rarely got home before midnight. Within weeks we were spending most of two days a week at the clinic.

It took me a while to understand why my initial discomfort disappeared so fast; it was because I realized that the job was made for me. From early on in my life, I had to be the fast thinking family consultant. This was just more of the same except for the strange variety of problems.

We quickly learned to give each family only twenty minutes whenever possible, including written assignments, just like Dr. Florene Young did years earlier. We also told them to come back so we could check their progress, but very few actually did. Later one of our supervisors told us about a study showing that in free rural mental health clinics, the average number of visits was about three. So Carl and I added this to our reality. Spend a few minutes with the parent and child, listen hard, think fast, make a plan, explain it in the person's own language, write out their assignment, and wish them well. Then close the door and try to make a quick therapy note before the receptionist opened the door again with our next "patient."

We rapidly caught on to the routine and heard stories from town and farm folk that we had never dreamed about. One sad-looking farmer complained that his wife was beating *him*. Two more farmers were referred by the sheriff who wanted us to settle a dispute not quite at the level of the Hatfields and the McCoys. Our kindly preacher showed his humility and support by having his wife bring in their sinful smoking teenage grandson.

One of my most memorable cases was an eight-year-old boy and his mother who complained that his father was beating him. All the boy wanted to do was make fires, which he thought was really fun but had produced some close calls. I got the receptionist to call the fire chief, and we planned for a bunch of screaming fire engines to surround their house at bedtime because they had heard that there was a fire setter living in the house.

As we had rehearsed, in front of the whole family the chief instructed the father to teach the youngster how to safely set and extinguish fires in the fireplace and then in the yard. The young boy would then be the family official fireman, big red hat and all. I wish I could've been there. Even in Jonesboro I mostly worked out of an office, but always did everything I could to know what was going on in the homes of our patients.

Many people confused us with physicians and came in with medical illnesses. We eventually found a nurse who volunteered a half a day a week for these cases. We often got stuck and had to be bailed out by Dr. Boardman, our Friday supervisor, but after a while I simply started imitating him with the tough cases. At the end of the year Carl and I were extremely energized and agreed that our boot camp internship gave us a lifelong head start. The next group of incoming interns were the really unlucky ones: they just picked up with what we had started, and never knew what they had missed.

Looking back, it's clear that my new philosophy of getting out of the office, psychologically and even physically, was taking shape. Many internship cases continued to point me in this new direction, but I never thought one of them would come from struggling to help an autistic child.

## When Sarah Started Talking Again

On Christmas morning shortly after her third birthday, Sarah was halfway down the stairs with a big smile on her face, rushing to join her parents and brother around the Christmas tree. Suddenly she stopped, got a blank look on her face and did not utter another word for over three years. Neither her pediatrician nor a consulting psychiatrist knew what to do.

It was as if within a heartbeat Sarah skipped from a normal-functioning child to full-blown autism, and what is now called *Childhood Disintegrative Disorder*. There is no known cause and it may or may not be a variety of classic autism, because the onset of near-complete psychological collapse is rapid and total, while autism usually progresses slowly. In the first month of my internship, Sarah was assigned to me and another intern for assessment and hopefully, coming up with interventions that could bring her back into the world. Here is what happened.

Because almost nothing was known at the time about successfully treating autistic children, my colleague and I, together with our supervisor scoured the literature and found a UCLA psychologist named Ivar Lovaas, who had invented an extremely controversial method of short-term painful stimulation following dangerous headbanging, wrist chewing to the point of bleeding, and other self-destructive behavior. Parents referred to his clinic were given the choice of watching their children self-destruct, medicating them into oblivion, or agreeing to participate in Dr. Lovaas' research. Many desperate parents reluctantly signed up, and most reported significant improvement.

Our little team, including our supervisor, gathered and debated the pros and cons of giving brief pain-induction a try. We decided to go for it, but added a reward to the treatment whenever tiny signs of desirable behavior were observed. Four mornings of the week we sat across from Sarah at a small table with a container of apple juice directly in front of her. It wasn't hard to train her to reach for the apple juice box, but she was completely nonresponsive in repeating any of our words. The opposite mostly occurred; she would try to bang her head or take a bite out of her wrist with any instruction to say "apple juice." Only if she copied any of our sounds could she get a drink.

My unhappy job was to keep a soft grip on her leg just above her knee, and anytime she started a self-destructive behavior I would give her a brief but sharp squeeze, which would be followed by unintelligible protest. We went so long without any progress that her parents considered stopping the treatment, and I was thinking along the same path because I did not like being a punisher of children. Also, others in the hospital protested when they heard about our experimental work with the negative-sounding name of "behavior modification."

Then one day, when she was about to bite her wrist, and just before my leg pinch, my partner held her face to his, placed the straw near her lips and loudly said "APPLE JUICE!" To everyone's amazement, including her parents, other interns, and doctors behind a one-way mirror, Sarah yelled "AJUUS" just in time to prevent my squeeze. He then put the straw next in her mouth and she vigorously sucked up the juice.

Except for her parents and others before she became ill, no one had heard Sarah speak a word until that moment. At least in our setting, we only saw rare self-destructive acts after that. My partner was greedy and wanted to keep working to have her say additional words correctly, but I wanted to move more slowly.

His more aggressive approach paid off in less than a month, so then I suggested we go to work on her saying "Sarah." Then at one point the "apple juice effect" seems to be wearing off and her mother suggested we try one of her old favorites, cotton candy. The tiny pinch of cotton candy placed on the tongue following appropriate behavior turned out to be the most powerful reward I ever found for training autistic and out-of-control small children. Within another month Sarah could say "Sarah want candy," and our supervisors were rushing to publish the case, which we did. I had my first clinical publication.

She also greatly accelerated her language learning with a very scary and accidental intervention of my own. We had constructed a thickly padded room for Sarah and other self-destructive children, and it didn't take long to learn that Sarah would laugh, another gigantic surprise, whenever I would hold her arms and swing her around in a circle in the safe room. However, one day while flying around in the air she jerked her hands away from my hold on her wrists and went flying against the padded wall. I was terrified but then she jumped up, rushed over to me and yelled "more!"

Voluntarily, Sarah had used a word that we never trained her to say. It was not until a year later in our UCLA autism research laboratory that I learned about the biological basis for the autistic child's need for increased external stimulation to feel and react normally. Also, with Sarah I could not use the outdoor jungle gym because she liked to climb to the top and then leap out into space, somehow safely landing on a thick sponge-padded foundation or in my arms. Fortunately, she was never injured other than the discomfort of my reluctant knee squeezes. But Sarah had rediscovered joy and we were about to discover the limitation of one hour a day treatment in the outpatient clinic.

The parents continued to report worrisome incidents of self-biting and headbanging at home. It was then that I put into practice the lessons learned from Dr. Young's parent instruction and Dr. Ward's out-of-the-office treatment. We had Sarah's parents sit in the room with us every day and gradually take over the training, which by then included the very effective warning signal "STOP!" when she made any move to bite herself. I put together a simple rating scale for the parents to score at home for Sarah's appropriate word use, response to warnings, and any observed self-harm. Each day they would bring

began nursery school. With the Jonesboro successes, Sarah's experiences, and many other great learning experiences during the internship, I was finally very clear about how I wanted to earn a living, and again was struck by luck, and again Sid made it happen.

## Westward Bound

I had a girlfriend in my last year in graduate school, and we continued to see each other even though she moved to a school in her hometown of Jacksonville, Florida, about six hours south of Atlanta. One Friday morning I decided to take off early from the hospital and drive to see her for the weekend. I was literally backing out of my parking space when Sid came rushing up, waving his arms, and knocking on the car window. We knew all about each other's work, and he had just gotten word of an exciting all-day conference being held in our auditorium. I didn't care because I was headed south to see Linda, but Sid would not take no for an answer.

I learned that Dr. Lovaas, the very same expert in the experimental treatment of autism whose work got us started with Sarah, was one of the speakers and it was too much to miss. We went to the meeting and on the schedule for the afternoon was also the beginning pioneer in parent training, Dr. Gerald Patterson. Suddenly Linda had to wait. In one of the most stimulating days of my entire training, I quickly came under the spell of these two world experts, and everything came together.

At the end of the day I met both speakers and asked them if there was any way I could apply for a postdoctoral fellowship to study with them, even though I was already accepted in two other postdocs on the east and west coasts. Dr. Patterson had no openings at his Oregon Research Center in Eugene, Oregon. But Dr. Lovaas told me about a colleague in the UCLA Brain Research Institute, Dr. Martha Bernal, who was studying physiological reactivity in autism and also doing research on parent training. He gave me her name and address, I sent her my resume which she liked, and four months later I was in Los Angeles. My entire life was about to take an unexpected new road to the future.

Everything was in place for me to bring together my hunt to learn all about out-of-the-office child psychotherapy. I could continue my doctoral thesis work in psychophysiology, have a laboratory to study the biological basis of sensory impairments in severely autistic children, and help develop a home intervention program for parents of overaggressive and defiant children.

## Dr. Young, Once Again: Darlene's Story

Thanks to Dr. Bernal, I was allowed to have one day off per week to pursue my own interests. A social worker in Loma Linda, California, almost two hours east of Los Angeles, had spent a summer learning about our work and asked if I would help them get started with their own parent training program. So every Monday for several months I used what I was learning in our laboratory to train her and the staff of their rural community mental health center. The patients who came were mostly from within the local area, with one large exception: one parent training case took place on a desert ranch with two foster parents, eleven foster children, and a lot of farm animals.

One morning a woman came into the clinic with a most strange-looking little girl named Darlene. She looked very childish but at the same time was well on the way to becoming sexually mature. I asked the mother to come in alone and tell me how I could help. She started by describing how for many years she and her husband had brought the most troubled children to live at their ranch. Most of these youngsters had been abandoned or had flunked out of previous foster homes because of unmanageable behavior. The foster parents managed with state funding by having some of the more mature children help the younger ones, and each child had a job on the ranch that they could handle, no matter how little it contributed to the family's needs.

When I commented on the responsibilities of their chosen career, she said something like "I don't want to waste your time talking about the others, my husband and I can take care of them all. Darlene is the one I'm worried about because boys keep bothering her and she could get pregnant." The problem was that Darlene, a very shy and withdrawn child, was suddenly getting a lot of attention because of her blossoming appearance, and she really liked it.

Darlene was eight years old and had been on the ranch since her previous foster home had closed two years earlier. About six months before I saw her they began noticing the onset of puberty, which started with Darlene's growing breasts and her foster mom noticed pubic hair and widening hips. She had been told by the previous foster mother that Darlene's mother had a severe seizure disorder and that taking Dilantin, or phenytoin, to control the seizures might one day cause physical problems.

At Emory I had heard a lecture on a very rare disorder called *phenylhydantoin syndrome* which could occur when the pregnant mother was taking large doses of Dilantin for epilepsy control, which could produce many developmental problems like Darlene's. However, there were other causes of precocious puberty and it was unlikely that anyone would ever know for sure. I was surprised to learn that the visiting nurse had not yet suggested medications that could at least slow the progression of her physical maturation.

The desert ranch was forty miles from the clinic, which would ordinarily be too far for me to make a home visit. I had never heard of anything like this family's situation so I imagined something like an unorganized zoo with handicapped children wandering around with the animals. But then the foster mom showed me her photo album in which every child and animal looked really happy, leaving the impression that they all were very comfortable living together. I was determined to find a way to go out and see for myself where and how my patient lived.

The foster mother had brought in Darlene because she was unable to stop a few of the other boys from trying to touch her, and Darlene wasn't helping the situation. I wasn't sure how I could help. I spoke with Darlene, who was indeed quite shy but described her life on the ranch in a very positive way. She had average intelligence and seemed to know a lot about taking care of animals. I asked her if she had noticed her physical changes and she said she liked the way she looked.

It occurred to me to ask the foster mother if there was some youngster on the ranch who might be protective of Darlene. She told about a fifteen-year-old boy named Sammy, who had Down syndrome and always seemed to have his eye on her. This behavior initially had bothered the parents, but lately he had been telling them whenever someone was bothering Darlene. This is what I was looking for. I set up a time the following week for the foster mother to bring in him Sammy.

I had spent some time in a clinic for developmentally-delayed children at the Emory Medical Center. There I was reminded about what everyone had long known about these remarkable Down syndrome kids. As a group they are kind, well-behaved, love routines, and are always eager to learn something new. If Sammy was willing, my plan was to officially put him in charge of Darlene at one of their after-dinner family meetings.

The following week Sammy showed up in the clinic, nervous and looking at the floor, even though she had told him that he was there to help Darlene, and not there to get a shot of some kind. I shook his hand and we went into my office with his foster mom. She explained what it was all about and asked him if he wanted to be Darlene's big brother and keep her safe. Very appropriately, he agreed to help Darlene, saying, "Tell me what I have to do." I had his jobs printed on three pieces of paper, one for each of us.

Even with his below average IQ Sammy easily read what I had written. After each of the three items, his foster mother asked if the idea was okay with him. First, I wanted him to be with her when she told Darlene about the plan. Second, Sammy would immediately tell one of the stepparents if anyone did not do what he said.

Finally, I wanted him to stand by his foster mom when she made her most important announcement: she would tell everyone at the next after-lunch meeting that Sammy was now Darlene's big brother and was going to keep her safe. She would tell the older boys that they would lose one of their privileges for a time if they did not obey Sammy about keeping their hands off Darlene. We did a make-believe rehearsal of each of these ideas and Sammy, still a bit shaky, promised to do his best. I asked him if he would like for me to come to the ranch for the meeting, and he said yes.

The next week, I drove to Darlene's ranch and sat in on our rehearsed session with the entire family, which went surprisingly well. Darlene's foster father had built the house, and the large dining room was a masterpiece of craftsmanship, filled with Native American art and comfortable chairs. The parents introduced me to all of the kids as a friend of the family who was there to see how everyone was doing. The food was great and everything went smoothly.

My visit turned out to be a good decision for two reasons: I was able to visit the beautiful desert ranch and meet lots of kids and animals and also support Sammy in his new job as Darlene's personal guardian. Before I left their home, I told the stepmom to call the nurse again and ask her to get a doctor's order to administer hormone-controlling medication that would reduce Darlene's premature release of female hormones. These medications do not reverse precocious sexual development, but are very good in preventing further early changes.

Following my visit, the stepmom called in to the clinic each week to report on our plan's successes and problems. Two months later, when the time came for me to return full-time to UCLA, all was well on the ranch, which I mostly credited to the family's remarkable Samaritan parents. She would never know, but I'm sure that Dr. Young would have finally approved of her once bumbling student.

For years at UCLA I told every incoming group of psychiatric residents and psychological interns about this case, hoping that a few of them would one day have the courage to get out of their office and go see what was really happening in the lives of their patients. What could be more important for beginning child therapists?

# THE PARENT TRAINING CLINIC: AN ALTERNATIVE TO PSYCHOANALYTIC CHILD THERAPY

*How paramount the future is in the present when one is surrounded by children.*

—Charles Darwin

## Getting Started: From Outpatient Psychiatry to Navajoland

I WROTE EARLIER how I went straight from my postdoctoral fellowship to the faculty at the UCLA Child Outpatient Department. From the beginning I was determined to put together, for the first time, a hospital-based Parent Training Clinic with a focus on turning the homes of disturbed children into more healthy environments.

It never would have happened without the overindulgence of Dr. Jim Simmons, the chief of child psychiatry, who for some reason believed I could make a contribution to the department. In what I have already described as a major academic mistake, I told Dr. Simmons about my dream instead of my superiors in the Department of Medical Psychology. After all, he controlled the budget and at that time Departments of Psychiatry everywhere were flooded with funding for anything remotely related to helping those with developmental disabilities.

Drawing on those funds, Dr. Simmons provided me with two large rooms right next to the child outpatient waiting room, a secretary, and a research assistant. It still did not occur to me to consult with my superiors in Medical Psychology; I had other priorities. So I went to work with what I had learned from my postdoctoral supervisor Dr. Bernal and visits to Dr. Patterson's parenting group in Oregon, together with my own schemes for the future.

The possibility of creating a full-time facility devoted to better parenting seemed like the next logical career move for me. I didn't know it at the time, but my zeal to do something about dysfunctional families had a deeper motive. I needed to prove something. I needed to prove to myself and the world that what happened long ago to sensitive kids like me didn't have to be that way. I needed objective, scientific evidence about what goes wrong when children learn bad habits and end up with poor self-esteem. Then perhaps I could prevent this unnecessary suffering for others. With my scientific background, I felt prepared for the job. Unconsciously I must have felt that if I could not change my past, perhaps I could change the future for others.

In the early 1970s, there was no widely accepted practice or training about the psychotherapy of children other than traditional Freudian psychoanalysis. Yet back then, there seemed to be no limits in my search for a more efficient alternative to traditional psychoanalytic child therapy. Within a few months the Parent Training Clinic was up and functioning, accepting families and trainees for the next ten years and beyond.

Because we were so close to the child outpatient reception room, I got permission to use a screening procedure for every child who came into the outpatient department clinic. If the primary presenting complaint had to do with behavior problems or parent-child relations, our clinic could have access to these families for both treatment and research. Trainees from all mental health fields were encouraged to attend the clinic to get experience with children's in-home disturbances.

First, we had to carefully define desirable and undesirable actions in a child or parent, using as a baseline the daily lives of healthy nonclinic families that we also studied. Then we compared their styles of parenting with what was happening in the clinic and in the homes, using home-based interventions and measurements.

What was especially valuable was our inclusion of the parent and teacher ratings of the child's improved self-esteem and self-confidence as the parents became more positive and less negative in their home environments. These results also helped us understand more about the crucial details of parent-child interaction that got the family in trouble in the first place.

The following years were the most exciting and productive times in my career as a clinical psychologist. It now seems like almost each of those days was filled with eager students from not only the Neuropsychiatric Institute but from Europe, South America, and even Australia. Equally exciting were our new discoveries and successes with children and families. Like Darwin's law of variation and selection, we tried everything to experiment with new ways to provide effective short-term child and family care, hold on to what worked, and then take our methods to workshops across the country and abroad.

After showing that the measurements of desirable behavior were reliable up to one year after the family was discharged from the clinic, I summarized the findings. Then, after a little more than three years after the clinic opened, a book publisher showed up in the clinic and asked if I would write a manuscript describing our methods. I put all of the theory and results into *Systematic Parent Training: Procedures, Methods, and Cases.* Nancy, my clinic co-director, immediately followed with a published handbook containing all of the assessment and treatment materials.

It's amazing what a reader-friendly and useful book can do for a young academician: more invitations than I could handle in America, South America, and Europe, living out of a suitcase, and feeling like I had finally arrived. Pediatricians gathering at their annual conventions and looking for alternatives to stimulant medication for attention deficit hyperactive disorder showed great interest in the work of our clinic.

In many places with only a small but well-funded staff, I was able to construct a parent training facility from the ground up using our clinic at UCLA as a model. Because, thanks to my father, I had some construction experience I designed and helped build rooms with observation windows and communication devices for trainees and parents. Even clinical settings with groups hostile to behavioral interventions, such as St. Anne's Hospital in Paris, wanted to have a look at what their Director of Psychiatry Dr. Pichot called "the American obsession with doing things quickly." To some extent, I agreed with him but he seemed stuck in the past.

My ultimate home visit took the better part of two summers on the Navajo reservation. Our home base was the village of Chinle, Arizona, where our good friend the town sheriff warned us that nothing the white man ever did on their lands survived the sands of the Navajo desert for very long.

There I and Nancy, with her social work students went into Navajo six-sided huts, called hogans, where we were asked to study and help their autistic children. We had enough success to be asked back to build a Parent Training Clinic in their school for special needs children. I used everything I had learned at UCLA and helped them construct their own facilities for training parents. What we didn't know was whether any of our efforts would last.

One of my proudest moments ever took place many years later when my mother wanted us to show her the Indian reservation where we had worked. Late on the day of our arrival, we found the school open and ventured inside. At the end of a hallway in the new Navajo school was a "good behavior chart" full of happy faces showing the children's successes, just like the ones I trained native teachers and parents to use decades before.

Our contributions on the reservation took away any doubts I had that our methods and theory were useful for a broad population of troubled families. Yet somewhere inside I knew that I had other challenges to face in my work with parents before I could fully come to grips with my own upbringing.

At last I began to feel like I was following the childhood missionary dream of my early teen years to spread the gospel. Almost everyone was impressed with our research and home-based child therapy. In fact, once it became clear what we were able to do, the previous fifty years of doing only Freudian-based, one-on-one intensive child therapy for every troubled child seemed downright unreasonable. It's always better and more natural when children and their parents can solve problems in their own home. But in most cases, this is not included in the training of today's therapists.

In a few places, clinic staffs complained that no one had time to make home visits, a key ingredient in our successes. Even these complaints paid off, because they were the motivation to improve on our "parent daily reports," in which a student or staff member or even volunteer mom would call the home every day of the week each month with a brief checklist about the family's progress. It turned out that these results closely matched with the observations of our home-visiting staff member.

I then had a ready answer for clinic staffs with limited means. I never visited a clinic that could not get student or parent volunteers to gather home data using the parent daily report. Overall, the Parent

Training Clinic methods worked beautifully for another half-dozen years and it was all I cared about. The word about therapy in the home with children was getting out. And my search for what it takes to make a happy family was getting closer to the goal.

## The Parent Training Clinic's Greatest Challenge and Discovery

For years, we were able to consistently show that between 70 and 80 percent of the parents who came through the Parent Training Clinic dramatically improved their family life and that the gains lasted at least over a year, based on repeated measurements. This improvement rate at the time was far above the 60 percent success rate for any form of measured child treatment. Then, a strange thing happened in the early 1980s.

Unexpectedly, an increasing number of our trainees began to complain that their families were not making progress, and were becoming frustrated with their work in the clinic. Our success rate plummeted, down to the successful outcome averages reported for traditional child therapy. I knew something had to change, and with the help of a research assistant and a computing consultant, I spent one summer working on the problem. I looked everywhere to find out what was going on.

The first thing that stood out was that our children could no longer depend on their parents' ability to maintain positive responses for their desirable actions. As a result, our clinic children's frustration, aggressive behavior, and low self-esteem ratings continued to rise. Too many parents were also inconsistent in supporting each other's parenting. Overall, our success rates were changing because the parents' commitment to use what they learned in the clinic at home was changing.

We also knew from other research that whenever a clinic parent made more than three excuses for not following suggestions for improving parental skills in the first few weeks of training, the outcome was going to be very poor. But we still needed to know *why* some parents were making more excuses. What was needed was a way to accurately estimate each family's needs *prior* to treatment so that we could better customize the interventions, and assign the most difficult cases to our more experienced clinic staff and students.

One day we got an important clue. I should not have been surprised to learn that a big part of the answer came from the results of the personality test describing the primary caregiving parent, who was usually the mother.

I used the test results to develop a prediction formula that eventually let us know *in advance* what a clinic therapist could expect in treating any family that came into the clinic. Fortunately, the personality test was available in many different languages. This allowed our students and staffs in clinics everywhere to treat their incoming patients with either direct behavioral interventions or refer them for more costly traditional psychotherapy. I was very happy to see that our clinic students did not shy away from being assigned high risk families. Many were even eager for the challenge.

Knowing ahead of time how a child, especially if adopted, would succeed or not in a given home caused something of a stir when I presented our results to the Los Angeles County Department of Adoptions. The predictions of adoption outcomes were dismissed as unethical and unfair for families looking to adopt. I did not anticipate this, but should have.

We got many calls from clinic directors around the country wanting help on how to best use their resources on limited budgets. This was the easy part. The only thing a clinic needed to do was to administer the personality test to the parents and then use our formula to estimate the time and effort needed for successful outcomes. But for some, less than positive predictions created new challenges.

It did not go unnoticed that the successful use of our predictions in many different clinics provided further support for our theory about what makes parent training succeed or fail. We knew that the outcome of training was heavily dependent on long-standing personality traits of the parents. What we did not know was what trait was missing, or what was responsible for this very disturbing new trend, or what to do about it.

I met with the psychiatry department guru of personality testing Alex Caldwell. With his expert eye, Alex described how our test results were now showing, for the first time, an increase in "narcissistic personality disorders" in our clinic mothers. He said that it was not surprising I had missed this. There was no "narcissism" scale on the test.

The bottom line was that we were seeing more and more moms whose priority was their own needs rather than what was in the best interests of their children. Even with their occasional *initial* successes in our clinic, it was no wonder these mothers and fathers couldn't maintain their progress, which required teamwork and selfless efforts.

At last we had a starting point in our search to understand what was going wrong in our clinic. The new wave of failures seemed to result from the appearance of a new kind of "average" mother in our clinic and possibly, in our community!

What could parent training clinics do for the most disturbed families, who needed help the most? I decided that since parent training was still a recent invention, we should come up with a new way to help these self-occupied moms and dads become *more empathic* with their child's needs.

I had been taught well, but my overtrained scientific, measurement-crazy methods had caused me to miss the whole point of parenting. Children do need active guidance and discipline. But without empathy, without feeling understood by their moms and dads, emotionally neglected children *have* to act out. This was not just bratty behavior; it was a necessary protest and demonstration of the child's rightful needs. Our clinic had been rewarding kids for being more civil, compliant and keeping a clean room; we should have also been rewarding the parents for being more understanding and patient. I later understood my mechanical approach to parenting as an early wish for order amidst the emotional disorder in my own family.

So we started something called "empathy training," which raised many eyebrows in our Department of Psychiatry when the word got out. How do you make someone more empathic without years of intensive psychotherapy? A parent's empathy is about staying in touch with whatever his or her child is thinking and feeling. Empathy is necessary for caring, but without demonstrated caring about the child's unique and personal experience, little that is good can happen.

The new intervention was based on our assumption that parent's poor empathy habits could be *unlearned* with enough direct empathy training, and then replaced with increased emotional sensitivity to the child's *reasons* for unwanted behavior. *What did the child need that he or she could only get by being oppositional or manipulative?* What could we do to help parents learn the answer to this question? This was unknown territory, so we had to invent an entirely new kind of parent training.

In the observation room, one troubled clinic mom would sit on the floor pretending that she was her own oppositional, acting out child (Jenny). She was instructed to behave exactly like Jenny does at home. Another clinic mom would role-play the frustrated and disgusted parent who was trying to get Jenny to pick up scattered toys and place them in a box. She would completely ignore Jenny's attempts to communicate something about her feelings. For example, the Jenny might loudly protest, "I don't want to!", "You're mean!", or even ignore the pretend mom altogether just as her feelings had been ignored. Then a nearby "father" would then criticize the "mother" for not getting the job done.

Afterward, the real mother would be asked how her child must feel with this style of parenting. She would be given much group support for any display of sensitivity about what her child was emotionally missing. Then she would be helped to role-play expressing warmth and a full understanding of her "child's" needs before she acted. These real mothers would almost always talk with great emotion about how inadequate they felt as moms, which always brought lots of hugs and encouragement from the other mothers. These sessions required many boxes of Kleenex, not only for the moms but all of us watching the action behind the mirror. On an intensity scale of soothing, this was over the top.

Later I would discover how close our empathy training was to Adele Faber's book, *How to Listen so Your Child Will Talk and How to Talk so Your Child Will Listen*. Others were picking up on something critical that was missing in many families. All of our parents in empathy training were asked to read Faber's book.

A few, but sadly only a few of our high-risk mothers with poor responses to standard clinic training had dramatic breakthroughs in understanding their child's inner world. Some parents refused to participate and dropped out; many of these were referred for individual therapy in our department and were lost in the system. The dangerous personality trait of rigidity had struck again, this time focused on children as troublesome little machines.

During our empathy training sessions, we had some unforgettable and publicly reported breakthrough moments. However, they did not touch what was beginning to look like a major culture shift in the apparent growing personal entitlements of our Los Angeles clinic parents.

Eventually, I felt compelled to follow the trail wherever it took me to understand more about parents who were good enough at providing the material, but not emotional needs of childhood. For whatever reason, they were too busy with their own lives, leaving many children feeling emotionally abandoned. Just as in the empathy training clinic rooms with make-believe children, many real children acted out their frustrations with opposition and defiance. Others, like little Hans in his earlier years, turned their anger and harsh judgments inward.

But after my experiences in the parent training clinic, my life was no longer such a mystery! My well-meaning mom did not seem to know much about empathy (unless her children were physically ill). But I was going to make sure that working toward greater empathy would be my primary goal for the parents of children who never really felt understood.

Overall, our work in many parent training clinics had been shown to be a new, effective way of providing the tools needed for child therapy. But it was time for me to move on. Treating a wide population of children and their parents within the family context was beginning to look much more difficult—needing individual attention far beyond what a short-term behavioral training clinic could offer.

At that time my biggest concern was about the clinic itself. For years I had noticed how, when a clinic director left the hospital, the clinic's sign on the door was replaced by a new clinic name—usually *on the same day.* But years later I got a surprise.

## You Can Go Home Again

The original facility for the Parent Training Clinic in a section of the old UCLA Neuropsychiatric Institute was destroyed to make room for a new building in the 1990s. A few months ago, while visiting a patient in the new Neuropsychiatric Institute, now a major fixture in the UCLA Ronald Reagan Medical Center, I ventured over to what was left of the old building with more curiosity than comfort. The building was mostly the same, but the ground floor hospital wing that once contained our clinic meeting rooms and research laboratory was long-gone dust.

It was late on a Friday afternoon, and I was completely alone, wandering the quiet halls with a creepy sense of being in a time-warped dream. In the first chopped-off hallway, the doors were labeled with names of current psychiatric residents, psychological interns, and postdoctoral students. I walked around to the second hall and got a shock.

There, over the entrance to a suite of offices, very close to where it had once been, I saw this: *The Parent Training Clinic.* I had left in 1982 and here, before my eyes in 2015, was what remained of my mind-child. For a second, I had to reconsider my quick dismissal of the creepy dream that suddenly felt very real. Yet one of us, the PTC sign or me, was out of place and out of time.

It so happened that the next day I attended an all-day meeting required for updating ethical and forensic standards and laws. I always go early for these sleepers to get the last seat in the last row, and try to hide my laptop from the speaker's view. Just as I was settling in, two very old friends came up and greeted me. The social worker Nancy, and Steve, former head of the Neuropsychiatric Special Education Department from days gone by, were also required to take this course. We went to lunch together and I learned that they both still had connections to the new Neuropsychiatric Institute.

I told them about my previous day's experience wandering the ghostlike remains of my old workspace and my astonishment when I saw that something like a Parent Training Clinic still existed. They knew about this and each grabbed an arm, saying "Hans, your legacy is alive and well." It was too much.

# Private Practice

*The world breaks everyone and afterward many*
*are strengthened at the broken places.*

—Ernest Hemingway

AFTER YEARS OF being a university faculty member, immersing myself in the scientific study of families and growing questions about myself, I was ready for private practice and the freedom that I had long wanted from academic constraints. I knew I would always focus on the problems of parents and children, but now I had to find a way to be successful with all kinds of troubled children, parents, and other adults as well.

When I first began, I was filled with concern but also excitement. For the first time, my career and my income were completely dependent on me, but it felt right; I don't think I was ever meant to be an employee. I was also not meant to live the life of a psychoanalyst. Sometimes deep analysis is necessary, but I am a problem-solving consultant at heart. When I am doing well, my patients are learning to solve their own problems.

Yet it was exciting to know that I had been well trained in psychoanalytic, behavioral and cognitive therapies. What this meant was that my approach for any patient was flexible, based on what the patient needed. For many patients, I would first attempt to reduce troublesome symptoms using direct interventions and guidance. This required some creativity, because there is no therapy blueprint for everyone. Then, only when it became clear that a treatment blockade arose from a patient's traumatic past would I need to consider more time-consuming, intensive therapy. Sometimes people living in isolated despair just needed to find a good listener with whom they could share their story. There are good reasons why Freud's "talking cure" has been and still is the favorite method of psychotherapists. But even then, psychoanalytic insights did not automatically translate into new habits, which are in a very different part of the brain than newfound self-knowledge. In most cases, self-soothing and relationship skills still needed to be taught and learned.

So I continued to provide parent training for most of my child patients, but with a new focus on the intensive treatment of parents and other adults with severe personality disorders. And I still wanted to find out what to do about our declining Parent Training Clinic success rate in the small space of only two years. Also, I had learned the hard way that by the time an older child develops habitual and serious symptoms, it may be too late to intervene only with parents who have their own unresolved emotional problems. Another difference from the Parent Training Clinic procedures was that regular home visits with more disturbed private patients were no longer appropriate.

So why have I made a life of trying to provide care for unhappy children of all ages? Because they are our future and they need it the most. I also do this work because a wise teacher once instructed me to practice an ancient wisdom: "If there is something you need and don't have, give it away."

The therapy cases I will describe here mostly track my own learning curve as a therapist. They are grouped by similarity in the types of interventions used to reduce symptoms and promote well-being. For example, "Lynda" and "Ava " are bookends for my most challenging cases. "Charlie," "Renaldo," and others show details of the treatments I had to invent first for my own symptoms that also helped them and many others.

At one point a friend who read some of the early case descriptions said, "All you did was to tell me about people you were able to help, or not. I need to know what you did to make them better. How did you know what to do that might make a difference?" I took this as a useful challenge and sometimes describe in detail what happened in the therapy.

Finally, child psychotherapy is no longer a clear-cut specialty. In today's insurance world we can think of ourselves as specialists, but basically we take all comers. This is rarely an issue because the therapist often spends a lot of time talking with "the inner child" no matter how old the patient is.

The nine cases here show the wide range of psychotherapy patients that come into the care of child psychotherapists everywhere. Except for changed names and possible identifying circumstances, they are based on my therapy notes and the way I remember them.

## DR. MILLER! *Honeymooning in Maui*

As I was thinking and writing about the large part of my life I have spent practicing child, family, and individual psychotherapy,

I mentally revisited an oddball event from my early years when my lifelong "help everyone in need" mantra was not so unflagging.

Honeymooning with Nancy in Hawaii. Isolated beach at sundown, just north of Hanalei Bay in Kuai. Nancy is napping back in the beach house. Beginning to unwind from overwork at UCLA and private practice. Waves gently sloshing against the shoreline and giant palm fronds rustling in the warm late-afternoon breeze. Eyes closed, no responsibilities, full control. I thought this moment would never come, yet here I am, wonderfully close to a seven-year-old boy sleeping in his grandmother's warm lap. Perfect.

I hear noise in the distance, coming closer. The last beams of sunlight suddenly disappear behind shadows with new sounds of shuffling in the sand and I hear "*DR. MILLER!*" followed by a giddy barrage of adults and children.

I survive the shock, open my eyes, and gathered all around is the Karloff family from only one week ago. The rest is a cacophony of "Can I ask you just one question?" by the Mrs. and "I need to talk with you about our bill" from the Mr. My patient Alex is mercifully silent.

I didn't lose my cool, though it may have been one of the all-time great moments of bathos, an "abrupt transition from the exalted to the commonplace, producing a ludicrous effect." It felt more invasive than ludicrous. I don't remember everything that happened next but I would like to think that I put a towel over my face and ignored them until they went away. So much for unflagging devotion.

Back at the beach house, my bride laughed so hard that she could offer no consolation. Perhaps only a psychotherapist who saw the movie *What About Bob?* with Bill Murray will understand. This was one of Nancy's all-time favorite comedies. But I identified with

Richard Dreyfus, the psychologist tormented into helpless silliness by Bob's relentless stickiness.

Hilarious or not, recalling that scene on the beach I learned something very important. The Karloff family might have had some genuine need, but they broke a rule that I unknowingly lived by. Their insensitivity made it impossible for me to care for them at all, much less show compassion. Worse, I wasn't even nice about it. No matter how many therapists might have also been irritated, I saw how conditional my caregiving was. It was like a light switch on the wall, on or off with no middle position. I seemed to live by the standard "I'll be fully attentive and overly available for whatever you need as long as you show some consideration. I will probably not put up with anything else."

My honeymoon awakening put me at a loss, and showed how much I needed a way to bring my professional and personal life together, but at the time I did not know such a thing existed. Then one day I met a young man who pointed me in the right direction. Afterward, I had the opposite problem: keeping my two lives apart.

### David: A Professional Tragedy

*There's always some relief in giving up.*
— Lauren Oliver

We normally do not think of child psychotherapy as a life or death matter. Yet early in my career, I lost David and continue to wrestle with this question: what do you do with the memory of a child lost because of poor professional judgment, even when it is not your own?

I first saw David when he was eleven, brought in by a mother who had the look of a woman with more tension and guilt than she could handle. She said that David had been reporting increased anxiety and wanted to talk to someone. Sadly, she was using her hypersensitive youngest son to unload her own daily stresses, and much of my time was spent trying to get her to let up on him.

The previous year I sent Eli, the oldest son, to a wilderness camp to hopefully learn some ways to control his out of control oppositional behavior, and also to get him away from the temptations of Los Angeles. Lisa, a daughter, was doing well, but David's father was an obsessive, mechanically-minded person.

Early in our work, David described his "first love" as extrasensory perception, and wanted me to help him learn all kinds of special mental abilities. He became obsessed with the subject, and it wasn't long before I saw this as a search for superpowers that might control the extreme tension at home.

Nothing I did ever changed the verbal abuse by his mother. She could see the damage that she was causing and repeatedly promised to change, but could not. David liked our sessions and often would just lie on the couch and talk about whatever was on his mind, especially parapsychology. He was bright with good imagination and humor, which made our time very pleasurable. We seem to be on the right track for a while as he reported feeling much better in my office where he was able to relax.

I first suspected a deeper problem when I noticed that whenever he became very relaxed, he began to lose coherence in his sentence-making, almost as if he was speaking from a dream. As usual, when I had a question about any serious mental illness I administered the Rorschach inkblot test, the mental x-ray for diagnosing thought disorders and potential psychotic conditions. David's eccentric way of thinking, and that of his father, had already got me thinking about a possible schizoid personality with in-and-out connections to reality.

The test findings were strongly suggestive, but not conclusive. In the inkblots David perceived many rare and odd perceptions such as "It's a crying pink elephant with ears all over. All that red stuff on the card is blood—look, it's bleeding a lot." Psychologically, the interpretation might have been straightforward: David was identifying with a large but normally gentle creature which was emotionally distraught and victimized by too many deformities and too few self-protective defenses.

But the larger problem was that his inkblot perceptions suggested poor containment of unusual and fragmented thoughts, and he gave his imagination too much actual reality. David was aware of his unrealistic perceptions but tried to rationalize them by saying things like, "The inkblot maker guy made it this way to confuse people."

This response raised the possibility of a paranoid style of thinking, which for David was new in our therapy. His "elephant" was a popular perception on that particular Rorschach card, but David "contaminated" it with extremely rare and gruesome details not seen by healthy minds. Here David showed how he maintained more or less normal mental life, but just under the surface lurked unusual thinking. David did attempt to self-correct and maintain a good connection to the real world, while trying to convince himself that his troubles were caused by outside forces.

It was only when I pushed him to find new images in the cards that I understood how disturbed his thinking was. With increased external stress, his perceptions became more fragmented. At the age of only thirteen, David was showing a risk for having a serious mental disorder, not caused but very likely triggered by inescapable stresses in his home. I called for a parent meeting.

Neither parent was receptive to what I had to say. His father said, "I was that way and I'm okay now." His mother added, "It's just stress, he will grow out of it." I was troubled by their lack of being troubled. But I needed more evidence, such as hallucinations or delusions to be confident of David's diagnosis.

Also, because David's only clinical signs of unusual thinking were the Rorschach results and his obsession with possessing special powers, and because he liked coming to the office so much, I continued to engage him in whatever he wanted to talk about. He was a very good student in school and he had a lot to say about what he was learning.

Then a little over a month later, what I had tried to warn the family about actually happened at home. He called in a panic and said he had to see me right away. I made room for him to come in and he did, bringing with him a terrified look. He told about a fantasy that he often had, except this one had not gone away. It was about the Devil's voice whispering for him to yell out curse words in public. David's mild symptoms of a thought disorder had turned into his first paranoid delusion, indicating a potential "psychotic break" and fragmentation of his personality.

I knew the importance of responding aggressively in cases like David's, and set up a medication consultation with a colleague psychiatrist to reduce his anxiety and mental confusion. The treatment then and now for someone's first psychotic break is to immediately begin antipsychotic medication trials, which in many cases can prevent further decompensation.

I also directly warned his parents about his risks for serious mental illness. They responded by stopping David's therapy and sending him to a rabbinical school in New York, against all of my judgment and advice. The parents did agree that David and I could correspond. He wrote many letters, to which I would always respond with support and attempts to answer his questions. He hated the school, but seemed to like the structure of his daily life and being away from home. His antipsychotic medication appeared to be working.

When he came back to Los Angeles, I lost contact with David for some time. One day he called in another panic and said he had to see me. I told him to put his mother on the phone and was able to talk her into bringing him to my office. She was also in a panic.

David arrived red-faced and sweating, this time describing a heavenly voice threatening him with death if he did not follow frightening commands, such as sneaking up behind others and hitting them in the head. I did the usual test of asking him to point to the source of the voices, and this time he pointed upward, outside of his head. David was actively hallucinating, not simply broadcasting his own thoughts as he had before.

I canceled my other patients and told his mother to take him to a nearby emergency room, where I talked to the psychiatric resident and suggested immediate hospitalization for observation and new medication trials. David was admitted and his medication management was taken over by a psychiatrist in private practice who was also on the clinical staff at the hospital.

Without any consultation with others, the psychiatrist strictly forbade any future psychotherapy with me or any other therapist. And against David's loud protests, the parents suspended therapy and said my treatment of their son had come to an end. I, the messenger, had brought an intolerable message and was dismissed as a result.

Three months passed with no word from David or his therapist. Then I got another call from David. He frantically said, "I'm schizophrenic! They won't let me come to see you. What can I do?" I said I would call his mom and try to get him permission to see me at least one time.

Again she was guided by the psychiatrist who had told David's parents that "Insight will kill him—no more therapy. You may never take David to Dr. Miller again." This was quite strange because supportive psychotherapy, new self-soothing cognitive skills, and stress management are almost always part of the treatment of patients with acute schizophrenia. The psychiatrist would not return my calls, so I never had a chance to discuss alternatives to his rigid plan.

I agonized about David's condition, knowing that there was great personal liability attached to going against the parents and making further attempts to contact him. Nevertheless, one week later I called "just to see how he was doing." David's mother, strangely calm, said, "Last night David killed himself and that's all I have to say," and then she hung up.

David was an innocent and brilliant, lovable teenager, perhaps fated to have a mental illness, but not to die from what I will always believe was gross professional mismanagement. A visit to my past therapist was only partially helpful. He said, "I can't help you other than to say that things like this happen and come with the territory. Sometimes you can care too much about your patients, and you'll get over it. If you don't, call me again."

As I was preparing through the years to begin a private practice, I was neither taught nor warned that psychotherapy events like this came "with the territory." Perhaps I should've known better. But how does one integrate the death of any patient, especially one with my feelings for David? At the time, anything like integration was impossible. Had my own past therapist, with his decades in the business, found a way to minimize his feelings and simply not "care too much?" Or was my hypersensitivity acting up again? If I did one day have the wisdom to integrate the facts of private practice life with my own disturbance in cases like this, would I also get over my anger about the unnecessary loss of a child? I don't think so.

## Lynda, Who Taught Me How to Do Therapy

Not long after David died, forty-year-old Lynda came to see me, describing a lifelong history of panic attacks. Over a long and difficult course of treatment, she showed that if I could help her, I could also help many others. Every therapist sooner or later encounters such a patient: one who either burns you out or makes you stronger than you thought you were.

For me, "stronger" has come to mean allowing myself to become a determined student of my patient; influenced by what learning specialists call "shaping." It worked like this with Lynda. I gradually noticed that certain actions of mine were being "shaped" by her signals that I was on the right track. I began to develop confidence that I was learning what she needed in order to feel understood and start taking risks in her therapy. Lynda was very good at shaping my behavior; her blunt and often dramatic actions always let me know what was *not* working. So I felt free to copy or invent whatever worked to deepen the therapy and make progress.

Lynda had been in psychotherapy five times a week for several years with a well-known psychoanalyst. She described him as the only man she had ever been able to completely trust and recently felt strong sexual feelings for him. She was beginning to wonder if her feelings were shared by her therapist. He then developed a life-threatening illness and had to close his practice which led him to refer Lynda to me.

Here is what it took to get Lynda from multiple hospitalizations in Los Angeles to a new happy life on a farm in North Carolina: nine years, three sessions a week, powerful antidepressants, many outside professional appeals to help me, and most of all, learning whatever was necessary to help Lynda, who had been diagnosed as having a "borderline personality."

What is this soul-wrecking and interpersonal malignancy called borderline personality disorder? While in training at Emory University, I was told many times that severe personality disorders were untreatable with psychotherapy, but I took this as a challenge. The therapy cases that I used over the years in every workshop and article on "Treating Impasse with Borderline Patients" told a lot about this historically hapless syndrome. Lynda's case in particular was always guaranteed to wake up and sometimes frighten some of my seminar attendees.

One day in our early years together, Lynda came with pretty good spirits. Then, after about twenty minutes she suddenly put her head between her legs and began to sob, refusing to speak or look at me. But by then I had learned, after much trial and error, how to bring her out of it. I said, "Lynda, something just happened in this room and I can see how it has hurt you. You don't have to say much, but when you're ready, please tell me what happened, or point to what bothered you."

After another long silence, Lynda pointed to the ficus plant behind my chair and then to me, with a look of total devastation and abandonment. I said, "Okay, it's something about this plant and it's my plant so it's something about me." Suddenly she sobbed, "That dead leaf on the floor fell off your tree. If you cannot take care of your plants, *HOW THE HELL CAN YOU HELP ME?* Lynda then stood up, and before she reached the door I managed to barely get in, "I'll call you tonight." She mumbled, "Don't bother" and slammed the door behind her.

In psychotherapy, there is a general guideline some call the "50 percent rule," which means that the patient must do at least half the work in order to get well. Therapists are discouraged from going over the line and getting overly involved in the patient's life. But many patients live the lives of insecure children and need, for a while, a kind of therapeutic handholding.

That night I called Lynda at home; she answered with, "What do you want?" I said, "That was very hard for you today in my office when you saw the dead leaf fall from the ficus tree. You seemed to wonder if you are going to be neglected like that ficus plant, but you're not, and I'm not going anywhere." After a pause I asked, "How do you feel?" Lynda said, "You're asking me? I'm not here to teach you how to do therapy!" Before she could slam down the phone, I squeezed in, "I'll see you tomorrow."

The next day there she was, alone in the waiting room, greeting me with: "You have to help me with George (her husband). He says he's getting tired of my moods and doesn't understand me at all."

What happened here? What could account for her 180° switch from the rage of imagined abandonment to someone in good contact with reality?

Several weeks later, Lynda walked in smiling but immediately was troubled by something in the room. Most of the session was spent on a quarrel she just had with George. Then, about five minutes before the session was over she said, "I've been waiting for you to tell me why all those chess pieces are out of place over there." In the far corner of the room there was a marble chessboard, on a table nearly hidden behind a chair. I had been running late and didn't have time to straighten things up before she came in, because I was busy losing another game to a smarter-than-me teenager.

Lynda began to cry, but once again, I knew what to do. I said, "Okay, thanks for telling me that. When my last patient left I didn't put things back in place before you arrived, and then you became aware that I was talking to someone else." This was followed by a long silence and then Lynda sat up straight and said, "I think it's time for Cindy (her daughter) to have a checkup with you. Can I bring her in sometime next week? She doesn't mind waiting outside while I have my regular session."

It took quite a while for me to make sense out of these repeated meltdowns and lightning-fast recoveries. All therapists are trained in the treatment of traumatizing attachment disorders that usually occur in early childhood. Yet I was not prepared for the intensity of Lynda's need for a guaranteed, unfailing bond with someone who could contain her terror of abandonment.

I first got the full "picture" about Lynda's dependency on me when she showed up one day with her new camera, which without warning she pulled from her bag and rapidly snapped a series of photos of me in my chair.

After many false starts, Lynda was about to take her first lengthy absence from therapy in the form of a cruise with her husband and children to China. When she returned, her husband called to say that at some point on the trip, he had seen a worn photograph of me poking out of her purse. Later he noticed her taking it out at unpredictable times during the day and just looking at the picture. Lynda never mentioned this and I never brought it up.

Over the next several months, there was a noticeable change in her extreme shifting moods. Most impressive was her growing ability to notice that she was losing emotional control *before* she imagined that I was abandoning her, which meant that she needed less time and work to regain her composure.

How did I learn to respond therapeutically to Lynda's childlike departures from emotional reality? One of my very first lessons taught by Lynda, fortunately at an early time in my practice, was to invent something called "State A" and "State B" for patients with dramatic mood disorders. State A was about healthy emotional control and interaction with others. State B meant a loss of emotional self-regulation and regression to a traumatizing past. I got the idea on one of those occasions when she suddenly shifted from despair to a totally positive change in mood, which showed me that she was capable of interacting in a healthy way, and that her switch to health was becoming predictable. And for me, predictable despair and recovery meant potentially controllable, which meant potentially learnable by Lynda.

Unlike the rapid mood switches in individuals with bipolar disorder and the dramatic identity changes seen in so-called multiple personalities (often called "dissociative identity disorders" or DID), Lynda needed to start believing that it was possible that *a hurt relationship could be repaired on the spot* by a trusted other person. Only then could she function on her own out in the world, where relationship conflicts and disappointments are all too common. The key insight for me was to think of her as someone who had never escaped clinging infancy. I was treating a grown-up emotional baby, a description that quickly summarized moments of terrifying despair of people like Lynda.

So "State B" is where Lynda had spent a great deal of her life, and why she was coming for treatment; this was the so-called *borderline* state in which she was immediately incapacitated by any real or imagined threat of abandonment. Without intervention, she could stay in State B for days, sometimes hiding in a closet, sometimes cutting herself and causing us both to spend the evening in the emergency room.

Sometimes, it was trying to spend all of her husband's money in one trip to the mall, mostly on teddy bears. George once told me that there were hundreds in her bedroom. She actually got used to me laughing when she learned how funny it sounded to hear her describe how, while driving down some boulevard past a super mall, an alien force would take possession of her hands and force her steering wheel into the parking lot.

But then one day Lynda taught me something else about her fragile dependence on me. Unpredictably, once after I laughed she crashed and became very depressed. It was not obvious to me what had happened.

Sometimes when I was stuck with a new mystery about a patient, I tried to mentally role-play a dialogue with my master teacher Dr. Boardman. Here is how I imagined presenting this case to him:

Me: Dr. B., after sharing laughter with Lynda, she fell apart and I was unable to repair whatever damage I had done. I still don't know what happened.

Dr. B.: And you know what all of her tumbles into State B have in common.

Me: Sure, they all mean that she is terrified about feeling abandoned.

Dr. B.: So what's the big deal about a casual, mutual moment of mirth?

When I imagined him using the words "casual" and" mutual," all I could think was, Oh my! If I acted as if it was a casual friendship, to her that would be proof of my complete inability to understand her as a desperately ill woman.

Dr. B.: And what else?

Me: I think to her it might mean the looming end of her therapy – I must've scared the hell out of her.

Dr. B: Did it feel good when you laughed together?

I imagined myself saying yes, finally getting in touch with my feelings about Lynda and wanting her to get well.

Dr. B: Lynda gets to decide when she's ready to take the next step, not you.

Me: But we had shared that same laugh before.

Dr. B: Obviously, she could only handle a hint about improving.

In the next session, I asked Lynda if I made her uncomfortable by joking around in the previous meeting. She paused for a while and then, in another speedy about-face, asked if she should accept a volunteer position at a children's day care center that she had been talking about for weeks.

I used the same approach on many occasions with Lynda, and it almost never failed to produce a dramatic switch in her mood and reconnection with me. I still wondered if Lynda was having some kind of dissociative reaction because it was so fast and total. But then I learned that something very different was going on.

As I described above, "State A" was when Lynda was able to show her best and at times quite normal ability to function in the world. Again, after much trial and error and mostly errors, I found that all she needed to recover from hellish abandonment was for her words to be accepted *just as spoken* with no judgment.

The open door to State A was what I came to call "the therapeutic apology," which was simply a way of clearly restating, without opinion or interpretation, the events that led up to her separation anxiety and breakdown. It was as if what she really needed was not to learn something, but to have her very existence acknowledged.

There was no need for an actual "I'm sorry," so this was not a regular apology. And it was therapeutic because Lynda did not need an admission of my guilt, just reassuring proof that clear thinking about causes and effects was possible. This was my greatest lesson: that the health of patients with Lynda's problems depended directly on how well they were understood and treated by others, no matter how much work it takes.

Looking forward, the success of the treatment seemed to depend on two things: first, sustained empathy for as long as it took, and then, when the time was right, helping to transfer her new confidence and improved self-beliefs to relationships outside of the therapy.

What has always been a surprise to many people in my seminars is the idea that patients like Lynda are capable of living in opposite mental and emotional states. "Borderline personality disorder" has a terrible reputation in my field and is often talked about as the therapist's worst nightmare. But it is also a *"state,"* not simply a "trait" disorder. These patients want to be well; they just have never trusted anyone enough to safely grow up and think clearly about what is possible in human relationships. It never occurred to them that relationship ruptures could be repaired. Also, some therapists haven't discovered the value-free "therapeutic apology" as one pathway to sanity.

We usually take for granted that we can be both safe and open at the same time with someone we trust. But not so for those who go back and forth between babyhood and relatively good daily functioning. For them, there is no history or foundation for trust. If I could succeed in providing Lynda with a secure base, her next big insight would be that rare moments of emotional well-being could become more common and her positive self-beliefs could grow. I didn't know it at the time, but at that point in her therapy Lynda was years away from learning about taken-for-granted self-soothing.

Then on New Year's Day, in our eighth year, Lynda paged me and asked with some urgency if she could see me later that day about something very important. This meant I would have to give up watching a live broadcast of a University of Georgia bowl game, but Lynda suddenly had my full attention.

She came in with determined eye contact, and announced: "This year I'm going to have one good day, all day long." Lynda was at last taking charge of her therapy. That was the beginning of her new life in health, and by late February announced and celebrated her first anxiety-free day. Week by week, we had more complete "State A" sessions and less emotional meltdowns in my office and in her home.

She began to talk without fear about a desire to function more independently and asked me to help teach her new ways to solve problems in her increasingly complex daily life. She applied for and got a job at a local community college as a secretary for one of the deans. After a divorce a year later, she fell in love with a coworker and moved to a farm in North Carolina. For years she sent me Christmas cards, always asking when I could come to visit.

By the time I stopped seeing her for regular therapy, I realized that by helping Lynda achieve a solid state of wellness after so many difficult years for both of us, I was truly prepared for private practice.

I also learned that the doomsday label of "borderline personality disorder" was unfairly negative. The label said as much about a mismatch in the particular patient-therapist relationship as it did about an illness with a fixed handicap. I finally understood why fellow therapists would send me an "untreatable" patient whom I would find quite responsive, and why at other times I referred a difficult patient to someone else who was able to make a helpful connection.

With patience, determination, and creativity, any experienced therapist could do a great deal for patients like Lynda who, just like everyone, wanted to be understood on her own terms. Then, as Dr. Boardman would say, she would apply what she learned in therapy to her life out in the world when she was ready.

## *Andrew: The Joke Killer with a Rifle on the Roof*

I had never known a self-proclaimed joke killer before I met Andrew, but I could imagine what that might look like in action. People are having fun, and then they're not: someone spoils the party just by being him or herself.

When I met him, fourteen-year-old Andrew was a very gifted student at a top prep high school in West Los Angeles. His parents were already talking about the Massachusetts Institute of Technology before our first appointment. But they said for some time Andrew had been coming home from school looking sad, even though he got top grades in everything except the humanities. Also, he had exactly one steady friend and never wanted to talk to his parents about what made him sad.

One important job of a child psychologist is to collect clues about any possible social, emotional, or cognitive problem, and it begins with the first contact. But the psychologist must have one foot on the accelerator (look everywhere for clues) and one foot on the brake (keep a distance from any hasty diagnostic conclusions until all the facts are in). I already had an important diagnostic clue before meeting Andrew in my office. I had enough information from his mother to guess that he was gifted with his super-calculating left side of the brain, but weak in his right brain's specialty of social-emotional skills such as empathy. This is often seen in kids with social anxiety and low self-esteem. With additional clues along this line of thinking and a deeper look at his history, psychological testing, and storytelling, it could mean that Andrew had a serious developmental problem.

Early on, I began to think about *Asperger syndrome.* This is a lifelong condition at the most healthy extreme of autistic spectrum disorders. Earlier I described our interventions with Sarah during my internship at Emory University, who at the beginning of treatment was at the most disabled extreme of the autistic spectrum.

Children with Asperger syndrome show significant difficulties in social interaction and nonverbal communication because of a difficulty in reading others' minds and understanding intentions. They are socially handicapped, but they are famous for having precocious analytic skills. Asperger syndrome also differs from the autism because of normal language, excellent academic progress, and great sensitivity about their social impairments. They also have a normal yearning for an emotional connection with someone special, but little confidence and much fear about how to make the relationship work.

When these children are not helped to focus on their strengths and taught how to navigate the torturous social world of adolescence, depression is inevitable, and can show up as strange or angry outbursts. Their high intelligence can make everything worse because these boys and girls think too much, which can quickly turn into obsessive worry.

Most of the children and teenagers I see with this syndrome say things like "What good are grades if nobody likes me?" At one point in my work with Andrew, he asked, "Will I ever have a real girlfriend?"

Also, these young people feel helpless and sad because they quickly learn that they are always "a beat behind" the comprehension of spontaneous banter they hear every day at school. And this brings us back to the joke killer.

When Andrew's parents called for an appointment, I described the routine I always use before starting treatment. I would meet with the two of them for an extended interview about their son's early history, and especially what it had been like living with Andrew for the last year. I would have them fill out questionnaires that would summarize his development up to the present in physical, mental, social, behavioral, personal, and academic development, and set up an appointment schedule for Andrew's evaluation.

So I already had some hints about what Andrew could not do. All the testing was about finding what Andrew *could* do so that we could work together on his strengths and successes.

In our parent meeting about the evaluation, they said that Andrew preferred to be alone and expressed increasing concern about his darkening mood, but until recently thought it would pass because his school work was so good. I asked the parents how they would rate his current problems in terms of severity. The mom said "more concerned lately" and Andrew's father said it was just a stage that Andrew was going through just like he did when he was Andrew's age. He "snapped out" of his moodiness when he got his first girlfriend, and was concerned that having to talk to a psychologist might make Andrew feel worse about himself.

I described my plan, which involved administering the full scale mental status examination that I created many years earlier in the Parent Training Clinic. Afterward I would have a good idea about what kind of further testing and interventions Andrew needed.

In our first appointment, I greeted Andrew, a physically normal teen, who came into the office with no eye contact and took the most distant seat from me. Before I could speak, he said, "I'm a joke killer," and told about a typical event at school that very afternoon.

When classes were out, kids were hanging out in front of the school waiting for their parents to pick them up. Three or four boys he knew were standing around the school flag pole joking about something. He moved closer, trying to get the drift of what they were talking about. At one point one of the boys said something funny and they all began to laugh. Andrew joined in, and tried to add something to the humor. They suddenly became quiet, looked around, and slowly drifted away, leaving him standing there alone with the all too common feeling of being some kind of freak. When Andrew finished his story, he glanced in my direction and said, "I hate those guys. I hate myself. That's all I think about."

I asked if he had any notions about why all of this was happening; he said, "I guess I'm different." I asked if he knew anyone else with his problem, and he mentioned a younger girl who for some reason seemed to like him and often sat with him at lunch. They enjoyed talking about science and video games and college. Andrew said that she also was overly nervous around other kids and seemed to notice that he was rejected by his friends, which she had also experienced.

Andrew said she was the only person who made him feel at ease and wished he could spend all of his school time only with her. He also liked being teased about having a girlfriend and feeling almost normal. On one occasion when they were alone, the girl took his hand. He said he was very frightened and pulled away but hoped that it would happen again.

In the mental status evaluation, I was able to get a good idea about his sensory-motor abilities, his short and long-term memory, imagination, common sense, right and wrong judgments, wishes, and relationships with others as well as examples of social interaction. Andrew's answers were mostly in the normal range, except for two items: first was his answer to the question "If you could be any animal, what would it be?" Andrew said, "Raptor hawk, because they fly high above the ground and are free to do what they want and everyone is afraid of them."

Second, I had heard many of these answers before, but rarely his response when I asked "Have you ever felt so bad that you thought about hurting yourself or others?" Andrew said, "Yes," and described how he wondered if there was a nonmessy way to die without making his parents too upset. He then told of an elaborate plan to get his helicopter pilot's license so that he could crash into his school playground. I asked if he had talked about these things with others and he said he had not.

The odds against any youngster with any disorder carrying out such a plan are extremely small. However, in our country there continues to be incidences of disturbed young men creating mayhem and mass murders ending in suicide. These events often happened at the shooter's school, after feeling repeatedly humiliated and helpless. And, in nearly all carefully investigated cases, early signs were missed and I was not going to let this happen in Andrew's case. But because there was no specific threat, I chose not to tell him that if he began to give details about his homicidal plans, I would have to contact the authorities. Instead, I said that it was very good that he told me about his angry feelings, and that I could help him but that I needed to include his parents. Andrew was displeased, but I was able to take this approach because unlike the murderous cases I knew about, Andrew was highly motivated to get help.

He didn't like the idea of involving his parents at all. But I said that this might be his best chance to get the help he needed to change what was going on in school that was so humiliating. I also reassured him that I would always make sure that his parents fully understood his painful social life.

At that moment Andrew did something that would have seemed strange if I did not know about children with his kind of thinking. He started connecting his fingers in groups of two, three, and four. When he saw me watching, he said, "I've got a test tomorrow in calculus and I'm practicing the numbers I need to remember for some formulas."

I asked Andrew if it settled him down to think about doing math, and he said, "It's the one thing I can count on always working. I can predict what numbers are going to do next and I cannot do this with people." This revelation and a positive parent checklist for Asperger syndrome pretty much confirmed my diagnosis. Andrew was fairly incapable of knowing what was going on in other people's minds; he could sometimes *imagine* others' intentions, but mostly in a suspicious and irrational way.

When I met again with his parents, they mentioned something that had been earlier left out. Less than one year before, they came home and found him lying on his rooftop with his father's rifle pointed out at pedestrians passing by. He somehow convinced his parents that he was not serious and that he had made sure the gun was not loaded. His father took the rifle out of the house and nothing like this happened again.

But now in my office they took another look at how all of these stories were beginning to add up into something that could possibly lead to a disaster for many people. Andrew's mother began to cry; at first his father said nothing and was deep in thought, and then seemed to be searching for someone to blame for his son's "bad ideas." After a while, she asked, "Can you help him?" I told them that I thought the real question was, "Can we *all* help him understand and accept his differences, so that he can begin to focus on his strengths instead of his nightmarish social life? I may not be able to do much without both of you doing your part, and that will include getting him into a social skills group." They accepted this, but still could provide no answer about why Andrew could not share his troubles with them.

This was a most difficult moment because they had never considered that they were providing anything other than good parenting for their gifted son. But now they understood what was at stake and agreed to follow my suggestions. I told them that I wanted to make a home visit and see how he lived, especially in his bedroom and at meal time. I wanted to meet with his older brother who understood that Andrew was different and often needed his protection. I wanted Andrew's mother to call me at least once a week and leave a message about his mood, and desirable and worrisome behaviors. I explained that my role would be to act as Andrew's personal advocate and help him find alternatives for his angry impulses.

For the present, their role was to read together Jeffrey Cohen's book *The Asperger Parent: How to Raise a Child with Asperger Syndrome and Maintain Your Sense of Humor*. I told them that any child's problem is also a family problem, and that when the time was right, we could think about all meeting together and talking about the book.

If our therapy had a turning point, it was the moment when Andrew found the courage to tell me why he could not talk to his parents. He had often noticed that his father avoided people unless they were talking about something technical and specific. He never seemed to have fun and enjoy others' company, even in family gatherings.

I didn't have to ask what this meant for Andrew. But after a while of sitting silently, he looked up at me with full eye contact and said, "Well, my dad is very good at his job and my parents get along great. Do you think that maybe one day I will be okay too?"

Andrew's case was a "typical" difficult one, heavy with time and effort. There were home visits (in which the parents seemed to get almost as much as I did), meetings with Andrew's brother and teachers, and many regular and sometimes urgent phone calls. But what made it all worthwhile was Andrew's increasing self-acceptance and new comfort talking about his feelings. Perhaps for the first time, he was learning about hope.

After the family meeting about Asperger's, Andrew became very angry in my office about why no one had ever explained to him why he was "such a social moron." He said he felt terrible when he finally learned about the cause of his social anxiety and poor social skills, but "that was a lot better than never knowing why I sometimes feel like the hunchback of Notre Dame."

Before long, I discovered Andrew's more healthy passions. His first was "becoming an astronaut" which he quickly learned would require close-quarter mind-reading with the space craft crew, and he abandoned this idea. But then he read about NASA engineers and decided that was it. This rang all of his bells because "engineers have to be very good at math and inventing and fixing important stuff."

I knew a bit about engineers (my brother and father) and was a member of the Planetary Society at the Jet Propulsion Laboratory in Pasadena. If we could somehow avoid talking about higher math, I might be able to keep up with Andrew's plans to be a spacecraft engineer.

Then after about a year, Andrew stopped coming regularly. He had willingly joined a social skills group led by an old acquaintance and master group therapist for socially challenged teens. Over the next several years I followed Andrew's progress and met with him every two months. There were no other threats or discussions about taking violent revenge on his school tormentors, who gradually became less important to him. It's also possible they noticed a change in Andrew.

After he graduated from high school, Andrew was accepted at Cal State University, the home of many great scientists. I never knew if he got that job at NASA or the Jet Propulsion Laboratory, but he did learn to like himself.

## Nobody Doesn't Have Scoldophobia: Sasha's Story

*Thou canst not think worse of me than I do of myself.*

—Robert Burton

*Mommy, I did something bad and I need a timeout.*
—Seven-year-old Maelannie, a friend's child

You can't afford for mommy to be bad, so when something goes wrong between the two of you, play it safe, blame yourself, and keep your shame inside—after all, if mommy gets too upset with you she might leave. Those are the benefits of self-blame. Yet the cost can be a terror of being scolded, even if it means beating mommy to the punch and announcing that you need a timeout.

It was not until I was at this point in writing that I stopped to ask myself: what is the opposite of being soothed? I thought about my therapy experiences, myself, many people I know, and this is what I came up with:

*The opposite of being emotionally soothed is being scolded, and a safe way to prevent being scolded or criticized by others is to first scold yourself.* The certain result of this strategy is the development of scoldophobia; you simply cannot handle being criticized and there is no such thing as constructive criticism. There may be as many opposites of soothing as there are synonyms, but I got the idea about scoldophobia from a woman named Sasha.

Long before Sasha, I thought that Lynda had taught me what I needed to know about extreme sensitivity to imagined reprimands. But Sasha took the fear of being scolded to a new level. At age forty-seven, she was increasingly afraid to leave her house, which meant missing work and finally getting serious about therapy. Here are a few highlights from Sasha's life.

- Eight years old, third grade. Sitting on the back row behind a larger person by choice so she would be the least likely person for anyone to notice. Sasha made good grades because she was so attentive and had good teachers, but few friends, and preferred staying in the teacher's room during recess. In what was a classic "model scene" she described a time when the class was getting noisy. The teacher loudly cleared her throat and Sasha shot her hand up into the air yelling, "*I DID IT! I DID IT!* She was certain that when the teacher cleared her throat, she was being scolded for some wrongdoing; it did not matter that she had done absolutely nothing.

- Sasha often woke up screaming in the night, and when awakened by her mother, told about a dream in which she was running away from some kind of punishment.

- She had always love to write and her friend encouraged her to finish her story about a twelve-year-old girl who overheard her uncle John Wilkes Booth plotting the assassination of Abraham Lincoln, which she called "The Secret in the Family Tree."

Sasha's husband told her that her novel was a perfect story for preteen girls because of its strong character, scary moments, and how it provided a crucial clue that the federal agents actually used to track down Booth. Another friend also loved the story, and talked her into submitting it for publication, which she did. After a long wait, she received a tentative acceptance letter that required her to make many changes. Sasha became extremely depressed, tried to destroy the manuscript and never again submitted it because she was certain it was no good.

- Anytime I failed to greet her with a warm smile and friendly look, Sasha would not be able to function in the session until I reassured her that she had done nothing wrong. This went on for a long time; she did not seem capable of learning that people were not just standing around waiting for her to mess up so they could humiliate her.

After many months I was able to help Sasha become more comfortable going out into the world. She made some new friends who were very supportive, but two of them moved away. Her one remaining trusted friend actually talked her into going on a date. The man seemed to like her, but at one point on the date he told her that she was pretty but that he preferred women with longer hair. She immediately swore off all men until later when her mother introduced her to the very passive and kind son of a friend, who became her husband.

As a final boost for her scoldophobia, Sasha's remaining friend stopped calling and returning her calls. She refused my suggestion to go to her friend's house and make sure she was okay. Shortly afterward, she called my office saying that she was "cured" and would tell me about it the next day.

Sasha announced that her relationship problems were fixed forever because *there would be no more relationships*. She would never again take a chance on being criticized or feeling rejected, and the only way to be sure was to keep her distance from everyone. She was very proud of her "guarantee." Fortunately, this social stoppage did not include me, perhaps letting me know that she knew she wasn't really "cured." Or perhaps she was just praying that therapists weren't allowed to criticize their patients. It was very encouraging that before long Sasha's instinctive need for companionship resurfaced, and she found a new friend.

Later in our work, Sasha asked if she would ever be able to understand why she was so full of shame for things that she had come to recognize as irrational and unprovable. I suggested that we go over her background again to see if we had missed anything traumatic in early life that left her with feeling responsible for whatever went wrong. Sasha thought it might've started with that panic attack in the third grade, but I assured her that was only a replay of something earlier.

It was time to find answers to the questions "What is so bad about being occasionally scolded? What's the worst thing that can happen?" Whatever it was, it had to be something traumatic. At last, Sasha was very open to the idea of finding some answers, which were very similar to the ones that came from my own therapy.

At about the same time, I was referred by a friend to Dr. Don Dorsey, a very well-known therapist who might have some new ideas about my own sleep-wrecking anxiety. Dr. Dorsey turned out to be an expert in trauma treatment who used a technique called EMDR, or "Eye Movement Desensitization and Reprocessing."

Actually, the therapy does not require side-to-side eye movement at all, only that the two hemispheres of the brain are stimulated in an alternating way, such as the therapist tapping on the back of one hand and then the other until an important memory about trauma is recovered and made available for verbal analysis. The idea behind the treatment is that trauma is stored in the body, not the brain. The "thinking and talking" *left* side of the brain could not access the trauma because the *right* side of the brain was blocking conscious information about the trauma from the body.

In successful treatment with EMDR the pathways for information sharing between the two brain hemispheres are reopened by the alternating stimulation. When the original cause of the trauma can be safely talked about, the brain's natural self-soothing tendency takes over and gradually diminishes its power over the patient's unwanted emotions. Memories stay the same, they just don't mean so much. Fears become accessible to insightful self-awareness and speech. In many cases, this procedure can end the domination of terrifying flashbacks. EMDR has proven to be the most effective treatment for many traumas and PTSD.

In my case, anxiety may have served the purpose of keeping my attention on a problem even though I didn't know what it was. All I know for sure is that after Dr. Dorsey's use of EMDR, I was increasingly free of anxiety for the first time in my life.

I was so impressed by EMDR that I took a series of courses and learned about the different ways to improve the communication between the two sides of the brain, so that verbalized insight was more available for self-help. With Sasha, I could either refer her straightaway to a trauma specialist, or see how she might respond in my office to the techniques I learned that were so helpful for me. Here is what happened.

Using Dr. Dorsey's technique, I asked her to place a pillow on her knees with her hands side-by-side, palms down. After suggesting that she speak about whatever came up in her mind, I gently tapped the back of her hands in a very slow rhythm, back and forth. At first nothing happened, so I just waited.

Then Sasha began to softly cry but said nothing. After a few more moments she said, "I don't know why I'm crying," and I stopped tapping so she could concentrate on her thoughts. After a few more minutes, she again started speaking.

"On my father's horse farm in Kentucky, he used to ride all over the place in his pickup truck with me in his lap. I think it was when I was about seven years old and I really liked the bouncing. While you were tapping I remembered one time when he told me to hold the steering wheel and drive the truck. We hit a big bump and I lost control of the truck. My dad grabbed the wheel just as we were about to run into the side of an old barn. Nobody got hurt but I think I had a nightmare that night. Does any of that mean anything?"

I only said that it meant enough to come up at a time when we were beginning to understand what was going on back then. I asked her if anything else came to mind about her memory. She said her feelings were all jumbled up but something about the memory seemed important because it made her anxious. Again she asked about my thoughts.

I decided to leave her with the question and not take a chance on influencing her with my own many ideas about what this all meant. Often the fewer the words the better, and the most lasting insights often come from the patient, not from the therapist. So before we stopped I just said, "If you'd like, we can continue this next time and see what else comes up."

That night she had a troublesome dream of bouncing up and down on her father's lap. She liked it but again said something about it scared her. Later in that session, she said there was something she didn't quite get to while I was tapping the back of her hands, and wanted to try it again. After only a few seconds of tapping, Sasha suddenly jerked back, tightly wrapping her arms around herself.

She was silent for a while. I just waited. Then she opened her eyes and asked in a stern voice, "What are you thinking about?" I said, "I am thinking about how you described bouncing in your father's lap as enjoyable, but in your dream it felt different. What you make of that?"

Very irritated, Sasha said, "You know very well what this is about. Right after you started tapping, a picture of my father jumped into my mind and it scared me. I don't want to do this anymore. Besides, he didn't do anything." I said that just like the tapping could open things up that had been locked away in our minds, it could also let us think clearly about our past and perhaps lessen the disturbance of the memory. Then I added, "Many people have some version of your story. We're in no hurry here and you have nothing to fear in this room."

Throughout this entire exchange, I knew I could speak in psychological code about what might have been inappropriate physical stimulation by Sasha's father. Because she already had the crucial insight, there was no need to be explicit except for my reassurance about the boundaries in her relationship with me. The problem was that she had once taken for granted this kind of safety with her father. Now I, as a possible stand-in for him, might be suspect also.

So the next question was, "Who seduced who?" In almost every case I have seen in which there was a question about inappropriate sexual stimulation of a child, even imagined or unconscious, the child-then-adult always blamed him or herself for submitting or participating. Often, the victim even set things up for this to happen again. So the "victim" was sometimes also the seducer. But why would this be? From everything I've learned and have seen in my own patients, I believe the patient "seducer" keeps it going in hopes that one day she or someone else will have the strength to put an end to it, forever.

Sasha and I spent many long sessions, without any tapping, looking for connections between childhood memories and her inability to tolerate disapproval. When the time was right, I asked Sasha if she ever felt responsible for anything that happened back on the farm. Because she was more comfortable with her memories, she said she was sure that she had kept up the bouncing on her father's lap because it felt good. It was only much later that she started feeling that something was wrong about what happened in the pickup truck.

Over the years growing up, she managed to put the memory out of her conscious mind altogether, where it stayed until she had the courage to go deep in her therapy. But until then, she had lost the connections to her childhood and was left with a life of nameless guilt and anxiety.

At last I could begin to see clearly how scoldophobia worked. The mildest criticism from anyone created a lightning-fast reflex to escape from unbearable guilt coming from somewhere early in life. After a while, the reflex is so automatic that it loses its link to its conscious source. And then there was the matter of Sasha willingly taking the heat herself rather than blaming and perhaps destroying the only father she would ever have.

Gaining insights about this is important, but it is rarely a complete cure, and that was the case for Sasha. One day on her own she said that overall she was feeling better but still had intrusive, disturbing thoughts, and nothing we had done had changed them. This was familiar because I have seen few people who could have an "Aha!" insight powerful enough to defeat a lifetime habit of self-loathing, no matter how insightful the realization was at the time. What Sasha needed were some everyday tools to counter her overlearned and extreme reactions to criticism, and I had some ideas about what to do next.

What first came to mind was my version of cognitive therapy. In this therapy, insight is also important, but for very different reasons than it is used in psychoanalytic treatment. There, insight is about a deeper understanding of the historical sources of present emotional illnesses, such as Sasha's pickup truck memories.

In cognitive behavior therapy, insight means *mindfulness* and the goal is to be aware of mental and emotional experiences as they are occurring in the moment. Only when the patient can learn to ask, with the mildest disturbance, "What's happening right now?" is the brain free to come up with options other than the old reflexive habit. With this insight about one's momentary emotional state, negative thinking can be willfully replaced with more positive ideas about one's potential strengths.

Also, working back from the theory that fears of being scolded started with overwhelming guilt about real or imagined personality flaws, I knew that the therapy could only make a real difference when it also changed lifelong negative self-beliefs.

The solution was to use the cognitive technique which I called "left-page, right-page." Sasha was asked to become more immediately aware of negative thoughts (left page) and then try her best to counter them with more hopeful ideas (right page).

So the goal was to find positive ways to think about negative thoughts and beliefs. But in the left-page, right-page exercise, there was a crucial addition: *a test of whether the reframed positive thought was truly believable and lasting.* Since Sasha's negative thoughts were all symptoms of her deeper poor self-esteem, she seemed to be a perfect candidate for this approach.

Our interaction over the next several sessions went something like this.

Me:      What's an example of a troublesome thought that you had today?

Sasha: I don't know where to start (long pause). Okay, I was thinking that you are disappointed because of my slow progress.

Me:      That's a good one. Did you ever try to stop the thought or come up with something positive to counter it?

Sasha: I sometimes try that but it never works.

Me:      Want to try something new?

Sasha: Sure, what is it?

Me:      Let's call this the "left page – right page" game (handing her a small pocket notebook with left and right pages). Just open up this notebook then notice the empty pages. Take a pen and write at the top of the left page something about your thought that I'm disappointed in you—you know, like "Dr. Miller thinks that I'm not making enough progress." Then take a minute and try to think of some way to counter that negative thought with something new on the right page. What could you write?

Sasha: I don't know. (long pause) I can think of some stuff but I don't know if I believe it.

Me:      Like what?

Sasha: Maybe you are not very judgmental so maybe this worry just comes from me.

Me:      Write that at the top of the right page. In a few minutes I will show you how you can test the power of positive thoughts like that, so they will become more believable and really sink in. Now try to come up with a new left page negative thought, write it down and answer it by yourself. You're new at this game and I'll help if you want."

Sasha caught on quickly and seemed pleased that she was capable of reframing an unwanted thought. I said, "Keep your little book with you and look for solutions on your own. Bring it with you next time. Keep in mind that not all of your negative thoughts can be quickly repaired on the right page, at least not yet, but that's where I can help.

Sasha was highly motivated to move on from her insight about her childhood and get suggestions about what to do every day about constant self-doubt, and she rapidly learned the basics of 'left page-right page'. If she found the game useful, she could be on the way to healthy self-soothing. Then as expected, she had a few bad days and showed up in a state of despair, doubting her new tool and her therapist.

Sasha: How do I know if this will work? I'll never be able to write down all of my negative thoughts and work out an answer and write that down, especially on my own. This is too much work.

Me: Here's the good news. New habits do take work, but this one could be worth it because it gets right to the heart of the habit that has caused you so much grief. Once countering negative thoughts becomes an automatic habit, you'll just use "left page – right page" naturally without having to write anything down. Also, don't be surprised if you end up with only a few major complaints that cover most of your self-worrying. If you think about it, this is what most people do automatically to get through the day and feel okay about themselves. Try to think of something else to put on the left page.

Sasha: Okay. (long pause) I forgot that today was my day to pay for lunch with a friend until she had to remind me. I was so embarrassed.

Me: So what could happen?

Sasha: What if this happens again? She'll start having bad thoughts about me.

Me: That's a good one—put that last thought about your friend on the left page and think about what would make you feel better or even solve that worry. And remember that she is a good friend, and how quick you are to forget about her little mistakes.

Sasha: This is hard (another long pause). How about, "Knock it off, Sasha. You have no reason yet to distrust Kim."

Me: That's how you play this game. You're better at this than you think you are. I especially like "knock it off" because it shows how tired you are of beating yourself up. Don't leave anything on the left page not answered by something more soothing, even if it is just a wish. Remember the most important rule for this game: *Never leave a troubling left page entry in your notebook that is unanswered by a more positive thought on the right page.*

Just so you know, later on I'll ask you to find a time alone with only the right page notes in your little book. You'll learn how to test how much you believe each positive thought. As you build up confidence that you can find acceptable solutions to every worry, at some point your brain will get the message that you are not so bad after all.

For most of my patients, it takes a while for them to get into a rhythm of becoming immediately aware of self-putdowns and then reframing them in a more positive way. Patients who are already practicing mindfulness meditation almost always do well. There is something about the left-page-right-page game that appeals to a lot of people, and I have seen many patients make remarkable shifts from negative to more positive self-beliefs. Most learned that their self-doubts boil down to two or three self-critical thoughts and only write things down for a few months until the tool becomes automatic.

For Sasha, it took a lot of encouragement because on her own, every time she came up with a right page response it was countered by "yes but" and back she would go to the left page, so it was tiresome. But she stuck with it and slowly began to experience the soothing feeling of being able to control her negative thinking. In the end, Sasha would win or lose the game depending on how committed she was to self-loathing, or its opposite, a determination to feel better. That is why traditional cognitive behavior therapy alone is often unsuccessful. For many patients, the tool must include some way to build in gut-level self-appreciation.

"Left-page, right-page" is far from a cure-all. First, too many of my patients, like Sasha, need much deeper work before they can fully accept the thought, "Yes, I now believe I can find solutions for most of my daily problems." But a larger problem is the lack of follow-through with the homework. I commonly hear comments like Sasha's "Oh please, not one more job for me to do every day."

Here's a way to get a small feel for what Sasha was going through. Imagine you are taking a survey of things and situations that sometimes disturb people, and you're asked to rate four different items from 0 to 4 levels of anxiety, for a total of five levels. If you check off a "zero", this indicates "No sweat – that's easy for me". If you think "Very troublesome but I can handle it" your score is "2". A maximum self-rating of "4" indicates "I hate that – it makes me extremely anxious". Now judge yourself on these four test items that relate to scoldophobia: *"being criticized"*; *"feeling disapproved of"*; *"feeling rejected by others"*; and *"making mistakes"*.

Your maximum score is 20 (4 items, 5 levels of disturbance). A total score of 8 or less means that scoldophobia is not a major problem for you (in my career I have never seen anyone who scored "0" on these four items). But any score of 14 or above strongly suggests that you are one of the many whose insecurity and fear of shame can be very troubling.

I had a chance to partially test this idea. An assistant randomly pulled out the scores of over 50 of my child, adolescent and young adult patients from the test, called the Fear Survey Schedule, with a total of 108 items. Then, she added up the scores for the four items above. The average score was 13, revealing significant and disturbing insecurity and sensitivity to shame. No big surprise here, because these young people are in my office for good reasons. But assuming that the readers of this book experience more or less typical daily disturbances, I would still predict that there are a large number of people out there who are sensitive or even hypersensitive to various forms of criticism.

Here is how scoldophobia has worked in my life. It's what is going on when someone says to me, "You're being too sensitive," which points out a failing of mine and adds to my resentment toward the speaker, even if it is my best friend talking. It's rarely helpful and almost always adds to the hurt. I think being scolded can feel that a lifetime of self-doubt and personal flaws are being made public. It's the fear of being dismissed as somehow inferior, which in areas of my city can be deadly if you should happen to "diss" someone who is carrying a weapon.

One morning, while driving down my narrow canyon road, a woman on my right was pulling out of her driveway without slowing down when she came to the road, so I tapped my horn to get her attention and avoid a crash. I then noticed with increasing concern how close she was to my bumper until we got to a stop sign.

The next thing I knew she was banging on my window, screaming at me with heavily accented words that could only be verbal bullets. I then pulled over so she could pass, but instead she also pulled over and stopped behind my car. It was only when I was close to my office that she apparently decided that she had evened the score. That happy ending was soothing for both of us, but for very different reasons.

Something similar happened many years ago on a back road in southern France, when an ancient, busted and rusted Citroen jammed with kids and a smoking hunched-over Frenchman took exception to my attempt to pass him. His car seemed to be struggling along at a very slow speed. But when I pulled up alongside of him to pass, he hunched over his steering wheel even more and the car sped up into my lane, preventing me from passing. I tried once again and then decided to show up late in San Tropez rather than get us all killed. That night, on the patio of the old French innkeeper, I learned all about scolding on a national and historical level.

My friend graphically described how, after three humiliating and castrating German invasions, nearly all of his older countrymen found that their only reliable source of manly erections was when they were driving their cars, especially when their wives were watching. He explained that my encounter that afternoon was a life or death matter, at that moment even more important than his children. I wanted to yell out, a la the tennis great John McEnroe screaming at the umpire, "You canNOT be serious!" but I came to believe what he was saying.

Stories like this one got better as the hour grew later and his fabulous red wines took hold. Years later, when I learned to safely talk about the devastations caused by toxic shame early in my life, I sometimes flashed back to my all-night lessons about scoldophobia on that seaside patio in France.

As for Sasha, if she had not come for therapy and could have had her way, it is likely that she would've never left home. The old Sasha would say there is just too much hurt out there, waiting to strike.

# GONE! HOW CHARLIE STOPPED COUNTING AND STARTED LIVING

*I'm an obsessive. When I get a problem, or a*
*question in my mind, it can take me over.*
—Barbara Ehrenreich

LIKE ANDREW, CHARLIE was a troubled soul, a sweet and shy fifteen-year-old. But he had missed many school days because of a crippling case of "checking." He could not do anything once; if he closed a door or flushed the toilet or closed the lock on his school locker door, he had to make sure, up to at least five times that the job was properly done. Medication had not helped much.

Charlie had a severe obsessive-compulsive disorder (OCD), which comes in one of two (or both) flavors: inescapable compulsions to repeat some behavior, or mentally obsessing about the same thoughts over and over. The brain is locked in a fixed loop until some arbitrary standard is met, and any attempt to interrupt the compulsion brings on unbearable anxiety.

One patient, a nine-year-old girl, had her OCD mixed up with separation from her mother. It took me and the mom a half year, including home visits, to make her daughter feel safe while having her mother moved gradually away from her, foot by foot, room by room.

Another child was plagued by a fear of contamination by household products, which of course were everywhere. He went through the day labeling things as "this is for the good" or "this is for the bad." The lives of all these patients are filled with despair which almost always spreads to those who care most about them.

Even though OCD is often an inherited biological illness, for many of these patients a partial cure is now available thanks to the combination of anti-anxiety medication and cognitive behavior therapy, described in the previous case. This approach was the first psychological treatment of any kind to clearly show how the brain changes during psychotherapy. The neurological basis for the rigid behavioral cycle is literally a locked-up brain, in which its normal ability to detect danger is in overdrive. For OCD patients, danger lurks almost everywhere. Any unexpected change in routine is followed by attempts to self-soothe with repeated thoughts and behaviors.

Yet by gradually being helped to confront these repetitions in a semi-relaxed state, many individuals can learn to feel safe. Charlie was greatly encouraged when I told him that he had done nothing wrong, but had a brain problem that could be helped. He became a perfect patient, saying that he would do anything to be free from what we called his "puppet-master brain."

Charlie quickly mastered the ability to become deeply relaxed with minimal hypnosis, with the help of a handheld biofeedback device that produced a rising tone when his anxiety increased. Any time the tone went down, it meant that he was learning to control his anxiety not by trying hard but by just letting go of tension.

Also, because Charlie had such a good imagination, he quickly mastered our "surfer scene." Here the patient mentally places him or herself out on the pier watching surfers either ride a wave to shore or let it pass. It's all up to the surfer to control what happens. While

Charlie watched and using my hands, I demonstrated a vertical hand rising and falling like a surfer waiting for an oncoming wave, while my other hand mimicked the approaching wave.

I had Charlie imagine a rising impulse to check whether or not he had fastened a lock on his yard's gate, just as the surfer would feel the impulse to take a wave rising in his mind. Then he could picture himself rising with the wave, but deciding not to ride it and instead move straight back down to the level of the water and rest again. With his eyes closed, Charlie imagined the scene over and over until he felt confident that he could picture the lock, feel the impulse rising to check the lock one more time, but relax and let the impulse, just like the wave, pass away on its own.

Charlie even learned to imagine hearing the "click" of his school locker, and then pretend that he was taking a few steps away without having to look back or go back to the locker. Also, he became quite good at consciously postponing imagined urges while counting up to fifteen seconds before giving in to them. This kind of progress was very encouraging for both of us.

What Charlie 'the office expert' could not do was apply his imagined tools to compulsions in daily life. The most troubling of these occurred every day when he came home after school and made his mother sit in front of him, while he felt "forced" to recount the day's events. His mother was very concerned about him and his troubles, but became increasingly frustrated with his lengthy afterschool ritual that took a good deal of her time away from her chores and other children. I had a decision to make: give Charlie more time with the often successful cognitive therapy, or find a new approach for OCD.

As far as I knew at that time, the EMDR treatment that helped Sasha in the previous case had not been used on children with OCD. The idea for trying EMDR in Charlie's treatment came quite unexpectedly from my own experiences with the EMDR. This story will require a brief detour, revisiting Dr. Dorsey and his help with a new problem of mine.

In our decades-long UCLA neuroscience group, which meets weekly in my office, I once presented a paper on imagination which was part of a book I was writing. I loved this piece of work on the brain's ability to create mental images and was confident it would be well received. Traditionally, this is a most friendly and open-minded group, even when it includes intense debates about evolution and the brain. The unspoken and only rule for the group is that attacks are about the ideas at hand, never about the person.

But that day, some members of the group, including a good friend and brother-like Ben went after my paper and me with razor-like venomous gusto. At first I had no idea what was going on and retreated into unbelieving shock with only feeble and failed complaints. There was no precedent for this in the group.

I had two choices: angrily confront what must've been a much deeper group issue than my paper, or take some time and think about what had happened and what I needed to do about it. I chose to avoid dragging us all into group psychotherapy but missed several meetings with lame excuses. When I returned, there were no apologies from the group, only one member who outside of the group said, "Hans, you're too sensitive." I felt betrayed in the worst way; these were supposed to be my most dependable friends.

The incident gradually faded, but later when I told Dr. Dorsey about this, he suggested EMDR with the alternate tapping on the backs of my hands, and here is what came up.

While describing the event about Ben with eyes closed and Dr. Dorsey alternating his tapping on the back of my two hands, I suddenly had images of my over-idealized older brother humiliating and physically abusing me when I was in junior high school. I described how I felt helpless to stop him, and even weeks later many warnings by our mother did not change anything.

It wasn't until much later that I aggressively retaliated, which ended the abuse forever but didn't make me feel any better. Dr. Dorsey later said that even the most heavily repressed betrayals can't sleep forever. But I wasn't so sure, since it took decades to find relief for what amounted to *re*-traumatization, which takes me back to the group and then Charlie.

In our group, I wasn't going to change Ben and his co-conspirators the way I changed my brother's hostility when I was a teenager. Dr. Dorsey put it this way: "Bad things happen, and if you're persistent and lucky you learn to reprocess them and move on."

The group again came into play in a good way when I recalled that another member, Peter, once presented a short paper called "There Is No Delete Button." He was announcing the common sense knowledge that motivated all lengthy therapies: it takes a long time and a lot of work to rid patients of troubling feelings and thoughts and fantasies; there are no quick fixes. I thought about this for years as a challenge.

Then one day I had a new idea. If EMDR felt like a shortcut for psychoanalysis, which it did for me, could there be a shortcut for EMDR? It would be an intervention strangely close to a delete button, and it would be based on everything I knew about the biology of breathing and relaxation.

Breathing *in* activates the same brain-based hardware that drives the self-protective "flight or fight mechanism." Breathing *out* stimulates the brain's areas and chemistry responsible for relaxation. What if an extreme breath intake brings forth maximum tension that could be partially "deleted" by an equally strong outbreath? I see this in yawning, everyday deep breaths and in every sport. Watch any major league baseball pitcher: you'll see him take a slow deep breath followed by a big exhalation just before he throws the ball. Then fully relaxed, he leaves the past behind and is ready for the coming moment.

There's more. What if, at the peak of intense and stressful fully-inflated lungs, I intensely concentrated on an extremely troubling fear for three or four seconds, and then blew out the air with a mentally loud "GONE!" Could the radical breathing technique lessen or perhaps even erase the feared emotional experience? At least in theory it might work. Perhaps an extremely relaxing out-breath at the moment of maximum discomfort would be the complete opposite of (and block) anxiety, especially if it was accompanied by a strong self-assertion.

This procedure, which I have been most reluctant to share professionally because of its likely dismissal (at best) from colleagues, not only continues to wipe out many of my own irrational fears and unwanted thoughts, but those of most patients with which it has been used. In other words, if a fear is not rational or immediately dangerous, it is flexible and may disappear, at least for a while, in a flood of relaxing neurotransmitters and hormones. Many times, only one or a few uses of GONE can do the job. And if this sounds crazy, it is a crazy cure like nothing I have ever seen. *There may actually be a delete button.*

In the years since I first began experimenting with GONE, other techniques have been shown to take away unwanted fears as if they were actually deleted from the brain. These *events* aren't denied, just the excessive emotional reactions. For example, people with long-term phobias have learned to safely approach objects that formerly terrified them by first receiving twenty milligrams of propranolol. This adrenaline-blocking medication is administered sometime before a phobic person approaches a feared object such as a tarantula or hypodermic needle. In other studies both external and internal brain electrical stimulation presented at the time of fear arousal can end the power of whatever was terrifying or obsession-causing.

One day, when Charlie came in with an extremely despairing mood, I suggested we try something new. I described and demonstrated GONE. He assumed that the procedure was part of everyday psychotherapy practice and followed it to perfection. He deeply breathed in, pictured himself fastening his school locker combination lock, then walking away, looking back at the lock, desperately needing to physically go check it, and then fiercely holding his breath before a noisy exhalation as he mentally shouted "GONE."

I had learned to test the usefulness of GONE by repeating it to see if the previous fear was lessened. Charlie was my first clinical test case, and after only a few practices with test repeats, I was stunned by his response.

When he tried to reinstate the fear, he started laughing, which seemed inappropriate. He then said, "That was funny! I didn't feel anything when I imagined the urge to check the lock again. It's really dumb to worry about something like that. Can I try it with the gate lock on the side of the house?" This he did with similar results.

I had him test and retest the attempt to re-experience the fears after applying GONE to other compulsions. He simply could not regain the original intense compulsion. After a few days of applying GONE at school, he was for the first time successful in walking away from his locker with only a brief glance. Charlie not only had a possible delete button, but one that worked out in the real world. This extraordinary kind of response to a treatment for OCD "brain lock" was unheard of, yet seemed to work for many of his troublesome thoughts and fears.

In addition, over time Charlie gradually found a carryover of his successes to old fears, such as obsessively counting the contents of his backpack or perfectly placing food around on his plate. Something important had happened, but it still took a long time before I shared this new tool with a colleague, and even then I was careful to base my description on the well-accepted biological facts underlying the respiratory theory of GONE.

I don't know of anyone else using this technique, but the logic and results seemed sound, at least with my patients and in my personal life. Now all I needed was a graduate student in search of a large research project who could track down the ingredients of GONE using a variety of patients and nonpatients with both phobias and normal worries.

Meanwhile, Charlie made continuous gains in most areas of his previously anxious daily life. He never again missed school because of anxiety.

As time went on, both the imperfections and other benefits of the GONE technique gradually became apparent. If a frightening, realistic event such as giving a speech was coming up in someone's life, the anxiety was never fully deleted—a good thing because moderate anxiety allows us to function at our best when tested in the real world. Yet even then, my patients reported a meaningful reduction of public speaking anxiety.

Also, actual troubling events deep in my patients' histories remained troubling, but less so. Perhaps combining GONE with EMDR would be more effective for problems like PTSD than using either one of these interventions alone. For some people, their anticipated doomsday fears and urges, no matter how irrational, required months of practice with GONE before they become less disturbing. This is what happened to Charlie's compulsive urges to pressure his mom about his daily events.

In another example, a seventeen-year-old girl with severe depression believed so strongly that she was inferior in academics and her social life (the opposite was true) that GONE had little effect beyond briefly calming her down. For some, the irrational *is* personally rational and resistant to quick fixes.

And then there's the anger problem. Therapists know a great deal about treating anxiety. But there is precious little known about treating deep bitterness and expressions of irrational anger, other than trying to discover the root causes. In my experience, insight plays a limited role in the actual self-regulation of angry behavior such as ongoing resentments and emotional explosions. For me and my patients, GONE can temporarily take the edge off of anger, but with some very encouraging exceptions, most often these feelings don't get deleted.

One man who came from what he called "a family of screamers" was about to be divorced by his peace-loving wife and kids. In another case, a physician was discharged from a major hospital in Massachusetts because he couldn't stop blowing up in the operating room at doctors and nurses members who made mistakes. I was unable to help either of these men with GONE.

I searched for a biological explanation for this anger mystery and quickly found that the brain areas and chemistry responsible for reducing anxiety are different from those that trigger various degrees of anger. However, brain areas sensitive to threat, anxiety, and hurt feelings are often activated *before* anger. I've often wondered if all anger can be traced back to hurt feelings. It is the fear of losing one's freedom and increased frustration that is the primary trigger for anger and aggression, while anxiety can be activated by any perceived threat to security.

Also, perhaps GONE is more effective for anxiety because anger evolved as a physical readiness for full-bodied battle rather than anxious, passive worry or despair. My best therapy tools for troublesome anger combines anger management groups, meditation, insight, and the adrenaline-blocking medication propranolol. I'm still working on direct behavioral interventions and variations of GONE for anger and anxiety which focus on breathing exercises.

As for my own situation, I can now count on even my most troubling nighttime worries usually going away with a few repeats of this strange tool. But there are large individual differences in patients using GONE, and as I just mentioned, sometimes it just doesn't work at all. For example, I got so excited writing about GONE that when I awoke at four in the morning, nothing helped. None of these rare events have been serious enough for me to hesitate when I felt that GONE might be useful for a patient.

For Charlie and his mother, I still have some sort of special status. Charlie is my only patient who stopped by to see me before he went off to college and occasionally writes about his progress. I will be forever grateful to Charlie for helping me discover GONE.

❧

## Getting Rinaldo and Ted to Sleep

*How do people go to sleep? I'm afraid I've lost the knack.*
—Dorothy Parker
*When I want to go to sleep,*
*I must first get a whole menagerie of voices to shut up.*
—Karl Kraus

There are two stories here, tied together by the miseries of what has become a nationwide epidemic: not getting enough sleep. But the stories are quite different, in that the second improved approach to insomnia described here came over ten years after the first, and showed my need to constantly learn new interventions and adapt to wide individual differences in psychotherapy patients. There are also two main kinds of sleep disorders: one is when the individual had serious problems *falling* asleep (Rinaldo), and the other with *staying* asleep (Ted).

### Rinaldo: Sleeping with Hypnosis

Rinaldo was seventeen when his pediatrician sent him to me for sleep therapy. I was seeing many patients at the time for other reasons whose symptoms were worsened by not enough nighttime rest, called "sleep debt". In fact, as soon as I started asking about sleep disorders, I found that over half of my patients were not getting enough sleep. It was truly an epidemic and always helped explain the intensity of whatever symptoms people were coming in with, from stress at work, ADHD, depression, and all forms of anxiety. Yet to my knowledge, few therapists even do a simple assessment of the patient's sleep habits. I probably wouldn't have started asking about sleep without my own sleep disorder—another example of how my patients benefited by a personal problem of mine.

Rinaldo made it clear from the start that all he wanted was help with sleep, with "no headshrinking," like many of his friends who were forced to be in therapy. In our first session, he said, "There is nothing wrong with me that I can't fix by myself except this damn sleep thing. How many times do I have to come here?" He repeated this later when I told him that I would like specific ideas about the nature of his sleep habits with a weeklong nightly sleep record. I especially wanted to have him record his daily alertness several times a day using the Stanford Sleepiness Scale, which assesses arousal on a seven-point scale from "wide awake to near sleep onset with dreamlike thoughts."

Also I needed some background information using my standard questionnaire about his general strengths and weaknesses. But none of these routine procedures ever happened. So for the first time in years, I accepted a case and began treatment without any personal disclosures or information other than what I was able to get from his father. The closest I ever got to hearing about a psychological problem was when Rinaldo told me that sometimes his worry about not sleeping actually kept him from sleeping. This fear has the exotic name of *agrypniaphobia*, which described Rinaldo perfectly but he refused to talk about his feelings again.

Another conflict arose when I tried to impress upon him the importance of basic sleep hygiene. He briefly looked at the handout that is essential for all patients in sleep therapy. The material suggested developing a workable routine, limiting daytime naps to thirty minutes, no video screens, caffeine, or heavy exercise for at least thirty minutes before sleep, and soothing self-talk while sitting on the side of the bed, such as meditation, prayer, or learned self-hypnotic exercises until sleep takes over. Renaldo rolled his eyes and said he didn't need any of this and besides, it was "too much work."

All I had to work with was that Rinaldo had been a difficult son to raise, but because of his excellent academics and good social relationships, his father was allowing him to use his therapy time anyway he wished.

It was with this introduction that I went to work. I told Rinaldo that few people who come for treatment of specific symptoms get well in my office. I said, "This is where my patients learn new habits, and when they get better it's because they practice them on their own, outside of therapy." Again, Rinaldo rolled his eyes.

For a long while, I really thought that my patients would do much better in treatment if they knew how and why the treatment works. But this was misguided and for many people actually slowed down the therapy. Much of the time it's much better just to stay with *more show* and *less tell*. Also, Rinaldo was a man of few words and had no interest in hearing anything that was not directly related to why he walked in my room. He was basically angry with us "shrinks," saying, "If any of the pills that you guys made me take actually worked, this is the last place I would be."

As I mentioned earlier, there seems to be two kinds of sleep disorders: first getting to sleep, which requires the brain to be in a state of low or neutral arousal, much like a car idling. The second kind of sleep disorder is waking up too soon and then being unable to get back to sleep. Midnight waking is much harder to treat for the simple reason that it occurs in the early morning hours when the brain's mental control systems are not fully working. On the other hand, at bedtime the brain is still aroused enough to be receptive to voluntary, relaxing suggestions.

At that time, I was using a mild hypnotic induction with very simple instructions that any patient could easily learn and practice at bedtime. But with Rinaldo, I had to find out if the therapy even had a chance, which meant doing some experiments to see if he could relax, and then if he had any motivation to practice a new habit. Being relaxed is the key to falling asleep; the brain doesn't care if it is pleasurable excitement or worry that keeps it busy.

By the time I saw Rinaldo, I had discovered new ways to get myself to sleep without medication. I found that these approaches were workable with many, but not all patients in my office. This was contrary to the declaration of a sleep physician I once spent time with, who said, "No one can put himself to sleep." But what would it take to get Rinaldo to relax using my instructions, in the office? This was the first order of business and I was pleasantly surprised to learn that he was willing to follow suggestions as long as they were only about sleeping.

I had Rinaldo place a small pillow behind his head on the couch and sit up straight. He would stay in this erect posture until he could not help himself from flopping backward onto the pillow because of sleepiness. Using the same procedure that is essential to patients being introduced to "GONE," I placed a small table directly in front of him and had him close his eyes and think about an imaginary small uninflated blue balloon on the table. He was to imagine himself slowly counting to 3 which his balloon would be fully inflated with air. Then when the balloon could be inflated no more without bursting, he was to keep the pressure on the balloon to the count of 3, and only then slowly let the air out of the balloon as he counted forward from *1* to *7*. At that point he would imagine that the balloon was completely flat and empty, with nothing left inside.

Next, Rinaldo was asked to repeat the balloon exercise, but this time using his lungs, gradually filling them with air until he felt very tense and then slowly letting out the air until he could feel absolutely relaxed and without any tension anywhere in his body. He would especially focus on any remaining tension in his jaw and shoulders while imagining himself sinking deeper into the couch as he sat upright. He would look for feelings of sleepiness, wanting nothing more than to fall backward onto the pillow. At first, Rinaldo complained that he didn't like the idea of being hypnotized, but then decided to follow my suggestions, and before long had to constantly steady himself to stay upright.

At the end of our first session Rinaldo surprised me again with a report that I fortunately don't often hear. I asked him to answer a few questions on a standard follow-up sheet that I use for many patients who are seeing me for direct symptom treatment. After he left, I read his comments, in which he scored himself as "I became sleepy during the session" but then in response to the question "How helpful was the treatment?" Rinaldo wrote "Not at all." On his open-ended comments, he wrote "I didn't get any sleep last night and that's why I wanted to put my head back: it had nothing to do with the exercise."

So that was the *modus operandi* of our therapy relationship, which lasted seven meetings. He was extremely compliant and in each session became drowsy to the point of falling asleep, but he refused to link his progress in any way with anything I was doing. At one point I could not stop myself from smiling and thinking, "Hey, what about this therapy?" Then, sooner than I wanted, Rinaldo announced that he had used my room to cure himself and didn't need to come anymore. At least that was something, and he got what he came for.

Renaldo also proved that another one of my "guidelines for good therapy" was wrong, at least for him. Because he claimed that he never practiced anything we did at home to help him sleep, I don't actually know what I did for him at home in his own bed. The only thing I'm sure of is that I regularly got him into a state of deep sleep in my office, such that I had to wake him at the end of several sessions.

According to his father, Rinaldo became a decent sleeper and got off most of his medications, and left my office for the last time with his final negative report. He was sleeping better but still insisted that it had nothing to do with the treatment. His father later called me, saying that Rinaldo was going right to sleep at bedtime and sometimes still had problems waking in the middle of the night. He didn't want to come back for additional treatment.

Some patients would rather get well than go to therapy! This was actually not a bad thing for me because at that time I did not *have* a treatment for premature waking; I was still dependent on early morning tranquilizing medication myself and had yet to find a medication-free behavioral cure that worked. Why is this important? Because a new behavioral cure could avoid medication side effects, and perhaps more importantly, free the person for life with self-regulating tools that could reduce all daily stresses. I spent years working on a medication-free cure for early morning waking.

### Ted: Sleeping with "Nothing" and "Four Sleepy Questions"

By the time I met Ted a decade after Rinaldo, my techniques for treating sleep disorders had improved dramatically. I had discovered some new and effective ways to get myself and many others back to sleep in the early morning hours. Then one day a patient showed up who I was able to help not only with sleep but also help in another way that I had only dreamed about.

On a typical day at the office, I went to the waiting room to bring in a new patient. Following him to my office, I checked his intake form and there was his age and profession: a twenty-five-year-old professional baseball player. I stopped and had to reorient myself to the business at hand. Really? A pro baseball player? Minor or major league? What could I do for him? The referring therapist had only said that the patient had an unusual form of anxiety but no known traumas, and he thought that I might be able to help.

Soon I knew the story: Ted wanted to know if I could get him to stop freezing in the batter's box and get his previously high batting average back up to above .300, or three hits in ten tries, which could earn him millions of dollars in the major leagues. The team psychologist had only helped a little. Also, Ted had just re-signed with his major-league team and needed to be ready for spring training in less than three months. Then, Ted told me about a major sleep disorder that left him constantly feeling tired, and hoped that I might be able to help him get more rest.

By this time I was completely comfortable. I had faith in my sleep therapy, and that's where we would start. Then, in all likelihood, whatever else was going on would probably get better along the way. This would also give me time to explore his "freezing" that prevented him from even swinging his bat, no matter how "fat" and good-looking the pitch was. Ted thought that he could probably sleep better if he was hitting better but was very open to the opposite idea: *first, learn how to sleep.* Like most of my insomnia patients, Ted was eager to begin a routine of sleep hygiene, to complete the standard hourly sleep record, and rate himself on the Stanford Sleepiness Scale.

Ted came from a healthy family, although his father had a history of childhood anxiety. However, he was very successful in his job as an airplane mechanic manager at a local airport. His mother was a physical therapist, which greatly helped Ted because of a recent hip injury. A younger brother had no psychological problems. Everyone in the family seemed to be happily progressing and moving forward in life except for Ted. Yet he even had the "look" of a very fit and successful professional athlete, with intense focus and initiative to follow through with everything I suggested. We were off to a good start.

It got even better when he noticed that my hypnosis narratives included a lot of very realistic details about what it feels like to be in the batter's box. He asked a lot of questions about my youthful baseball career and achievements, and it took some effort to refrain from talking baseball.

Meanwhile, as shown in Ted's self-report questionnaires and an overnight brainwave sleep study in a nearby clinic, Ted had one of the most distorted sleep records I had ever seen. It was amazing that he could be a successful athlete, much less have the attentional focus to hit a ninety-mile-an-hour fastball.

Everyone usually cycles through five stages of sleep, beginning with light sleep, full unconsciousness, the thirty-minute periods of Stage Four deep sleep, and the even more critical stage of rapid eye movement (REM) sleep. A complete sleep cycle takes about 1 1/2 hours and is repeated for four or five times in the night. Ted was actually getting a good bit of sleep in terms of total hours, but the record showed near-zero Stage Four sleep, which is essential for feeling refreshed in the morning and maintaining alertness during the day. Also, years earlier as part of my postdoctoral fellowship with neurology residents studying overnight sleep records, we learned that sleep medications of all kinds reduced Stage Four sleep to about 10 percent of what is needed. The modern flood of sleep medication aides are better, but not by much and they cost a lot more.

This was a further complication for me and Ted: we had to find a way to get him sleeping better without his sleep medication so that he would need this potential troublemaker less.

First, I introduced the "blue balloon" scene that I used for Rinaldo. One improvement in the procedure was to first have the patient breathe in for three seconds, hold the breath for three seconds, breathe out very slowly for seven seconds, and then add, "when all the air is gone, stop breathing for about three to five seconds while saying to yourself 'nothing is left,' and then with slumping shoulders and jaw, just think 'NOTHING'." Ted practiced this version of relaxation several times and then sleepily said, "I didn't think it was possible to feel nothing at all, even for a second, but I really like it."

Finding out about the mental state of "nothing" has been my most effective way of getting people to relax for whatever reason. But more is needed to get people to sleep and even more to get them back to sleep when waking too early. For this, after much experimentation on myself and a series of patients, I came up with "The Four Sleepy Questions." This is the standard method I used to get patients started with the questions:

"After sitting up on the bedside, when you can honestly answer no to these four questions, you will fall back on your bed pillow and go to sleep. When this becomes a habit, it will help you with early waking as well. If for any reason you have any doubts about the truth of "no" for these questions, then honestly answer "yes" and start over. Here they are:

1. Do I *want* to think about anything right now other than falling asleep? (Pause and think about your answer for a moment. When the answer is truthfully "no," just wait a few moments to see what else comes to mind on its own and repeat the question.)

2. Do I *need* to think of anything else right now? Again, pause and see if there any doubts.

3. Do I *have* to think of anything besides sleeping right now?

4. Do I *care* about anything more than falling asleep right now?

If there are still any *yes's* left, work backward from 'Do I care.' But anytime there are only true-feeling *no's*, then take one final deep breath and think "Don't care . . . nothing left . . . nothing at all . . . time to sleep."

That night, Ted practiced "nothing" starting with the blue balloon and then asked his four questions. He said that the first couple of times he answered "yes" to some of the questions but kept going until each of his answers was a convincing "no." He easily fell asleep; and when he awoke too early in the morning, he found that his new tools had helped him get back to sleep.

A few weeks later, he said he was having trouble holding on to the feeling of "nothing" after answering the questions. So I suggested two additional sleep helpers. One was GONE, which Ted rapidly mastered and found very useful. Then I asked him to keep a pad and pencil beside him in the bed on which to write down and "offload" questions like "What if I don't pass the team physical exam?" from his brain onto his pad for attention the next morning.

I also mentioned that strangely enough, there might be something deeper than *nothing*: a sudden awareness of surrendering that last bit of caring about anything when needing sleep. We practiced this in the office until he could find a sense of whatever "total surrender" meant to him, and he said he was feeling very sleepy.

Then two things happened. First, a limitation of direct symptom therapy showed itself. Ted said that everything was better, but something was still nagging him for which he could not find a name. In the batter's box in his practice batting cage, he noticed this new uncomfortable feeling and he was becoming worried again. Second, I began to think about EMDR.

As I showed with two earlier cases, this procedure can free the brain to access potentially soothing verbal labels to emerge about past repressed feelings. I wasn't thinking about trauma at the time, since his former therapist had taken a complete early life history which seemed to rule out terrifying experiences. But our therapy would be incomplete if there were still troublesome feelings at work. I decided to briefly use what I had learned about EMDR, and if he did not respond, I would refer him for more intensive trauma therapy as I had done on several occasions.

One clue to Ted's uncomfortable feelings was that they were experienced most intensely while in the batter's box. So I asked Ted to sit back and with palms down on a lap pillow and eyes closed. After he settled in, our interaction went something like this:

Me:     When did you start playing baseball?

Ted:    Little League. Even then I could hit just about anything.

Me:     Stay with that early image of being in the batter's box as I tap on your hands.

Ted:    (After less than 20 seconds of tapping) I'm remembering that once I got hit but I got over it with my dad's help.

Me:     (stop tapping) What did he do?

Ted:     He said that if I was going to be a serious baseball player, I had to shake it off and get over it.

Me:     Then what?

Ted:     Later in the season I got hit in the head but shook it off.

Me:     Stay with that. (tapping until Ted started talking)

Ted:     Well, that's strange. I suddenly pictured myself in the batter's box today. Coach turned off the machine and started pitching himself. He said it was time to make hitting more realistic. One of his pitches came close.

Me:     (quiet, not tapping)

Ted:     (opens eyes) Actually, now I remember the third time I got hit when I was a kid. I thought I was over all that, but maybe not. Is this PTSD?

Me:     What do you think?

Ted:     Maybe so—maybe somehow my brain added up all of those close calls.

Me:     Not all flashbacks are symptoms of posttraumatic stress disorder. Maybe those are the memories you needed to come up with. How do you feel right now?

Ted:     I think I'm okay. I'll know tomorrow in practice. Should I practice GONE right now?

Me:     Just do what you need to do.

Ted spent the rest of the session using the breathing exercises, and before long said that he was having trouble recapturing the "bothersome nagging feeling," which he decided was about "fear of being hit in the head." The following week Ted reported his hitting was back on track and that "brush back" pitches were part of the game. He would just stay loose, trust his swing, and put all of his focus on the location of the ball.

Another piece of news should not have been a surprise, because Ted was by then a full partner and coming up with his own ideas about therapy. One day he came in and said that he was now sleeping through the night without meds and with very few awakenings, and that he had discovered something new. It was the "going deeper than nothing" that made the difference in both sleeping and in hitting.

What surprised me was this: "going deeper" was designed to help people sleep. I never anticipated or suggested that this "deeper than nothing" state of mind would be useful in the batter's box. I assumed that it was not good to be that relaxed before trying to catch up with a fastball. Isn't some degree of tension necessary for an athlete about to run or throw or hit? Apparently not for Ted, or at least based on what he reported.

While in his batting cage at home, the improvement in his hitting was so remarkable that his coach asked him what he was doing differently to "smoke" the ball so solidly, time after time. Ted was getting what we only speculated about at the beginning: all-night sleep and the kind of hitting that could improve his batting average, and he was doing his way. *Two for the price of one.*

Ted was happy until it occurred to him that he had never frozen in practice, only in a real ballgame. One day he said, "Do you think that my therapy will automatically help with freezing?" I said, "Maybe, but why take a chance? You now have all of the basics. Next week let's work on freezing." To which Ted wanted to know *how.* I said, "We're going to practice freezing until you are completely in control of how it feels and how not to freeze. Next week bring your bat."

This was going to be tricky, but it had to happen. If he should ever freeze without a way to prove with confidence that it was controllable, our entire baseball therapy could be in doubt. On the other hand, if he could learn to confront the freezing head-on and survive, the unfortunate habit might be conquered. Ted was more than willing, but found it strange that we would actually practice such an awful thing.

To prepare, I asked Ted to write out the complete physical and emotional experience of his last freeze setback and bring it in. The following week, I asked him to read aloud his story about freezing, while practicing GONE any time he felt uncomfortable. This he did with a few pauses. For the first time, he was able to identify and describe the thoughts that triggered a freeze and then, with bat in hand in the middle of my office, take a full swing.

Now it was my turn to freeze. Ted swung with such power that had he let go of the bat it would have surely gone through the wall—or me. It was easily the most explosive drama my office had ever witnessed, but it was also very exciting to see. He said he felt no hesitation at all as he imagined a pitch coming his way. He said he wanted to try a few more to see if he could instantly dismiss any concerns about being hit or freezing. I pushed my chair back more than a few feet and watched the show.

Only one thing was left, and it was the most important thing for Ted. In spring training, could he maintain his near-perfect swing without freezing against experienced professional pitchers? Would I have to (or get to) go to his Arizona training camp to help him fine-tune his new skills? I wasn't worried and it turned out that I didn't have to be. Ted no longer had a problem freezing in the batter's box, but like so many other talented ballplayers he struggled to get in the lineup on a regular basis.

Overall, what I did was to find some ways to help Ted, a true therapy partner, get the sleep he needed and then get him unstuck in the batter's box. Perhaps other approaches would have worked, but I was happy with the outcome of our combined efforts. Sometimes the success of complicated therapies such as Ted's depends on an arsenal of related interventions.

Sadly, Ted ended up reinjuring his hip and the last I heard he was taking a break from baseball to recover. He was one of the thousands of good ballplayers dreaming of playing in the major leagues and who may never make it. For a while, I got to dream along with him.

Oh yes, I said Ted got two for the "price of one." In his last session with me, he made it three. Just as time ran out in our last session, he said something like, "Oh, yeah, I never told you about my needle phobia. Well, my doctor wanted additional bloodwork for my physical exam and I had to go in twice for what has always been torture for me. Guess what? All it took was a couple of 'GONEs' and 'nothings.' The nurse, who knows me very well, noticed my deep breathing but was surprised that I was smiling and asked me what was going on. I just told her that needles weren't a problem anymore." Such is the joy of working with someone so full of initiative.

### Ava: The Manic Defense and the Capacity to Be Alone

*All are insecure; the only difference in us*
*is the size of our security blankets.*

There is a widespread syndrome out there called the "manic defense," and it is very soothing. The syndrome is soothing because it allows an immediate escape from shame, depression, and even the inner terrors of psychosis that I described with "Bertha" at the beginning of this book. It has several parts, and I know them very well.

First, as in a dream when you're being chased, you can never slow down, especially when it means looking hard at yourself.

Second, there have been moments when you tried to relax and contemplate your inner thoughts and fears. It did not go well; afterward you were more anxious than ever, grabbing at your next mental or physical activity. Something had bubbled up from the inside that got you refocused on your endless jobs and problems. All of our self-distracting habits, such as unhealthy Internet use and substance addictions, qualify as *manic defenses*. With only a little practice they become automatic, dominating daily life simply because it is so rewarding to quickly escape from boredom, despair, and even panic.

Third, if you are in therapy, even though you really trust that your therapist can handle your awful beliefs about yourself, you always go prepared with enough collected symptoms and complaints to fill the therapy time. Your therapy is not about *you*; it's about your endless problems. He or she probably won't mind—therapists understand all this and partially make their living by going easy on desperately needed security blankets. Plus, your therapy ventilations may keep you from wearing out your mate and friends with complaints.

Ava's stonewalled message to me was "Keep your distance from my feelings—you have to help me with this crisis right now!" Her security blanket was great and she was an ever-busy collector of impingements. And she seemed to be completely dependent on her personal fireman, who happened to be me.

Several times a year I made a special effort to help her have a small look at herself, but it had no lasting value. I met with the same resistance when I tried to ask her about her childhood. I also tried to set a firm limit that the first half of each session we would talk only about her and not just about her handicapped son or some imagined calamity. For a long while, the closest I came to getting her to experiment with relaxing was when I interrupted her numerous complaints with "Can we talk about you little bit?" She would seem to make an honest effort for a moment, and that gave me hope.

Another source of hope was Ava's habit of showing up about every two weeks in a strangely quiet mood, not talking much or being frantic. Not wanting to change the mood, I just kept quiet and waited until she had something to say, wondering what it would take her to have more days like that. For a long time, I remained puzzled by these brief interruptions of her mania. Whether it was some self-correcting brain chemistry or fatigue from all her stress, Ava did have access to something all her own that was soothing. For whatever reason, I never commented on this.

Then after another week of Ava's complaining, I would wake up and realize that her dire suffering had again seduced me back into our status quo. She could keep her nose above water level, but not for very long. And we seemed to have a conspiracy of silence about her deepest yearning—to feel worthy of being cared for in spite of her self-loathing. Whenever I actually approached this truth about her, it was met with protests until she could get me to once again answer urgent questions and offer guidance. Nor would she follow through with my attempts to teach her tried-and-true methods for relaxation and anxiety reduction—or take her anti-stress medication. Her rigid defenses and doomsday thinking were defeating my skills and creativity.

Yet Ava herself was an excellent trainer: some part of her brain seemed to know about the power of unpredictable rewards that I described much earlier in this book. On average, about one out of five of her issues were actually about *her* therapy. Yet just like one of my lab animals from the distant past being trained to never give up pressing the bar for food, I could never give up on her. Why not? Because of being randomly "fed" with one of Ava's pro-therapy gestures one of every five tries, I could not predict when a therapy moment would occur, and this is why I kept trying. These meager rewards were enough to keep me focused on the hope for emotional growth rather than her next looming catastrophe. Here is how I got into this.

A special education teacher, who had once participated in the Parent Training Clinic, referred Ava and her ten-year-old adopted son Misha to me for therapy. While in the clinic, my former student had unfortunately been assigned a very high risk family, meaning that even with a great deal of time and effort, the likelihood of success was low. She actually got the mother to make some positive changes, but the later follow-up measures showed almost no maintenance of the treatment gains.

Ava reminded her of the family she had struggled with long ago, and she wondered if I had come up with any new ways to help difficult parents. She described Ava as extremely anxious and self-doubting about almost every aspect of her life, and said that Misha was the most hyperactive and out-of-control child she had seen in years.

So from the beginning, two things were clear to me. First, I could not begin treatment without knowing a lot more about both mother and child. What negative self-beliefs were holding back Ava from doing her job as a person and a parent? What was Misha's neurological diagnosis and how could I help him?

Second, this treatment case would go far beyond what we normally called "parent training." I would have to help Ava become more receptive to developing new habits, which was a psychotherapy issue. I also had both a responsibility and new incentive to answer the referring teacher's question: what had I learned about high-risk parents that we didn't know when I was in charge of the UCLA Parent Training Clinic?

Ava was a single mother who became extremely depressed and obese after her fellow actor and fiancé died many years ago. She decided that the solution to her grief was to pay a pregnant young woman to carry the baby which would then become her adopted child at birth. It was only later that Ava learned about the mother's long history of drug abuse. Ava's father also complicated the situation: he was Ava's sole source of income and extremely judgmental. He had set high standards for his daughter to raise a grandson of whom he could be proud.

Early in Misha's life, Ava had seen signs of neurologically-based attention deficit disorder with very scattered abilities, poor impulse control, and oppositional defiance. Ava's baffled approach to parenting only added to Misha's severe problems. When I made my first home visit during breakfast, all I saw was chaos and screaming. Ava loudly criticized Misha for being too skinny and yelled at him to eat; he would then throw his fork, seemingly aimed at her head. Looking in my direction, she would then say, "Do you see how he treats me?"

At first I thought this poor woman desperately wanted and needed my help with her son. Not so, she wanted me to reduce the danger, not stop the conflict. I came to this conclusion only after helping her find solutions to many of her son's problems, but then found that no amount of good news ever soothed her for long.

I think Ava was one of the most overwrought and apprehensive persons I've ever met. She literally lived from one crisis to the next, and to make it worse, was completely noncompliant with her antianxiety medication and diet. The goal with her was clear, but the path did not yet exist: I needed to find a way to get her to say, "What's at stake? Not nearly as much as I thought." I tried this one time and she immediately changed the subject; I could not have been more off-base. If only I had a security pill! But then of course I might be out of a job.

Why would anyone *not* want to relax? Why did Ava play such a major role in keeping the battle going with her son? The answers to questions like these always seemed to be the same for Ava: *she simply could not afford to stop worrying*. That was the manic defense in action.

So this was the case before the so-called expert in parent therapy, who was confronted with a high risk for mother and child. In the early sessions with her, I said many times that she and her son were an unfortunate match, and that *any* mother of Misha would have great difficulty and require special training. Each time she would say, "Stop telling me he's handicapped—I'm not a bad mother" (another case of scoldophobia?). Nothing in my old parent training manual worked, but I had to remind myself that it was largely because of mothers like Ava that I went into private practice.

I did some testing with Ava, and my worst fears were supported: based on our original clinic measurements, she would have been one of our clinic high risk moms. She was very prone to experiencing episodes of extreme anxiety, shame, and seemed to be obsessed with conflict. The only thing she disliked more than herself was a constant fear of overwhelming shame whenever she did something wrong.

Fortunately, I had some experience with mothers like Ava and had an idea what I was in for when I took on this case. The biggest problem would be to get Ava to slow down her manic pursuit of allowing her son's problems to dominate her life. I had no choice but to also make Misha a priority, and hope that helping him might help her relax enough to talk about herself. So this case is about two patients, both of whom needed professional attention, which would complicate everything because she insisted that I also be Misha's therapist.

At one point I asked for a brain scan for Misha, and the results were like nothing I had ever seen. Both the front and underside areas of his brain had the look of Swiss cheese, indicating very poor blood flow to critical brain areas responsible for self-regulation and psychological maturation. With Ava I minimized the results to prevent more panic attacks. A well-known neurologist and I discussed Misha's scan results. He said, "Sadly, this is what I call 'The Ring of Fire' type of attention deficit hyperactivity disorder (ADHD)—too much of his brain is not functioning well; this boy will have a very rough life and he may not respond to medication."

Then after Misha was dismissed from a local private school, one morning at breakfast, he hit his target with the fork and put his mother in the emergency room with eye trauma. I had no other option but to send him away to a series of therapeutic boarding schools, all with poor results. Suddenly Ava had more to worry about: increased pressure from her father who didn't understand why his only grandson was in a "special school." I once had a chance to talk with him and he seemed reasonable, but I never convinced her that she was safe to tell him the whole truth about Misha.

Then three years later, together with a special consultant, we found a place in Idaho with a good reputation for helping troubled youngsters like Misha. This school was not for everyone: every privilege except eating and sleeping in a bed had to be earned. Also, any extreme defiance or aggression earned the resident the privilege of digging post holes for a new fence around the property, rain or shine. When Ava heard about this from her wailing son, she angrily demanded that I get him out of there, and send him home.

It took three consecutive days of debate for her to understand the good and bad news. This was a major crossroad in Misha's life, and if she rewarded his manipulation with a dangerously premature return to the streets of Los Angeles, she would risk losing him forever. Even with his poorly integrated personality Misha was fully capable of digging holes.

If she wanted me to continue treatment, she would have to give the facility a chance to civilize him no matter how much he complained. Fortunately, Ava made the right decision. She should forever thank hole digging for her son's beginning ability to function in the world.

About a year later, Misha became what I could only consider to be 'a real person' for the first time, with more socially appropriate behavior. In another year before he left the therapeutic boarding school at age eighteen, he had for the first time become a student, even interested in Shakespeare. The stories and poetry he proudly sent to me were surprising and impressive. Without success, I tried to prevent Ava from allowing Misha to return to Los Angeles but because of his adult status we had few options. So I drew up a plan for him to go to a series of transitional house placements for life-skills training, which at first seemed to be helping.

Most other mothers I know would find these new developments to be a source of joy. Ava only wanted her boy home with "some

freedom at last." What Misha wanted was an escape to Hollywood
and the Venice Beach boardwalk, where he quickly became somewhat
of an expert at LSD experimentation. At least, I thought, I could insist
on intensive therapy with mother and son and try to keep things
under control.

Everything failed, and soon Misha was arrested for possession of
drugs and brandishing a switchblade knife. And then the son of Ava's
friend in Washington State volunteered to take him to a small town
in the northwest and care for him with my long-distance supervision.
This satisfied the court but gave Ava a new cause of frequent panic
attacks when Misha kept trying to run away from life in the woods.
A few run-ins with creatures of the night quickly brought him back
to his house.

Over time, without the temptations of the city, Misha began to
settle down. Under intense pressure from his mother, he passed the
high school equivalency test and qualified for the local community
college, actually passing subjects with the intensive help of a local
educational specialist. By then, the therapist, fireman, and family
engineer had four patients: Ava, Misha, his caregiver, and the teacher-
mentor for whom Misha was an entirely new experience.

Remarkably, a new set of brain scans I requested from the
University of Washington Imaging Center showed tremendous
improvement in Misha's previously undeveloped brain areas. This
triumph of brain plasticity explained his academic progress and more
open, honest communication with me. But I knew better than to hope
that Ava would begin to relax.

When it came to the old "moving goalpost syndrome" which I
described earlier, Ava put my mother to shame. Nothing was ever
quite good enough because accepting good news could mean a threat
to her unconscious, busybody defense system. She meant well but she

just couldn't stop worrying. None of this was lost on Misha, who once asked with great insight, "Can you stop Mom from ignoring my good things and always pushing for more?"

For a long time nothing changed, including Ava's occasional one-in-five little gifts that kept me on board. But I began to notice that something else was happening: she seemed to really like the fact that I was not giving up on her. That was one of the reasons I really liked Ava. When not in a panic, she was smart, very friendly, most generous, a great lover of animals, and increasingly thankful for my efforts. For whatever reason, Ava was beginning to show mothering strengths that were not predicted by her personality test. About that same time, she reinforced this idea.

Ava made an intentional effort to self-soothe after she became so stressed in one session that, out of desperation, I asked if she ever thought about seeing a religious counselor. She made excuses, but one day a friend invited her to go with her to Mass and she accepted.

Ava then surprised me by joining a women's group in that Catholic Church. This was interesting because some of my Catholic friends tell me, perhaps unfairly, that their church is ground zero for guilt. Ava actually studied the catechism and became a member of the Church, but to my knowledge never went to confession or met with her priest. When I ask her about that she said, "I have nothing to be ashamed of."

There it was: her mind was filled with the dread that she had *everything* to be ashamed of, and this was what maintained her understandable but extreme defensiveness. It was as if the last thing she wanted was to see a priest who might either increase or reduce her guilt and shame. I could lead her to water but I could not make her drink. At one point, a colleague again reminded me of the old adage,

"Better the devil you know" referring to her unhealthy acceptance of living with daily disturbances.

So on we went, a tenacious psychologist and an increasingly likable lady who still refused to abandon or even question her unhealthy emotional defenses. Ava was simply one of a great many people who need a guarantee that they can forever avoid the capacity to be alone. This guarantee is built-in for everyone anytime it's needed; if you are disturbed by the contents of your mind, all you have to do is just keep running toward any distraction that protects you from looking inward.

When did humans start running from solitude? I believe it was when we evolved the ability to feel shame, which is a very sophisticated social emotion. After that we had something dear to protect, at all costs. Perhaps I am a case in point.

For example, if I feel guilty after violating some social taboo such as parking illegally, I expect to be scolded by someone, which can keep me in line with my fellow in-group members. But if I humiliate myself with an untimely, insensitive and public remark, revealing my flawed self in a way that results in a catastrophic loss of self-respect, I will feel shame, lower my eyes, and wish to disappear.

Guilt is about behavior and *outside* punishment; shame is about hating oneself and *inside* punishment, and they can go together. With shame, my low self-esteem becomes transparent and my terrible self-beliefs are reinforced. In my case, the best way I found to prevent shame was to get smart, talk a lot, and try to convince people that I am a worthy person.

Ava's security blanket was to manically seek out and cling to problems about her son to prevent possible perceptions that she was a failed mother and person. Her very essence was at stake and her security blanket was not up for discussion. This meant that my suggestions that she go to church to talk about her failings or just rest quietly on the back pew were premature.

As my friend had suggested, the misery of endless crises out in the world was much less painful than the misery of conscious shame. It did not matter to Sasha how much she fed her obesity or how high her blood pressure rose; emotional safety had to come first.

I only began to make meaningful progress with Ava when I reread the work of Donald Winnicott, whom I have often mentioned. The author of the "true self" concept, he was for much of my career an adopted guide in understanding the emotional development of children and adults.

For years I led discussion groups focusing on all of his writings. But most of our time was taken up with his book *The Maturational Process and the Facilitating Environment*. It was there that he included a short lecture called "The Capacity to Be Alone," first presented publicly in 1958. This is how Winnicott described the development of the manic defense that prevents the feeling of being alone.

*We most often hear about the fear of being alone or the wish to be alone rather than the* ability *to be alone; a discussion of the positive aspects of the capacity to be alone is overdue. The capacity to be alone is one of the most important signs of maturity and emotional development. It is the basis for periods of relaxation, patience, tolerance of ambivalence, and knowing about the preciousness of solitude.*

*The ability to be truly alone, that is, alone in the emotional presence of another, depends upon the early experience of being in the presence of a continuously supportive other person, such as the infant with his or her mother.*

Gradually a secure base and "the capacity to be alone" can become fixed *inside* the child's mind. *Mental* reminders increase, including memories of the original, safe mother-infant bond, the crib, the father, and later on, other adults, fictional heroes, and friends. Fortunately, with the right therapist many can also have a second chance to learn why they are so frightened by solitude.

So the ability to be safely alone can be soothing even when someone is physically alone, because he or she has an internal, body-based sense of security to draw upon. In this way, the emotionally healthy individual is never psychologically alone at all. No escape into worldly busyness and no manic defense is needed.

On the other hand, lacking the capacity to be alone (not feeling the *emotional* presence of others) is a recipe for insecurity and emotional immaturity. Aloneness is feared and becomes a signal for depression about what was lost in childhood, and the only option for many is to keep busy and escape into restless defensiveness. As I mentioned earlier, this habit is so soothing that the manic defense is rewarded and quickly becomes a way of life. Anything more than fleeting contentment is impossible. The danger of being physically alone then *really* grows.

I had long ago thought about Ava as being controlled by manic defenses, but had lost touch with the deeper understanding that could make possible a more helpful approach. Putting into practice what I re-learned from Winnicott became an essential way to understand Ava and my own defensive need to soothe her panic.

It wasn't until I fully relaxed in her presence and stopped trying to single-handedly fix everything that we were able to form a partnership in problem solving. She learned that at least she had the option to slow down a bit. She acknowledged that not rushing headlong into the next crisis sometimes wasn't so bad. One day she actually spent a session and a half totally focused on her guilt-ridden and lonely life, and agreed to consider visiting a grief group for women.

It was during this discussion about Ava talking with someone else about her problems that I learned a surprising truth. She apologetically said that on those occasional sessions where she came in seeming calm, she had just come from her fortuneteller of many years. I took this in two ways: I was impressed that she had reached out and found a fairly harmless form of soothing. I placed no judgment on her fortune-telling consolation. Second, I could only wonder what role her two "therapies" played in her progress.

An equally pleasant surprise happened when Ava came in one day and said that she had not tried hard enough to be active in the church. An assistant to the priest heard her speak in a group and asked her if she would become a lector, or reader from the scripture, at Mass.

As a former successful actress, her anxiety did not extend to public speaking, and she accepted the offer. Ava said that there might be several benefits in becoming a lector. Perhaps it would get her to church more regularly and reading the Bible more, help others, hopefully build social connections, and even motivate her to lose weight. More remarkable was her timing: she was already occupied with looking for in-home care for her father, and her son was still having problems.

Ava was also proving something very important for me. As we had suspected, the carefully assessed high risk mothers we struggled with in the Parent Training Clinic could actually be helped. With psychotherapy and enough patience, they could become successful lower-risk mothers.

Ava's case may sound extreme, but today we don't have to look far to find stressed-out, hyperactive, forever on-the-run men and women and now four-year-old children with iPads in my therapy playroom. All I have to do is ask my young patients to leave their iPads with their moms in the waiting room during our sessions. I haven't seen such terror from the threat of a pause in self-stimulation since my early days working with severely autistic children.

Is there a foreseeable future in which parents again learn to enjoy solitude? Or even more important, could they become models for a healthy capacity to be alone in the presence of others? Perhaps someone will come along with a new Parent Training Clinic and make solitude and self-soothing a priority. My colleague, the psychoanalyst Dr. Regina Pally, has already started this approach with her Center for Reflective Parenting.

As for Ava, she may never have the natural ability to be alone with her mind and memories, but she did prove that she knew what self-acceptance and genuine empathy for her son felt like. And Ava was no longer afraid to spend a few minutes during the week on the back pew of the church. And to my knowledge, for the first time, I had a fortune-teller as a co-therapist.

## Monica: Protecting the True Self at All Costs

*"But what if we fail?" they ask, whispering the dreaded*
*word across the generation gap to their parents back in*
*the establishment. The parents whisper back: "DON'T!"*
—Robert Blake

Most parents seek out and fully commit to their children's therapy, often eager to participate as needed. For this reason, my treatment with young people often succeeds. However, as I described David's parents early in these therapy cases, a parent can sometimes forget to keep their child's emotional needs in the foreground. This is what happened with Monica, a phenomenally gifted cellist.

For years, Nancy and I spent our weekends in a friend's mountain cabin in the small village of Idyllwild one hundred miles from Los Angeles high in the San Jacinto Mountains. We loved our life in the woods far away from city stresses.

But weekend jobs on the hill were scarce, and our private practice there could not survive the small payments and occasionally bartered home crafts, garden vegetables, and canned goods, even barnyard animals. What do you do with chickens in West Los Angeles? Then when we were offered part-time teaching and consulting positions at a music and arts school near the town, we got serious about moving. It was there that I was asked to help Monica, a fifteen-year-old student.

To her parent's great despair, Monica had slacked off practicing the cello and seemed depressed, for which they offered little comfort. She was there for a purpose and she would continue working toward stardom. But Monica found a way to get their attention when her teacher noted deep scratch marks on her wrist.

The parents found out about me, and instead of bringing her home for a needed inpatient evaluation as I suggested, they insisted that she stay with the program and for me to "get her back on track." They made an appointment to meet in my Los Angeles office and told about Monica's extraordinary skills as a musician. I was allowed to see Monica for one month, at which time I was expected to give them good news. My problem was that I wanted to go in a very different direction without getting fired.

The writer William Zinsser described my problem this way:

*One of the corrosive forces in American life, I think, is our obsession with the victorious result. Growth, wisdom, confidence, self-expression, dealing with failure and loss aren't valued because they don't get a grade.*

This meant that the *true* self of the young person must yield to the *compliant*, performing self. But this surrender almost always brings trouble. Humans want to succeed, but there always comes a time when they want to exist for something more important than what they *do*: they want to feel deeply accepted and understood by those they depend upon.

Here is how my dialogue began with Monica in my little Idyllwild office:

Monica: What's this all about? I don't need a therapist—I just want for people to leave me alone for a while.

Me:     And I just want to hear your story. Your parents hired me but all I care about right now is learning something about what you're going through.

Monica: Why should I trust you? I know you're only here because of my parents.

Me:     What do you have to lose by giving me a chance? I've spent a lot of years with kids like you who can't find someone who will just listen.

Monica (crying): I'll come to see you if I don't have to talk for a while.

Me:     It's a deal. Besides, I heard that you are very good at drawing. We don't have to sit in this office—I could meet you at school and we could find a place outside where we could

just sit while you are drawing anything you want. I'm still
a bit new here, maybe you could show me around."

Monica spent the rest of our first session slouching back on the
couch, eyes closed, silent. But before she left she said, "Do you know
where the library is? I can meet you there around ten o'clock next
Saturday." I agreed to accept her plan if she would agree to take my
card and call me anytime she thought about hurting herself. She said
OK and then rode her bike back to school.

I was not completely honest with Monica. In our early weekend
trips to the mountains, Nancy and I took long walks in the woods
surrounding Monica's school. We got to know the campus quite well.
I developed a habit of making my morning run from our place to the
campus, filled with the sights and smells and animals of the wild.

One morning while jogging through the forest I heard the sounds
of a cello in the distance somewhere down in the woods. Quietly
approaching, I saw a teenage boy sitting on a tree stump, eyes closed,
beautifully playing a Bach solo suite that I was struggling with at
the time. This was one of those perfect surprises that can make your
whole day. All doubts I had about making a serious investment in
Idyllwild ended, and we started looking for a cabin of our own.

Monica was waiting for me when I arrived at the library, but
brought no drawing materials. For a moment I was concerned that
she wanted to call the whole thing off, but she just wanted to sit on a
bench and talk. Over the next few weeks, I got the history I needed to
answer my biggest question: where was Monica on a scale of "*I want
a life. If I they ever make me play the cello again, I will die*" at one end

of the scale. At the other end was *"If I ever play the cello again, it has to be because I want to, not because I have to."*

I learned about her being given a choice at age five between a stringed instrument or the piano, with her mom playing recordings and taking her to many music stores. Like a good little girl, Monica never asked why. She said she chose the cello because she liked its mysterious, buzzing sound. She was immediately sent to a private and well-known teacher after school every day.

Most fortunately, her wise teacher played a few simple songs and let Monica decide which she liked the best. She said that her first experience playing the cello was about fun, not the hateful note reading, scales, and finger positions which imprison most music students, including me, a total musical dyslexic.

For Monica, not a word was said about actually reading music notation until she could play her song well. We'll never know what might have happened if she had started her career with a conventional straight-laced teacher.

Monica was a very fast learner and remembered being described as "a natural." After two years her teacher passed her on to a more skilled cellist. Monica never understood the change, and her parents ignored her complaints. By the time she was nine, the cello had become nothing but work and a robber of afterschool playtime. But her parents began to have her play for friends and relatives, and Monica enjoyed the acclaim and reputation as "a very gifted child." So she continued to practice and perform.

When it came time for high school, the parents were told by an orchestra cellist that local private schools had too many distractions and would only retard her musical gifts. Because Monica did not want to go to a music academy far from home, she was enrolled in the mountain music and arts school and had been there one year before she hit the wall. This is close to how she described it:

"One day I was in the middle of practicing a very difficult piece, with my teacher watching closely. Suddenly my mind went blank and I was completely disoriented. I was sent to my room to rest, but I didn't recover. I got into a zombie-like state where I was doing what I had to do but without any feeling at all. They said that I was in a depression because of a problem with my boyfriend, and to stick with the program. But I became more and more cut off from everything and felt kind of dead inside. That's when I started scratching my wrist, sort of a reminder that something inside of me was still alive. My teacher, who I really liked, told the headmaster about that, and here I am. But I don't see what good talking about this will do me—nothing is ever going to change and my parents would kill me if I dropped out of school."

I had to look hard at my options. Based on my one conversation with Monica's parents, I knew they were perfectly capable of ridding themselves of any obstacle to their dreams and expectations of their daughter. Meanwhile, my entire life as a psychologist had been based on a commitment to help parents find a way to guide, and then support, their child's healthy self-expression and true self. Monica knew nothing about this possibility, and if she had known, she would not have any confidence about deciding on a path for herself. All she knew was the cello, but she was experiencing the woes that someone once asked of the young cellist prodigy Yo-Yo Ma: "How do you keep your interest up?"

So in this case, my approach about helping her find herself had the potential of having a bad outcome for Monica, her family, and me.

I also needed to understand if Monica's relationship with her cello had become a full-bodied trauma, connected to a feeling of being emotionally abandoned by her parents.

So I called the parents and got their permission for additional time, telling them that their daughter was beginning to open up about what caused her to break down. They also agreed for me to see Monica twice a week, on both the Saturdays and Sundays we were in our mountain home.

Monica quickly learned to self-rate her disturbance on the 1-10 anxiety scale (nine is a total panic attack; ten is passing out) that I used for many of my patients. At one point I asked how she felt when I said the word "cello." She gave it a score of 7 or 8. Curious, I asked, "Why not a 9 or 10 ?"

She said every now and then she had a dream about publicly playing a beautiful duet by Saint-Saens called "The Swan" that I had always loved. I told her about this and let her know that if she ever wanted to play it for an audience of one, to please keep me in mind. She said she would think about it but did not like the idea of anyone else ever pressuring her to play again. I apologized and told her again that my first hope was that she would find something to do that felt like a happy hobby and not just a job.

Then things became even more difficult for me. Monica wanted me to talk her parents into shifting her school focus on to art for a while and maybe come back to the cello later. I needed an ally that the parents respected, and talked with the school director about drafting a letter to the parents, asking them to be patient while Monica was regaining her self-confidence. The director also emphasized the great acclaim that Monica had been receiving for her paintings and drawings. As expected, the parents rejected this idea.

Another problem popped up: Monica was scheduled to be part of the spring recital coming up in only six weeks, and she wasn't ready. Her parents were planning for many of their friends to come up the mountain and hear Monica's brilliant playing. It was desperation time and I needed to do something with a chance of working, so with the parent's approval, I met privately with the music director.

In the most direct way, I described our dilemma and told her about Monica's love of the Saint-Saens duet. Could Monica and her pianist friend play "The Swan" in the recital? The director wasn't happy because she wanted Monica to play a number of solo and ensemble cello favorites, which required a great deal of preparation. But when she learned what was at stake she consented.

Then all I had to do was get Monica to focus on playing for her own pleasure. It may have helped a little when I reminded her that what an audience loves most of all is hearing music that the performer loves and plays with great feeling.

For the next several weeks, Monica and I focused on tools to self-regulate her breathing and the meanings that she attached to playing. She gradually learned to dismiss unwanted thoughts and feelings with the repeated deep in-and-out breaths I described earlier that were so helpful for Charlie and Ted, whose minds were also filled with doomsday thoughts. As I described it, this intervention is almost always successful when the unwanted thoughts are irrational and without physical consequences.

Doubtful at first, Monica was able to accept that it was not really reasonable to fear playing a piece that she had always loved. It didn't take many role-plays for her to play "The Swan" with confidence and beauty, no matter who was going to be in the audience. Then one day she asked me to listen to her play with her accompanist in the recital auditorium, and I experienced a wonderful side effect of our work.

As I sat there alone on the back row, I thought about a time when I was in front of friends playing "The Swan," though not in any way close to how Monica was playing. This scene brought up memories of identifying with Ted when he talked about smacking a baseball and swinging his bat in my office, and then similarities with other patients over the years.

A long time ago we were taught to be very careful about identifying with our patients, lest we lose our objectivity. So it was a nice feeling to know that allowing myself to connect with patients where there were common interests seemed to help the therapy. Perhaps my personal and professional lives weren't so different after all.

This would be a good time to conclude with Monica's continued and smooth progress toward realizing her personal dreams, supported by all those who cared for her. But it didn't quite happen that way.

The recital was a big success, but the parents took advantage of their visit to call for a meeting with the school's music directors, Monica, and of course, me. Monica's mother used her outstanding performance at the recital as ammunition for her immediate return to "the plan we are paying you people for." But fortunately, she was outvoted by her father. Somehow, he was the only one of her parents who noticed that he had not seen his daughter so happy in many years, and wanted to support anything that would keep her feeling good about herself. And he wanted to know how Monica felt about continuing with the cello. Monica later told me that this was the first time either of them had asked that question.

Then it was Monica's turn to speak, and it took a while. She finally said, "There's something I would really miss if I completely gave up the cello and I know you would hate me, but what I really want is to have some time to only play the music I really like. And I want to stay here." The school and music directors then had a minor squabble about how much Monica should continue to practice basic skills, but they finally decided to put that issue aside for a while.

I suppose it was inevitable that Monica's mother, who continued to question my motives, would then ask for my opinion. I put on my political hat and said what I had rehearsed for the occasion: "The only thing I'm sure of is that Monica is determined to have a happy and successful future, no matter what she does. As an amateur cellist, I can say that Monica has a unique sound that is very satisfying for anyone who hears her play, and in this situation I trust Monica's judgment."

Against her mother's continued protests, Monica did stop playing the cello—for many months, and then was playing better than ever. Yo-Yo Ma's son Nicholas once described a similar period in his father's life playing the cello: "Through the process of going away he found himself at home again." I was again reminded how many times I have seen a young person such as Monica return to their earliest and most beloved values when given a chance to do it on their own.

# PART THREE

# The Mockingbird

*When you wake up, you notice that you're here.*

—Annie Dillard

# Searching for Integration and the True Self

*This book tells two stories that are braided*
*so tightly they cannot be separated.*

Adam Frank, *Blending*

I BEGAN THIS book with four quests. First, I would rescue soothing from its status of triviality in our daily lives and promote it to the respect it deserves, as a requirement for life itself. In the second quest, I would try to find the important events that pieced together my personality, especially those parts that at times were desperate for soothing. A third theme would be told in the stories of inventive habits I and my patients created to find reliable sources of self-soothing for us all.

In the final quest, I would try to make sense of my lives as an often confused, hypersensitive person and as a successful therapist. I would search for ways to braid together these two conflicting parts of my personality and perhaps solve the mystery of self-compassion. I wanted to find a true self and a bigger picture of my place in time.

So how did I do? Feeling fully satisfied with a compelling case for the importance of soothing is going to take a while, and as I noted, will need its own book. I now know myself much better than I did before I started writing, and I'm happy with the results of the second quest. And there is no end to the stories describing mutually helpful partnerships with my patients so I'm going to continue writing about that. The search for a broader perspective on my life is also a work in progress.

So the job is not finished; many quests but few conquests. And this is the way it should be: what life would be like if the business of putting ourselves together ended? Besides, what if every achievement in integrating our inner and outer lives is followed by an even more interesting challenge? There is no end to these life challenges. Shortly I will describe how the Dalai Lama once talked about integration and enlightenment as a matter of daily practice.

Yet "integration" only seems to plague those of us who think about it: always looking for ways to zoom out from little and local moments and grasp the larger meaning of life on earth. Can anyone do this? Unless you are naturally gifted, living each moment to its fullest like the potato digger I will soon describe, it always seems incomplete.

Our greatest minds are those that understand the challenge of integration, and struggle just like the rest of us, often because of, or with the help of, some personal malady. The extraordinary memoirist and dyslexic Eileen Simpson finally gave up: "Enough! Whatever I might write in the future would be objective, external, outside myself . . . No more memoir!" Other famous suffering dyslexics, Jean Jacques Rousseau, Jean Paul Sartre, and especially Leo Tolstoy kept up the search for integration their whole lives. Each of these brilliant minds had one more thing to integrate; they were all orphans. What about us lesser minds with our own Achilles' heels?

I did finally figure out what searching for "a bigger picture" might mean, or at least what the goal is. For me, integration means having the intention to take the little pieces of my personal and professional lives as they come and accept them both for what they are. It can sometimes be very soothing to surrender and accept what cannot be changed. Pema Chodren put it this way:

> *Things fall apart, and then they come together. And they fall apart again, and then they come together again.*

I had a totally new idea about integration after I read Pema's quote. If she's right, then I could have been wrong from the beginning about living two separate lives. A deeper truth might be that my personal and 'helper' lives have always influenced each other. There have been private moments when I found peace of mind, and there have been moments when my attempts to help others have been wrecked by personal distress. Perhaps integration and non-integration are always in the background or foreground. Perhaps integration, at its best, is just a wish, or an intention. Perhaps the real goal is in the words of Rudyard Kipling: "If you can meet with triumph and disaster and treat those imposters the same."

Each of the stories in this book has contained a lesson about integration for me, something that probably would not have happened without writing them down. In one unforgettable lesson, just when I was getting the UCLA Parent Training Clinic off the ground in the early 1970s, I met a father named Robert. His chronic worry and self-loathing rendered him helpless to soothe his hyperactive son Robbie Jr. This man described his whole life as unfinished business because as a university professor of philosophy, he craved his daily struggle with ambiguity and the deepest questions about the meaning of life.

Robert's problem was that he did not know how to leave his work at the office. He felt oddly detached from most everything else.

Then when he got home, something in Robert triggered his most unfinished business, which was finding a way to feel emotionally connected to his son and wife, the way he felt connected when facing intellectual challenges. For a long time, Robert was the easiest patient for me to identify with.

Then one night while driving home from the office, for some reason I started thinking about Robert. I found myself time traveling far back to summers with my grandparents. I remembered a man somewhere in those years who falsely thought he had the answer to problems like Robert's, and I decided to write about it.

## The Potato Digger

*When you start your journey to Ithaca, then pray that the road is long, full of adventure, full of knowledge...*

C. P. Cavafy


I always looked forward to long visits at my grandparent's country home in south Georgia. I had discovered Grandpa's small bookcase in the dark hallway leading from the front door to the back porch. Many warm summer evenings I sat under the dim ceiling light bulb reading from his collection. I took for granted that these were just books from his years at Mercer University in Macon (where I would later begin college), so if he kept them I should read them too.

Over several summers I read from *A History of the English-Speaking Peoples* by Winston Churchill, which my grandfather explained was really the story of our own people in previous centuries. Parts of *The Decline and Fall of the Roman Empire* by Edmund Gibbons became a lesson for how civilizations, like people, sooner or later struggle to survive. This book was also the beginning of a long love affair with everything Roman. There were others, but my favorite was *The Great Physician* by someone named Josephus. For many years I didn't know why it had such appeal.

*The Great Physician* had a faded pink cover, was much worn, at least three inches thick and very heavy. I always look forward to reading more, but not to lifting and stuffing it back onto the shelf at bedtime. The book was about a man who lived in ancient times, before science was invented and physicians and philosophers had pretty much the same job. He roamed his world endlessly puzzling about everything.

I have not been able to recall the fictional philosopher's name, and after all these years finally gave up trying to find a copy of the book. Even the Web's books out-of-print failed me. The only thing that I'm sure about was the philosopher's reflections on his life toward the end of the book, which for some reason became a source of endless pleas from Nancy to be retold whenever we went out with friends. This is the way I remember the passage from grandpa's book.

On a typical afternoon while walking from one village to the next on the old road, the mind-wandering philosopher, shifting his attention from compelling events in nature to timeless mental absorption, noticed a broken-down shack off to the right of the road.

From a distance, he could see a peasant woman out front who seemed to be struggling with the hard earth to give up its potatoes. He noticed that her old garment was ragged but clean. It seemed strange that she was softly humming, and he then saw there was no struggle at all; she was just cleaning and caressing her latest discoveries. As he came closer, for a moment they made eye contact and she smiled as if she was utterly content with her life and everything in it, including strangers on the road.

The thinker and worrier became seriously conflicted by what he saw and felt. Her demeanor fit no pattern he had ever seen, so he thought to himself, "How can this destitute and ignorant woman be smiling unless she has lost her mind? All she does, every day, is the same thing over and over again with nothing to show for it except perhaps a meal. She discovers nothing original and contributes nothing of importance. Perhaps the poor woman can't read and will never find out what she's missing."

The philosopher had always believed that if he learned enough and thought hard enough about everything, new compelling mysteries would always come. He loved his endless foraging for mental stimulation and found long ago he could accept his loneliness if he just kept thinking and moving.

But at that moment he could not escape what the potato digger had exposed in him, which was an ancient yearning for the kindness and peace of mind that she seemed to take for granted. For the first time in his life, it occurred to him to ask: "She seems to have the lasting happiness I have always wanted, even though I do not understand it. *Would I trade places if I could?*"

This old woman had the peaceful glow that he had given up finding for himself many years before. As he passed her, she seemed to offer him one of her freshly-dug treasures. He had a momentary impulse to approach but kept moving.

He spent the rest of the afternoon on the road to the next village where he could perhaps find food and a bed. But he couldn't understand what happened back there with the old woman until he reached the crest of a hill overlooking the settlement below.

Deciding to rest a bit, the philosopher settled himself on a large stone. He possessed a foolproof method for solving what he expected to be just another philosophical puzzle, and was confident that he could sort it out.

First, he would try to imagine that he was the old contented woman, who seemed to always be in the present moment, fully accepting whatever was happening, just as it was. He also knew that it was neither logical nor honest to deny what had struck him as appealing about her state of peace, quiet and freedom. The next step was to review and examine the peak experiences of his never-ending mental discoveries. Finally he would complete his analysis by systematically comparing the pros and cons of the two imagined scenes, and using his powers of logical reasoning to reach the proper conclusion. His method almost never failed, so he relaxed and went to work.

Suddenly he had it: first, he had to accept that for some few people, a soothing peace comes with just knowing what you need to know, moment by moment. Before he encountered the potato digger, he never imagined that kind of self-soothing existence was possible, much less desirable. Yet that option was now an established fact. But then the obvious solution presented itself; for the first time he knew the truth about the only thing that had lasting value for him. It was the search. It was *not* knowing.

He could never stop being curious if he tried, and even if he spent the rest of his days worrying about the meanings of life. He would rather die struggling with some compelling philosophical puzzle than live the earthy existence of the potato digger, empty of new insights about grand issues. Satisfied with having resolved his most important existential crisis so far, the thinker rose and headed down the hill to the village.

No matter how many times I recount this story, I always learn something new. The latest insight is a new kind of clarity about my achievements that sometimes help others and the ever elusive self-acceptance. Now I am thinking that there may be another way, different from the beliefs of the smiling potato digger or the heady philosopher, both of which have always been extremely appealing. Now, one is too simple and the other too familiar.

If as I believe, all books are in one way or another autobiographical, Josephus painted his characters in stark, all or none colors to reveal his own dilemma. We will never know if he left it there or found a middle way. Perhaps like his philosopher, he was soothed by accepting that uncertainty, mixed with distant yearnings to feel connected with others and live in the moment, can make a good enough life. Or perhaps he was one of many people who never stop searching for ways to integrate all their joys and sorrows into a self that somehow makes sense.

## The Bagpipe Professor

When I showed up as a seventeen-year-old freshman at Mercer University in Macon, Georgia, I got in line with everyone else registering for fall quarter classes. The elective courses about science were full, and when I asked the registrar about my options, she wondered what I was interested in. I told her "psychology" and she again said the beginning courses were full but that there was a senior level class for people interested in clinical psychology, and I could attend if I thought I was up to it. I jumped at the chance.

The class only had about 15 people in it, probably because the psychology majors had already taken the course. The instructor was someone named Professor Simpson, who surely was the oldest man on the faculty but still had bright eyes, a sharp focus, and a warm smile. He said a few words about the class, and then introduced the textbook, *Clinical Psychology: An Introduction to Phenomenology*, which meant very little to me. We were to get the book and read the first three chapters for the following day's class.

I had already been 'rushed' by SAE fraternity and when I returned to the frat house after class I learned all about my famous professor. My fraternity big brother, a guy named Lewis, said something like, "You are very lucky to get in his class—there's no one like him on the faculty. Take lots of notes. Last year a bunch of us took his class, and at the end of the quarter we made a bet that we could find a question Professor Simpson couldn't answer. I'm the only one who bet against him because the question was about who invented the bagpipe. There was no way he could know that.

So when we all went to his house that night he invited us in, served tea, and we got his permission to ask him anything. After hearing our question, without a word he went into his hallway, reached high on some shelf, and brought down a bagpipe, on which he proceeded to play what he later told us was the Scottish national anthem. He then told us the inventor's name. I lost five bucks. Nobody wanted to believe us, but you can ask the other guys if you want."

Remarkable stories like this were repeated many times during the fall semester in his class on phenomenology and clinical psychology and this time I got to see him in action close up. Of course no one 'tested' him in class, but he brought life and great personal knowledge to everything he told us.

Back then, what he taught was interesting, but not compelling because I didn't understand "phenomenology." In psychology, it was something about how healthy people find a way to bring together and accept all of their experiences, good and bad. This was completely counter to my own personal reading of Freud's books, starting with the *Psychopathology of Everyday Life*.

Freud taught that there was no way to consciously integrate everything because most of our experiences, especially the really important ones, were repressed due to trauma and made unavailable to consciousness. Professor Simpson talked about this and acknowledged the difficulty of integrating old experiences of guilt and shame and hate into an acceptable view of oneself. But he insisted that it should be the ideal for anyone wanting to live a contented life. As a clinical psychologist, he believed that the best approach to treatment was to help people learn to more fully accept themselves.

But I still didn't get it. I was seventeen at the time and just assumed that maybe some people out there got it all together and felt great most of the time. I doubted that this could happen to me. *The Great Physician*, which I had finished reading several years earlier, was still on my mind. What reminded me of Professor Simpson was the way the philosopher found comfort in accepting that his life was about the journey, not about getting somewhere. Today I believe that if Professor Simpson had summarized his approach to clinical psychology in four words, they would have been "more integration, less complaining." The big picture can sometimes make the little picture, no matter how painful, seem less important.

Now, after a half-century, it feels like I'm beginning to close the loop all the way back to where it started with Professor Simpson, but this time with less thinking and more body-based feeling. There's a big difference between a goal, no matter how wonderful, and putting too much pressure on oneself to reach it or else. A lot was lost when very early on I became obsessed with just accumulating knowledge for the purpose of impressing others. I must have been a very late bloomer to finally grasp what now seems like common sense.

Also, I've learned that "integration" doesn't mean complete self-understanding. It's not true that when the wisdom-seeking masters like the great physician and Professor Simpson have moments of clarity, they can finally relax. The writer Cheryl Strayed put it this way:

> *Two things can be true at once—even opposing truths. It*
> *could be true that you will suffer forever because you were*
> *abused as a child—it can also be true that you can overcome*
> *that and not let that experience define your life. And you*
> *can hold those two truths in two hands, and walk forward.*

In early 2014, the Dalai Lama agreed to be interviewed for Time magazine. The correspondent asked him ten questions, and at the end of the meeting wondered how he had been able to deal with the slaughter of so many of his people in Tibet in the Chinese invasion of 1950. She suggested that with his accumulated wisdom and enlightenment, he must have found a way to integrate this tragedy into his personal life and teachings so he could carry on. The Dalai Lama said, "I try to take the wider view. Enlightenment is what I strive for and I have to work at it every day."

## The White Oleander

*When you learn how big the universe is, how old the universe is, what the contents of the universal are, you realize how fleeting your presence on earth really is. It helps you refocus, gives you a new point of view on your problems.*
Neil Degrasse Tyson.

Most mornings I jog up and down my winding canyon road for a few miles. Uphill is a slow jog, but downhill on a perfect, clear day running hard against the oncoming ocean wind, is my time to bellow out the opening lines from Vivaldi's *Gloria*. Especially on Sundays, I have to compete for road space and watch out for the bee-swarm sounds of racing professional bikers. I've done this for years.

One Sunday morning not long ago, just after a close call when I had to jump off the road next to the fence, a brilliant white flower on the grass grabbed my attention. After only another jog or two, without knowing why, I stopped in my tracks and walked back up to have a closer look. What first struck most of all when I picked it up was the perfectly clean and fresh brilliant white surfaces on each of the five petals. I had no idea how a flower on the grass had the power to interrupt Vivaldi and I could not stop inspecting its parts.

Suddenly the flower was familiar. I remembered the bushy and extremely poisonous oleander flowers and leaves that I had planted on the hill behind my house when I moved in many years ago. Eat a flower like two Los Angeles toddlers did in 2000 and you may die a most unpleasant death. Once after a close call with a major brush fire, a fireman working on the hillside hotspots told me about a rattlesnake den about fifty feet above my fence, and said that I should plant some oleanders, which rattlesnakes avoided. Now my white and pink bushes are fully grown, just like the summer snakes that really seem to enjoy being around them.

Then something very weird happened between me and the flower. For a few seconds it was all a mystery: how could indescribable beauty be in the same hand as death itself? Then I had the thought of beauty *and* death, and finally, *what's the difference?* It was all about the impossible merger of existence and nonexistence. Odd as it may sound, the dichotomy between these two categories had disappeared. In *Pilgrim at Tinker Creek*, the poet Annie Dillard felt something similar when she wrote this: "The sight held awesome wonders: power and beauty, grace tangled in a rapture with violence."

Then I thought about our old Professor Zimmer in graduate school, who never could seem to find an audience for his mantra, "There are no dichotomies in nature—all dichotomies are created by people to reduce anxiety." After he killed himself doing electrical experiments in his creepy basement laboratory one night, we all decided that since he was probably crazy, so must his mantra be nonsense.

When I got back home, with flower still cradled in hand, I tried to write about what happened and see if I could figure out what it all meant. A tiny temporal lobe stroke? Did "runners high" squelch all my worries and dichotomies for a moment? A dissociative reaction similar to what happened when I took my father to the mental hospital all those years ago? One of those spiritual "transcendent moments" on the way to great understanding, which I had always written off as brain hiccups? And I wasn't high on some interesting chemical; no mushrooms or marijuana for forty years.

It took a few days before I decided to just go with what seemed right on that strange Sunday morning; a moment of clarity had brought together an important truth about my personal and professional lives. I recalled Pema Chodren's poem about the balancing act between coming together and falling apart. What if I had been living with a false dichotomy?

But this was just the beginning, thanks to black Monday nights when I roll the trash cans down to the roadside garbage pickup area. I think of this as my personal "church," and stand for a while just looking up.

In most late nights here in the Santa Monica Mountains, the skies become clear and full of planets and stars. Long ago I made a habit of imagining myself on a familiar planet or far away galaxy looking back on Carl Sagan's "pale blue dot." Like Sagan, each time I mentally detached from my grounded existence, I had new thoughts about our earth. Some were about the horrible harm done down there. Most were about the great stamina of life on earth, no matter who wins the battle between the angels and demons in every person.

I end my mental space travel back home, right where I was standing, feeling lucky to have had all the inner troubles that made possible a useful life as a child therapist. Now I have come full circle, all the way from a little boy who first learned about higher levels of abstraction from his father to an endlessly expanding, bigger perspective about life.

Perhaps this is why "ultimate" reality is so elusive for even our greatest cosmologists, or, as the science journalist John Horgan put it, "When we peer out to the farthest edge of the universe, we see, finally, our own puzzled faces looking down at us."

So every time a new "truth" about reality or human limits is discovered, the available space for new realities of human potential to see a bigger picture widens again. And the same thing must be true about my attempts to understand almost anything. From childhood, this curiosity to somehow go beyond whatever I encounter has been one of my greatest mental soothers. After all, way out there in the cosmos, there's no one to care, and that's okay. If what we have here is only a momentary, shifting point of view, and if all I can do is make the most of it, that's okay too.

So as I begin to get some closure in this memoir about my most important quest, the search for wholeness, I can sometimes see my entire life in a single glance and feel good that my two lives are becoming one.

With this simple collage of endless cosmic beauty, roadside garbage and a new acceptance of ambiguity and self-compassion, I could get a glimpse of Professor Simpson's "integration" and my one true self almost anytime I was willing, like a mockingbird, to make the effort.

# The Mockingbird

## Mary Oliver

*All summer*
*the mockingbird in his pearl-gray coat,*

*flies*
*from the hedge to the top of the pine*
*and begins to sing, but it's neither*
*lilting nor lovely,*

*for he is the thief of other sounds—*
*whistles and truck brakes and dry hinges*
*plus all the songs*
*of other birds in his neighborhood;*

*all mimicking and elaborating,*
*he sings with humor and bravado,*
*so I have to wait a long time*
*for the softer voice of his own life*

*to come through. He begins*
*by giving up all his usual flutter*
*and settling down on the pine's forelock*
*then looking around*

*as though to make sure he's alone;*
*then he slaps each wing against his breast,*
*where his heart is,*

*and copying nothing, begins*

*easing into it*
*as though it was not half so easy*
*as rollicking,*
*as though his subject now*

*was his true self,*
*which of course was as dark and secret*
*as anyone else's,*
*and it was too hard–*

*perhaps you understand–*
*to speak or to sing it*
*to anything or anyone*
*but the sky.*

# ACKNOWLEDGMENTS

THIS BOOK WOULD not have been written except for a long-standing series of emotional disturbances about Nancy's well-being that I could not understand without taking a hard look at my life and work. For as long as she lives and beyond, I will forever thank my soulmate for her tolerance and teaching me about true love.

Nancy was also the greatest soother I ever met. Except for the losses of two of our grandchildren, no matter how bad the news, Nancy could always find a way to spin it in a more positive light and find the silver lining.

This book could also not have been written in its present form without the guidance provided by William Zinsser in his books *Writing Well, Writing about Your Life,* and *Inventing the Truth.* I owe him a great deal, including apologies for his ideas and even phrases that gave voice to my searching mind. I eagerly borrowed "Escape to Baseball," "the fever that struck a young man," and other perfect solutions to my imperfect articulations. Thanks to Zinsser, I was able to make the difficult transition from objective scientific reporting to writing with feeling about the essence of being human. It was also Zinsser who introduced me to Annie Dillard, who in *The Writing Life* taught me what *not* to write, and who can inject compelling vitality into the work of any author, and to Russell Baker, whose writing style I can only hope to find.

Thanks to Sid Jordan, who is a permanent influence in my life and a constant in this book, and for introducing me to William Zinsser.

Thanks to Jane Monteagle, Jennifer Soliman, Dale Atkins, Jonathan Salk and Susan O'Hara for their support, ideas, and much needed corrections, for Linda Circado who taught me about momentum and flow by reading the manuscript out loud, and especially to Dallas Jones for looking over my shoulder from beginning to end.

Special thanks to my sister Martha for the unwavering support that I needed to tell my story, and to Don Dorsey for teaching me how to live free of excessive anxiety.

Thanks to all the study group members I debated with over the decades, who shaped my expressions of concise and interesting thoughts.

And also, thanks to Pippen Properties for permission to use the Harry Bliss cartoon.

And special thanks to the support team at Xlibris who shepherded my manuscript all the way to publication and marketing. Any flaws in the book are mine alone.

# INDEX

## A

abandonment, 69, 175–76, 178
ability, 36, 50, 52, 54, 83–84, 94,
  113, 121, 129, 155, 208, 238,
  241–43
abstraction, 74–78, 270
ADHD (attention deficit
  hyperactivity disorder), 51,
  217, 237
Adler, Alfred, 122, 124, 134
Adriana (Joanie's mother), 1–2
Africa, 20–21, 23, 29, 51
agrypniaphobia, 218
Andrew (patient with Asperger
  syndrome), 182–90, 207
anxiety, 2, 5–6, 19, 42, 51, 126, 170,
  195, 198, 204, 208, 212, 214,
  216–17, 223–24, 244, 269
*Asperger Parent: How to Raise
  a Child with Asperger
  Syndrome and Maintain
  Your Sense of Humor, The*
  (Cohen), 189
Asperger syndrome, 183, 187, 189
Atlanta, 42, 56, 72, 79, 135–36, 143
autism, 43, 138, 142–44, 183
Ava (woman with manic defense),
  165, 231–45

## B

Basch (doctor), 128, 130
baseball, 86, 89–90, 92–95, 101,
  105, 231, 253
behavior, 19, 42–43, 52, 100, 132,
  139–40, 146, 152, 158, 168,
  173, 207–8, 238, 241
  self-destructive, 129, 139
Ben (Hans' friend), 210–11
Bertha (schizophrenic), 11–12, 231
Bethany (depressed patient), 116,
  119–22, 124–25
Boardman, Bill, 42–45, 51, 138,
  178, 182
Bobby (patient with social
  withdrawal), 104–5, 112, 114,
  134
borderline personality disorder,
  174, 180, 182

## C

Charlene (lawyer), 61–62
Charlie (patient with OCD), 165,
  207–9, 211, 213–16, 252
Chicago, 48, 61
child psychiatry, 149
child psychotherapy, 99, 102, 165,
  167

child therapy, 102–3, 105, 161
  intensive, 154
  traditional, 155
cognitive behavior therapy, 199,
    203, 208
Cohen, Jeffrey, 189
creativity, 9, 51, 66, 107, 125, 164,
    182, 233

**D**

Darlene (patient with physical
    development problem),
    144–48
David (patient with anxiety),
    167–73
depression, 123–24, 184, 215, 217,
    231, 243, 250
*Diary of a Baby, The* (Stern), 12, 67
DNA (deoxyribonucleic acid), 20,
    23
Dorsey, Don, 194, 210–11
Down syndrome, 146
Dreyfus, Richard, 167

**E**

EMDR (eye movement
    desensitization and
    reprocessing), 194–95, 210–
    11, 215, 227
Emory University Medical Center,
    42, 104, 110, 134–35, 145–46,
    174, 183
empathy, 54, 107, 112–16, 158, 160,
    183, 245
Europe, 22, 151–52

**F**

Freud, Sigmund, 5, 8, 99–101, 107,
    122–23, 266

**G**

Gehrig, Lou, 92
George (Lynda's husband), 175–76,
    178
Georgia, 11, 22, 29, 35, 46, 59, 61,
    72, 79, 81, 102, 264

**H**

Hitler, Adolf, 115
hospital, 46, 49, 57, 80, 135, 140,
    142–43, 161, 171, 215
  mental, 79–80, 269

**I**

imagination, 74–75, 77, 90, 168–69,
    186, 208, 210
insecurity, 19, 24, 31, 111, 204, 243
*Interpersonal World of the Infant,
    The* (Stern), 66

**J**

Jimmy (toy thrower), 23, 102–3, 112
Joanie (patient with
    trichotillomania), 1–9, 24,
    108, 116, 123
Jonesboro, 136–37
Jordon, Sid, 37–41, 44, 50, 136, 143

Justin (patient with moving goalpost syndrome), 82–83

**K**

Kimberly (paranoid patient), 128–33
Kohut, Heinz, 114–15

**L**

Larson, Don, 91
Lindsay (patient with dissociative disorder), 109–12
Los Angeles, 36, 43–44, 61, 144, 160, 168, 171, 174, 238, 246, 268
Lovaas (doctor), 139, 143
Lynda (patient with panic attacks), 165, 173–82, 191

**M**

manic defense, 231–32, 236, 242–43
mantra, 269
medical psychology, 47, 149–50
Michael (depressed patient), 125–27
Miller (doctor), iii, 49, 165–66, 172, 200
Misha (hyperactive patient), 234–40
missionary, 29–30, 60
Monica (suicidal teenager), 66, 245–54

moving goalpost syndrome, 82–83, 239

**N**

Nancy (Hans' wife), 28, 37, 52, 94, 130, 152–53, 166, 246, 248, 261, 275
NASA (National Aeronautics and Space Administration), 190
Neuropsychiatric Institute, 151, 161–62
North Carolina, 22, 174, 181

**O**

OCD (obsessive-compulsive disorder), 2, 35, 51, 207–10, 214
orange crates, 59–60

**P**

panic attacks, 35, 110, 173, 194, 237
Parent Training Clinic, 47, 49, 125, 150, 153, 155, 157, 160–62, 185, 234, 244
pathological dissociative reaction, 121
personality disorders, 129, 131, 164, 174
personality test, 156, 240
phenomenology, 265
phenylhydantoin syndrome, 145
phobia, 4, 6, 35–36, 213–14
potato digger, 258, 260, 262–63

psychiatry, 35, 46, 48–49, 149, 152, 158

psychology, iii, 40, 45, 61, 68, 101, 264–65

 clinical, iii, 99, 101, 264–66

psychotherapy, iii, 19, 42, 66, 99, 106, 116, 123, 125, 150, 165, 171, 173–75, 208, 217, 244

punishment, 192, 241

## R

Ray (Unitarian Church member), 27–29

Reeve, Christopher, 58–59

REM (rapid eye movement), 224

Richland, 22, 29, 61, 71–72

Rinaldo (patient with sleeping disorder), 217–22, 225

Robert (professor), 259–60

Rorschach inkblot test, 42–43, 169–70

## S

Sammy (boy with Down syndrome), 48, 146–48

San Francisco, 44, 81, 114–15

Sarah (autistic), 138–43, 183

Sasha (patient with scoldophobia), 191–204, 206, 210, 242

Savannah, 33, 36, 87, 92–93

Saver (doctor), 67–68

schizophrenia, 11, 172

scoldophobia, 190–91, 193, 198, 204–6, 236

sexual abuse, 131

Simmons, Jim, 44, 47, 149–50

Simpson (professor), 265–67, 271

sleep disorder, 217–19, 223

sleep therapy, 217–18, 223

solitude, 122, 241–43, 245

Solomon (compulsive buyer), 116–19, 125

soothing, 8–14, 18–19, 21, 84, 95, 101, 103, 105–6, 108, 111, 159, 191, 202, 205, 219, 227, 231, 233, 243–44, 257

Spain, 22

Stern, Daniel, 12, 66–67

symptoms, 2, 4–5, 50, 108, 164–65, 170, 199, 217, 219, 228

## T

Tara (teacher), 53

Ted (patient with sleeping disorder), 217, 222–31, 252–53

therapy, 2–4, 8, 18, 29, 42, 65, 71, 96, 102–5, 107, 111, 115, 117, 119, 122–25, 128, 130, 135, 137, 155, 160, 165, 169, 172–73, 175–76, 179–82, 189, 191, 194, 198–99, 206, 211, 218–22, 227, 229, 232, 234, 244, 253

 children's, 245

 cognitive, 120, 124, 199, 209

 intensive, 126, 164, 239

 office-bound, 134

 parent, 236

trauma, 5, 19, 36, 194–95, 223, 227, 266

trichotillomania, 1

# U

UCLA (University of California–
Los Angeles), 35, 43–45, 81,
94, 109, 125, 129, 148, 152–
53, 166, 210

# W

Ward, Rick, 104–5, 112, 134, 141
Winnicott, 56, 59, 65–67, 242–43

# Y

Young, Florene, 102–4, 134, 137,
148

CPSIA information can be obtained
at www.ICGtesting.com
Printed in the USA
LVHW092000180423
744631LV00027B/1227